STUDIES IN WELSH HISTORY

Editors

RALPH A. GRIFFITHS   KENNETH O. MORGAN
GLANMOR WILLIAMS

13

BUILDING JERUSALEM

NONCONFORMITY, LABOUR AND THE
SOCIAL QUESTION IN WALES,
1906–1939

BUILDING JERUSALEM

NONCONFORMITY, LABOUR AND THE
SOCIAL QUESTION IN WALES,
1906–1939

by

ROBERT POPE

*Published on behalf of the
History and Law Committee
of the Board of Celtic Studies*

CARDIFF
UNIVERSITY OF WALES PRESS
1998

British Library Cataloguing-in-Publication Data
A catalogue record for this book is available from the British Library.

ISBN 0-7083-1413-9

Typeset at the University of Wales Press
Printed in Great Britain by Dinefwr Press, Llandybïe, Dyfed

I FY MAM,
MARY,

AC
ER COF ANNWYL AM
KEITH,
FY NHAD

EDITORS' FOREWORD

Since the Second World War, Welsh history has attracted considerable scholarly attention and enjoyed a vigorous popularity. Not only have the approaches, both traditional and new, to the study of history in general been successfully applied to Wales's past, but the number of scholars engaged in this enterprise has multiplied during these years. These advances have been especially marked in the University of Wales.

In order to make more widely available the conclusions of recent research, much of it of limited accessibility in postgraduate dissertations and theses, in 1977 the History and Law Committee of the Board of Celtic Studies inaugurated this new series of monographs, *Studies in Welsh History*. It was anticipated that many of the volumes would originate in research conducted in the University of Wales or under the auspices of the Board of Celtic Studies. But the series does not exclude significant contributions made by researchers in other universities and elsewhere. Its primary aim is to serve historical scholarship and to encourage the study of Welsh history. Each volume so far published has fulfilled that aim in ample measure, and it is a pleasure to welcome the most recent addition to the list.

CONTENTS

EDITORS' FOREWORD   vii

PREFACE   xi

LIST OF ABBREVIATIONS   xiv

I   SETTING THE SCENE   1

II   THE NONCONFORMIST RESPONSE TO
       SOCIALISM, 1906–1914   31

III   LABOUR, SOCIALISM AND NONCONFORMITY   71

IV   THE TURNING-POINT 1910–1911:
       NONCONFORMITY'S SOCIAL CONSCIENCE   123

V   BUILDING JERUSALEM: NONCONFORMITY
       AND POST-WAR RECONSTRUCTION   165

VI   LOSING THE BATTLE   229

CONCLUSION   241

SOURCES AND BIBLIOGRAPHY   250

INDEX   261

PREFACE

Most Welsh social and industrial history written during the last twenty years has concentrated less on industrial relations, Nonconformity in religion and Liberalism in politics than on the doctrine of class war, Socialism and the politics of labour. This kind of history had its genesis in the early 1970s with the South Wales Coalfield Project and has been promulgated effectively by the members of the Society for the Study of Welsh Labour History and their journal *Llafur*. Working-class culture has been presented in terms of a thirst for knowledge which was generally secular, economic and political; the overwhelming influence of the union lodge and workingmen's institute, and the high priority given to sport and the public house. Oddly, little place has been given to religion, and this despite the 1904–5 revival which brought thousands into contact with the chapel. The history of the Welsh working class in the twentieth century has been presented as a migration from the chapels into the labour movement, with the latter succeeding in speaking directly to the social and personal condition of the working class. A corollary of this is the often implicit claim that the chapels had no relevant message for the working class or for social reform.

This study is based on my Ph.D. thesis, 'Nonconformity, labour and the social question in Wales, 1906–1939', submitted to the School of Theology and Religious Studies, University of Wales, Bangor, in 1995. Its aim is to look again at the evidence and to discover the pattern of social and religious development most likely to have occurred in Wales. In attempting to discover what religious and political allegiance meant to the working class and to find the ideological and theological basis to Nonconformist activity in the period, this study seeks to present the situation from both the working-class and the Nonconformist point of view, the latter having been neglected in recent social history. It will ask whether in fact the Welsh chapels were silent over the need for social reform or whether they had a unique contribution to make which, for whatever reason, the labour movement chose to ignore.

Several amendments have had to be made before the manuscript was ready for publication. The narrative and thematic structure of the thesis has been revised in order to give a clearer chronology, while concentration on the historical side meant the extraction of a major chapter on Welsh theology. My hope is that this will be published elsewhere in due course.

One of the major problems encountered in preparing this work for publication concerned the use of male-dominated language. The academic world has been made increasingly aware that masculine terminology is unacceptable when speaking on behalf of humanity as a whole. In an effort to accede to this, many of the original references to 'man' or 'men' have been amended. Many others have been left untouched for several reasons. Patriarchalism, perceived as a problem, is a recent phenomenon. In leaving masculine terminology in the body of the book, the reader will gain a greater insight into the debate of the time. The 'social problem' specifically concerned *men*. Agitators sought amelioration of conditions, and political representation, for working men. While it is undeniable that the term was used generically in the majority of cases, there was no explicit recognition that solving the social problem would also change women's lives for the better. It is also possible, for example, that when Nonconformists and labour spokesmen suggested that social reform would occur following the moral regeneration of 'men' and their commitment to live self-sacrificial lives for the good of others and society as a whole, they viewed the building of society exclusively as a male preserve. Such a proposition is all the more plausible bearing in mind that women did not have a vote and therefore had no public input before 1918. Because it is unclear, and because the primary concept was that of the 'brotherhood of man', the reader is presented with many of the arguments still in 'patriarchal' form, and can decide the meaning for him or herself.

It is appropriate here to record my gratitude to those who helped me to research and write my thesis and to prepare it for publication. Professor Duncan Tanner, School of History and Welsh History, University of Wales, Bangor, Dr Huw Walters, National Library of Wales, Aberystwyth and Principal W. Eifion

Powell, Coleg yr Annibynwyr, Aberystwyth, were all helpful in answering various queries as were the staff of the South Wales Miners' Library, Swansea. Mrs R. Atkin, Swansea, kindly loaned papers concerning her late father-in-law, the Revd Leon Atkin, without which I would have been unable to comment at all on his contribution to the question. Professor Gwilym H. Jones and the staff of the School of Theology and Religious Studies, University of Wales, Bangor, were constantly helpful and supportive, particularly during my year as Kirby-Laing Research Assistant. I owe much to my doctoral supervisor, Dr Densil Morgan, for his advice stretching back to my undergraduate days. *Mawr fy nyled, mwy fy niolch.* The editors of the Studies in Welsh History series have saved me from many errors of style and expression, and Professor Ralph Griffiths has been a particular encouragement as the book has been prepared for publication. My thanks are also due to the staff of the University of Wales Press who have steered the book to publication, particularly Ceinwen Jones and Liz Powell. These people have helped enormously to make the book what it is: my gratitude to them is immense. What remains, however, is mine, warts and all.

Finally, I must note my greatest debt which is to my family, without whose constant love, support and encouragement this work would never have seen the light of day. My father died while this book was being prepared for publication. Both he and my mother have always believed in me and my ability to a far greater degree than I have, their vision clouded by the greatest of virtues. For this, and for much more, I dedicate my book to my mother and to the memory of my father.

I

SETTING THE SCENE

The decline in Nonconformist numerical strength and social influence, together with the ascendancy of the Labour Party in national and local politics, are probably two of the most significant aspects of twentieth-century Welsh history. Both have affected the wider cultural, nationalistic and linguistic issues which have risen to prominence through the years. Both stem from a period when working men were challenged to support the Labour Party and break free from the chains of oppression which maintained the status quo, of which, it was alleged, the church was a major support. Ironically, the evidence in 1900 pointed, superficially at least, to an entirely different future, one in which Nonconformity, supported by a Liberal Party committed to preserve its interests, would go from strength to strength.

Nonconformity had achieved an unprecedented status in Welsh society during the nineteenth century. The religious revival of 1859 had brought many once more into its fold. But Nonconformist strength is not to be measured by the number of its adherents alone. C. R. Williams has claimed that 'religion probably exercised a greater influence on the lives of the people of Wales during the last century than was the case in England or in any other Protestant country'.[1] And that religion was largely Nonconformist. The influence of the chapel extended far beyond exclusively religious circles to society more generally, shaping the moral and political attitudes of whole communities.[2] This is not to say that the Anglican Church in Wales enjoyed no support, but, through its internal restrictions, it had been unable to take advantage of the population movement of the previous century-and-a-half. The result was a cautious and inward-looking polity

---

[1] C. R. Williams, 'The Welsh religious revival, 1904–5', *British Journal of Sociology*, III/3, (1952), 242; also R. Tudur Jones, *Ffydd ac Argyfwng Cenedl*, I, *Prysurdeb a Phryder* (Swansea, 1981), p.15.
[2] See Dai Smith, *Wales! Wales?* (London, 1984), pp.44–5; Gwyn A.Williams, *When Was Wales?* (London, 1985), pp.206–7.

which offered less theological and cultural variety than that of
Nonconformity.

It was perhaps Nonconformity's political influence and
allegiance that became most marked by the end of the nineteenth century. From cautious beginnings, the Nonconformists
developed an alliance with radical politics, which they viewed as
the only means to achieve not merely political goals but basic
rights. Writing in 1817, the Baptist minister and evangelist
Christmas Evans held that 'it is not the province of Christians to
debate and discuss politics but to behave humbly towards our
superiors'.[3] By mid-century this had been transformed in some
quarters into an almost seditious radicalism. David Rees,
Llanelli, writing in 1843, suggested that Robert Peel and his
Tory policies had directly caused the Rebecca riots. He called for
a mass agitation 'to petition the Queen to dismiss Peel and his
crew'.[4] As the nineteenth century passed, Nonconformity
became almost wholly identified with the Liberal Party, through
whose policies Nonconformist fears and grievances were
eventually allayed. When religious bodies used their influence in
order to ensure Liberal victory, this identification became
complete. The Monmouthshire Baptist Association in 1885 told
its members to 'be loyal to their consciences and to the Saviour
in the polling booth . . . and not to fail to record their votes in
favour of the Liberal candidates'.[5] David Rowlands (Dewi Môn)
told the Welsh Independents that 'our religious principles make
us of necessity Liberals in politics'.[6] D. Tecwyn Evans recalled
that as a boy almost all the children of his locality supported the
Liberal Party, while they believed that 'no-one but the Liberals
would go to heaven'.[7]

Nonconformists' support of the Liberal Party was not merely
the result of their social and political aspiration. They shared a
common ideology based on the importance of individual choice.
Nonconformist ecclesiology had depended on evangelical

---

[3] *North Wales Gazette*, 27 March 1817; quoted in Christopher B. Turner, 'Revivals and
popular religion in Victorian and Edwardian Wales' (Ph.D. thesis, University of Wales,
1979).
[4] David Rees, 'Gwleidiadaeth', *Y Diwygiwr* (1843), 288.
[5] Philip Jenkins, *A History of Modern Wales 1536–1990* (London, 1992), p.345; T. M.
Bassett, *Bedyddwyr Cymru* (Swansea, 1977), p.295.
[6] R. Tudur Jones, *Hanes Annibynwyr Cymru* (Swansea, 1966), p.274; Union of Welsh
Independents Reports, 1871–5, p.190.
[7] D. Tecwyn Evans, *Atgofion Cynnar* (Tywyn, 1950), p.24.

conversion and then individual decision to become part of a local congregation, the gathered church. The freedom to do this, both politically and in the theological sense of free will, was paramount in discussing churchmanship. Liberalism had seen this freedom in terms of the economy, the need to practise *laissez-faire*, and the consequent lack of government interference in any part of the life of the individual. R. H. Tawney argued that this kind of capitalism was a direct result of the Protestant Reformation when individual freedom and choice in a religious sense were transferred into social and economic fields. Although this had begun to change during the nineteenth century, and the Liberal government would introduce measures for social welfare such as Old Age Pensions in 1908, the so-called 'People's Budget' of 1909, and health and unemployment insurance in 1911, the Liberal Party continued to adhere to an anti-*Socialist* stance throughout the period here described. The relationship which existed between Liberal politics, on the one hand, and Nonconformist religion, on the other, was complex but intimate. This meant that as working men came to question the reality of freedom of choice in temporal concerns and to consider themselves as victims of social and economic structures, so too they questioned their ability to choose in religious matters.

The struggle for basic rights had characterized Nonconformity's witness since the days of the early Dissenters during the Reformation. It is hardly surprising that some within its ranks sought an identification with the oppressed in industrial society. The *Merthyr Express* could claim in 1885 that 'the history of Nonconformity is that of one long continuous fight of right against the oppressor'[8] and could do so without fear of contradiction. But 'oppression' would soon be interpreted in a more particularly social and political, rather than religious, sense. Socialist agitators such as Robert Blatchford and Keir Hardie toured south Wales in the 1890s expounding the class system which had been deepened by industrialization, and claimed that the oppressor was the capitalist who very often attended the same chapel as working men. It was how Nonconformists would deal with the advent of a highly vocal and

---

[8] *Merthyr Express*, 20 June 1885; quoted in W. R. Lambert, 'Some working class attitudes towards organized religion in nineteenth century Wales', *Llafur*, II/1 (1976), 4–5.

increasingly popular labour movement that would largely seal the fate of the chapels over the next few years. The success of the labour movement itself would be marked by the extent to which it could inculcate a class consciousness amongst the working men. This, possibly more than anything else, went against traditional Nonconformist ideology. The term 'working man' had been deemed unnecessary, Nonconformist ecclesiology being characterized by a classless *gwerin*, 'a country's residents of every grade and class'.[9] The word 'gwerin' reflected at best a prohibitive social moralism, one that required its adherents to recognize the fundamental equality of all men under God, and at worst a philosophy of denial. Such distinctions as existed in the mills and mines between owner, manager and workman, were not to be found in chapel meetings. Before the Great War, Nonconformists generally seemed to have accepted if not the propriety, at least the existence, of social and class distinctions in the world of industry and commerce. Their concern was that these distinctions should not enter the chapel. With such divisions becoming progressively sharper, especially as Socialist agitators advocated the doctrine of class war, it was only a matter of time before they impinged on chapel life itself. The *gwerin* did not officially constitute the working class, but there was a tendency in the work of some Socialists to make the two synonymous. The Revd T. E. Nicholas, Congregationalist minister at Glais in the Swansea valley and a leading Socialist agitator in the period 1904 to 1914, was perhaps the most notable example of this trend.

One of the most significant changes in attitude which occurred during the nineteenth century concerned the trade-union movement. In 1831 the Calvinistic Methodists, probably the most conservative of Welsh denominations, forbade their communicants to join trade unions.[10] But towards the end of the century individual ministers were encouraging the workers to fight for their rights by joining and strengthening a trade union. During the strike at the Brymbo steelworks in 1896, a meeting chaired by the Revd E. K. Jones passed a resolution pledging to support the trade-union cause as 'the best mode of improving the

[9] D. Wyre Lewis, 'Crist a'r werin', *Seren Gomer* (1920), 260.
[10] A. H. Dodd, *The Industrial Revolution in North Wales* (3rd edn., Cardiff, 1971), p.415.

moral and social conditions of its members'.[11] During the Penrhyn strike of 1900–3, Keinion Thomas advised the quarrymen to do the same as the south Wales miners, who were winning the day 'by forming a strong union'.[12] In 1900 Daniel Lleufer Thomas published a pamphlet which outlined the history of trade-unionism in Wales and he too recommended that the workers form strong trade unions, mainly in the belief that self-help alone would ensure social improvement.[13] Thus, some Nonconformists at least were attempting to keep up with social and industrial developments while also beginning to embrace ideologies and practices which had previously been considered anathema.

The advent of the labour movement coincided with scientific, philosophical and theological developments which would cast doubt on traditional Nonconformist mores and question the churches' adherence to Calvinistic theology. The 'higher criticism' was threatening the traditional view of the inspiration of scripture.[14] The popularity of Hegelian philosophy would have grave implications for theology, stressing as it did God's immanence, the general trend in history towards perfection and the ultimate unity of all reality. Darwin's theory of evolution questioned the validity of the creation narratives contained in the first and second chapters of the Book of Genesis. A sign of the times was the essay competition on the relationship of evolution to theology set in the 1893 National Eisteddfod, where David Adams and Ebenezer Griffith-Jones shared the first prize. Adams became the foremost exponent of Hegelian philosophy and Darwinian evolution in Welsh.[15] Griffith-Jones, who ministered for most of his life in England, published his Eisteddfod essay as *The Ascent Through Christ* (London, 1899), and the popularity of the subject was demonstrated by its run of nine editions in six

[11] Arthur Griffiths, 'B.I.S.A.K.T.A. in North Wales', in G. A. Hughes (ed.), *Men of No Property* (Caerwys, 1971), p.89.
[12] R. Tudor Jones, *Hanes*, p.273.
[13] D. Lleufer Thomas, *Labour Unions in Wales: Their Early Struggle for Existence* (Swansea, 1901), p.23.
[14] See W. Eifion Powell, 'Esboniadaeth Feiblaidd Ryddfrydol yng Nghymru', *Diwinyddiaeth*, XXV (1974), 29–39; also W. Nantlais Williams, *O Gopa Bryn Nebo* (Llandysul, 1967), pp.49–50; R. Tudor Jones, *Ffydd ac Argyfwng Cenedl*, II, *Dryswch a Diwygiad* (Swansea, 1982), pp.102–3.
[15] His essay was published as *Traethawd ar Ddatblygiad yn Ei Berthynas â'r Cwymp, yr Ymgnawdoliad a'r Atgyfodiad* (Caernarfon, 1893).

years.[16] As younger ministers were drawn towards social
concern, they looked to this new teaching to give it an ideological
basis.

With the religious revival of 1904–5 and the landslide Liberal
victory in 1906, Nonconformists generally assumed that their
dominance in national life was assured. Thus, they entered the
twentieth century in confident and optimistic mood, convinced
that they would achieve greater prestige and prominence in the
nation's life. In fact, these events foreshadowed the decline of
both. The recognition that they had very little political influence
would soon dawn on the Nonconformists, while the advent of the
labour and Socialist movements threatened to turn the masses
against them. All this offered a potentially damaging challenge to
the propriety of the theological, ecclesiological and social status
quo.

1. THE ADVENT OF SOCIALISM

The Socialist message, as proclaimed in the 1890s, threatened to
strike a blow at the very heart of Nonconformist culture. Not
only did it require Nonconformists to reappraise their political
allegiances, but it also challenged their traditional emphasis on
the importance and responsibility of the individual. Socialism's
compatibility with their religious faith was thus the most
important question facing Nonconformists, but it proved to be a
difficult one to answer due to the ambiguity surrounding the
term 'Socialism' even amongst its protagonists. Although the
term had first appeared in the *Cooperative Magazine* as early as
November 1827, its meaning had never been precisely defined
and by 1924 there were at least thirty-nine different definitions.
The original Socialists in the south Wales coalfield were
principally agitators fired by a semi-religious zeal for righteousness and dedicated to revealing the injustices of the industrial
system. They inspired the working-class imagination with a
vision of a better tomorrow. The provision of a definite economic
and political policy was consequently of secondary importance.
Where agreement existed, it chiefly concerned the replacement

---

[16] See R. Tudur Jones, *Congregationalism in England 1662–1962* (London, 1962),
pp.347–8.

of private ownership with collectivism and nationalization.[17] Despite this imprecision, Socialism offered the working class a cause akin to religion, yet one whose vision would bring social and material rather than specifically spiritual rewards. The term 'religion of Socialism' was in use by 1885,[18] while many of the early agitators drew on a store of imagery and language inherited from their religious upbringing.[19] They spread the 'good news', added 'converts' to the 'cause' and ensured that men underwent a 'conversion' to Socialist principles, thereby opening the way to its interpretation as a 'faith'. In order that the labour movement should be a force in politics, these agitators recognized the need to draw Nonconformists, with their traditions of political radicalism, away from the Liberal Party to the Socialist message. They set about achieving this by advocating Socialism more as a moral force than as a political and economic doctrine.[20]

The question was how far should such a 'religion of Socialism' go? Both Richard Whiteing and Fenner Brockway advocated Socialism as a secular and even semi-pagan religion. For Whiteing, Socialism was an all-consuming spirit in society whose expression required the development of a specifically Socialist art and literature as well as a Socialist church with its own cult which would be inaugurated by a Messianic figure yet to be born.[21] Fenner Brockway based his religion on certain moral doctrines which, he claimed, all Socialists held in common. These were the sanctity of human life in a society orientated towards service of human need, and the expansion of the individual self-consciousness into the 'whole-consciousness'.[22] Co-operation would replace competition, and fellowship, good-will and unity would replace the division and suspicion currently rampant in society.

There was something vaguely sinister about such quasi-religious spiritualizing. Whiteing's message in particular was characterized by fanaticism. Excesses apart, however, it seems

---

[17] A. J. Davies, *To Build a New Jerusalem* (London, 1992), p.32; Ronald Preston, *Church and Society in the Late Twentieth Century* (London, 1983), p.13.
[18] Leonard Smith, *Religion and the Rise of Labour* (Keele, 1993), pp.25, 83.
[19] G. Foote, *The Labour Party's Political Thought: A History* (London, 1985), pp.34–7, 52–6, passim.
[20] A. J. Davies, *New Jerusalem*, p.23.
[21] *Labour Leader*, 24 February 1911, p.116.
[22] Ibid., 30 April 1914, p.4; 7 May 1914, p.7.

that the early attraction of Socialism included its appeal as a faith or a religious spirit which could encompass all men, requiring that they be 'born again' through conversion to a higher morality and ideal, and then demanding their complete devotion. What authority was enlisted to support such assertions, apart from an appeal to consensus morality, is unclear. But the preaching of Socialism as a faith rather than an economic philosophy ensured that its mission would be understood if not as a cult, then at least as a spiritual or religious movement. To an extent, John Trevor's 'Labour Church' had already provided a cultic environment for Socialist ideology, but it was never strong outside Manchester and Bradford.[23] Some of its branches were established in south Wales, but it was never popular and had certainly disappeared by 1918.[24] This points to the probability that, for the Welsh, Socialism had to be perceived as being at least compatible with existing religious forms, and understood as being a natural outgrowth of chapel culture rather than a substitute for it. Welshmen required not so much an ideological definition but a language and strong personality to which they could relate. The irony of the nascent Socialist movement in Wales was that, while propagating a message which subordinated the individual's interests to those of society, its popularity depended almost exclusively on the strength of individuals.[25] It was the message of Keir Hardie which seemed more appropriate than any other for the working population of south Wales.

2. KEIR HARDIE

James Keir Hardie[26] founded the Independent Labour Party (ILP) in 1893 to promote working-class representation in Parliament. He was perhaps the most influential figure in industrial south Wales at the turn of the twentieth century, growing increasingly more popular than the native 'Lib-Lab' and

[23] Leonard Smith, *Religion*, p.93.
[24] Ibid., p.82; cf. Preston, *Church and Society*, p.13; K. S. Inglis, *Churches and the Working Classes in Victorian England* (London, 1963), p.221.
[25] A. J. Davies, *New Jerusalem*, p.5; Peter Stead, 'Working class leadership in south Wales 1900–20', *Welsh History Review*, VI/3 (1973), 352.
[26] For J. Keir Hardie (1856–1915), H. Hamilton-Fyfe, *Keir Hardie* (London, 1935); Kenneth O. Morgan, *Keir Hardie: Radical and Socialist* (London, 1975); G. Foote, *Political Thought*, pp.41–8, *passim*; Caroline Benn, *Keir Hardie* (London, 1992).

conciliatory miners' leaders such as the formidable William Abrahams (better known by his bardic name 'Mabon'). Hardie's call was emotive, prophetic and couched in a preaching style familiar to those brought up in the chapels. By emphasizing the moral dynamic of the Socialist message, Hardie set the religious tone characteristic of its early years.

> Socialism sets up a new standard of human relationships: it assumes the universal brotherhood of the race, and because the private ownership of the land and instruments of production, with its consequent outcome of class antagonism, stands in the way of the realisation of that brotherhood, therefore we demand that the entire system be swept away.[27]

Despite the religious imagery which characterized his speeches,[28] Hardie's connection with organized religion became increasingly tenuous. His conversion to evangelical Christianity in 1878 was soon followed by a rebellion against the hypocrisy which he perceived to be rife amongst professing Christians. He, like many others,[29] accused the church of preaching a dead faith, one which had not been allowed to affect social practice. From 1884 he ceased to attend church regularly. His name was linked with R. J. Campbell and the New Theology, and his religious views, though not identical with Campbell's, were certainly heterodox (see the next section). In fact, it appears that spiritualism, palmistry and astrology held more fascination for him than orthodox Christianity.[30] Nevertheless, by clothing his Socialism in religious garb he ensured that his message would be familiar to the working men of south Wales whose society was pervaded by chapel culture.

In his speeches Hardie applied the Christian moral dynamic to the specific economic context of an industrial society. He emphasized that the two fundamental aspects of both Christianity and Socialism were the Sermon on the Mount and the building of the Kingdom of God, though his interpretation of both aspects was more economic than theological. For him the

---

[27] *Merthyr Pioneer*, 23 April 1914, p.8.
[28] Cf. e.g. Emrys Hughes (ed.), *Keir Hardie: His Writings and Speeches* (Glasgow, 1928), p.84; J. Keir Hardie, *Can a Man Be a Christian on a Pound a Week?* (London, n.d.).
[29] E.g. *Llais Llafur*, 29 June 1907, p.1; 13 July 1907, p.4; 7 March 1909, p.7.
[30] Morgan, *Keir Hardie*, p.46.

Sermon on the Mount was a condemnation of private property, the existence of which diverted attention from 'life itself to the things of life'. Hardie advocated the abolition of private property through the establishment of a common store from which everyone could draw freely, and, as a result, live without anxiety for food and clothing. This, as far as Hardie was concerned, would usher in God's Kingdom.[31] Jesus, he said, was a member of the working class who had sought to raise men up from subservience, oppression and bondage. Obedience to his teaching would naturally establish Communism, as had already been seen in the life of the early church.[32] This revolutionary force had been obscured, however, by organized religion. Hardie's conclusion was that the church had departed from Christ's teaching and had thus prevented the establishment of a Christian form of Communism.

The Socialist message propagated by Hardie concentrated on the formative effect of environment on character.[33] Thus, working men living in slums and resorting to drunkenness and foul language were victims of evil rather than its perpetrators. As a result, Christianity's primary concern should have been the salvation of society and not the encouragement of individual morality. A corollary of this was Hardie's understanding of sin as a corporate phenomenon to the virtual exclusion of its individualist aspects, despite his emphasis on the responsibility of the Christian individual to the society in which he lived.

> . . . the Christian who professes the Christian faith is thereby under obligation to make whatever sacrifice may be necessary in order to remove sin, suffering and injustice from the lives of those around him . . . Make no mistake about this. The only way you can serve God is by serving mankind.[34]

Hardie did not merely advocate the embodiment of the principles of Jesus's teaching within the social system. He held that such a development was a necessary prerequisite for the creation of Christians. This was the natural consequence of his

---

[31] Hardie, *Can a Man Be a Christian?*, p.9.
[32] Ibid., p.8. He quoted Acts 4: 32–5 as proof of this.
[33] Ibid., pp.5, 9.
[34] Hughes (ed.), *Keir Hardie*, pp.141–2.

belief that environment formed character, but it subordinated the role of religion to that of the labour movement. Religion was a luxury that could only rightly be enjoyed after Socialism had done its work. It would not exist in a full sense until 'full, free communism' had been established.[35] Socialism, on the other hand, offered both an inspiring vision for the future and the sole means to achieve a better life. With the introduction of state ownership and the employment of labour in service of society's need, the working man would live a fulfilled life, rising 'towards that perfect manhood which is surely the goal of human existence'.[36]

Although many ordinary people listened avidly to his message, it was Hardie's personality and character which had the greatest impact upon them. Hardie's ability to convince the working class that he was 'on their side' was recalled vividly by Jack Jones many years later:

> 'Comrades', from his mouth that word fell charged with pity. At once he made closer contact with his audiences of Welsh-speaking miners than ever their own Welsh-speaking leaders had made. Twice, when only a boy of 14, did I hear him speak during the latter half of that six-month stoppage. Yet it seemed to me then that every word he spoke about the workers and their sufferings and struggles came from a bleeding heart, a heart that had always bled, would always bleed, for the suffering of mankind.[37]

Hardie certainly hit the right note with the working class of south Wales. His combination of Christianity's eschatological ideal with the challenge that it should be realized in the present, not only persuaded many working men that Socialism would lift them out of their bondage, but that through it Christianity would finally find a true embodiment. Whether we agree with Kenneth Morgan that Hardie had been able to 'translate socialist ethics into images of popular nonconformity'[38] or with Caroline Benn that Hardie had 'translated religious images into labour and socialist politics',[39] the effect was the same. His political message

[35] Quoted in Benn, Keir Hardie, pp.259–60.
[36] Hardie, Can a Man Be a Christian?, p.6.
[37] Jack Jones, Jack Jones' Unfinished Journey (London, 1937), p.86.
[38] Kenneth O. Morgan, 'The Merthyr of Keir Hardie', in Glanmor Williams (ed.), Merthyr Politics: The Making of a Working Class Tradition (Cardiff, 1966), p.67.
[39] Benn, Keir Hardie, p.261.

was made more accessible to Welshmen living and working in a
society dominated by chapel culture. More than anything else,
Hardie offered a new interpretation of religion which
emphasized social practice rather than belief in a definite creed
or particular intellectual formulation. While this inevitably
meant that some had 'left the Churches in order to become
Christians',[40] it also meant that for some time the labour
movement did not recognize the importance of formulating
specific economic policies.[41] Ultimately, his use of religious
imagery contributed to the chapel's loss of influence in the very
society whose values and standards it had largely formed. Some
men came to talk of Hardie in mysterious, heroic and almost
mystical terms. James Griffiths recalled that he looked like a
'prophet'.[42] W. J. Edwards, though convinced that he was 'one of
us', also saw him in the way in which 'the children of Israel must
have seen Moses; a prophet showing the way through an
industrial wilderness'.[43] These two men demonstrate the different
responses to Hardie's message which his critique of religion and
his particular presentation of Socialism made possible. Griffiths
and others were able to remain within the chapel, seeing the
labour movement as an essentially religious body whose goal was
the creation of an ideal society. W. J. Edwards for his part was
critical of the chapel and devoted his life to the labour movement, leaving organized religion behind.

Although completely honest and genuinely sympathetic with
the working class and their plight, Hardie was also an arch-
propagandist. There can be little doubt that he had great respect
for Jesus, but his Christ was a working-class saviour whose 'heart
beat in sympathy with the great human heart of the race'.[44] He
knew that religious talk was well received by working men reared
in the chapel. He knew, too, of the dramatic effect of an
apocalyptic sermon, or the call to establish the Kingdom of God
on earth. In fact, he used homely and familiar terms to convince
people that Socialism was the movement which deserved their
support. Typical of his rhetoric was the claim that in Socialism

[40] Address on 'Labour and Christianity', 5 May 1910, quoted in Benn, *Keir Hardie*, p.261.

[41] *Llais Llafur*, 18 July 1908, p.1; Morgan, *Keir Hardie*, p.290.

[42] James Griffiths, *Pages from Memory* (London, 1969), p.14.

[43] W. J. Edwards, *From the Valley I Came* (London, 1956), pp.90–1.

[44] Hardie, *Can a Man Be a Christian?*, p.12.

men 'may find . . . a realization of the meaning of the words they learned at their mother's knee when they were taught to pray, "Thy Kingdom come, thy will be done on earth as it is in Heaven" '.[45]

Following Hardie's election to Parliament by the people of Merthyr and Aberdare in 1900, Socialism was continually presented to the people of south Wales in religious terms, both in the imagery used and the loyalty demanded. Already the seed had been sown for the dissemination of Socialist ideas alongside unorthodox, if not heretical, theology inspired by an almost proletarian Jesus. Similar Christological developments were taking place in theology as the human, 'historical Jesus' became the subject of much contemporary biblical scholarship. The ministers who adopted this kind of theology tended also to develop social consciences, some of them becoming apologists for Socialism. Their very presence on Socialist platforms would encourage the tendency to present Socialism as a religious cause, with the implied assertion that its creed was neither atheistic nor would it lead to irreligion. Initially, at least, it was either non-Welsh ministers or those who had ministered to English pastorates who propagated Socialism. The brothers Ben and Stitt Wilson, for example, came from as far away as America to tour south Wales during 1909.[46] They were evangelists for Socialism, using specifically religious imagery to propagate their message. Thus, capitalism was the modern 'anti-Christ' and should be opposed, while obedience to Jesus's teaching made Socialism 'inevitable'.[47] Stitt frequently referred to Moses as the leader of the 'first great strike' of history, to the prophets as the critics of oppression and injustice, and to Christ's cross as 'a symbol of self-less devotion to men first, last and always, and to make them free and to deliver the world to righteousness'.[48] By accepting the status quo, both the churches and the mainstream political parties tolerated social injustice. As Socialism's primary concern was to secure for the working classes the benefits and produce of their toil, its 'unparalleled righteousness' was

---

[45] Ibid., p.6.
[46] Cf. T. Brennan, E. W. Cooney and H. Pollins, *Social Change in South West Wales* (London, 1954), p.149n.; also W. M. Davies, conversation with Hywel Francis, 4 October 1972, SWML; *Y Tyst*, 3 February 1909, p.9.
[47] *Llais Llafur*, 9 January 1909, p.8.
[48] *Aberdare Leader*, 19 December 1908, p.6.

assured.[49] Despite their weak theology the Wilsons, like Hardie, helped to relay the Socialist message as a cause akin to a religion. Although some young working men were initially impressed, the direct influence of the Wilson brothers was minimal. Even former devotees later came to see that 'there was a difference between the religion of Christ and the Wilsons' religion . . . I don't believe they were on the same line at all.'[50] For Hardie and those like him, however, Socialism was truly compatible with religious zeal and mission, even if that religion was unorthodox. This came to a head by 1907 in the 'New Theology' movement.

3. R. J. CAMPBELL, RHONDDA WILLIAMS AND THE 'NEW THEOLOGY'

Christian leaders were becoming increasingly concerned at the estrangement of certain classes from the church. On the one hand, there was the cultured or educated class, to which, it was suggested, the orthodox and Calvinistic interpretations of the faith had been a stumbling-block. On the other hand, there was the working class, which, it was claimed, had been frozen out by a largely middle-class respectability within the churches intent on maintaining the status quo. The 'New Theology' attempted to appeal to both groups. It was not an exclusively Nonconformist phenomenon, there being 'new theologians' in most communions,[51] but its most important interpreters for Wales and for the labour movement in general were the Bradford-based Congregationalist minister, the Revd Thomas Rhondda Williams,[52] and the Revd R. J. Campbell[53] of the City Temple in London, one of the foremost Nonconformist pulpits in the country. On account of his status and extraordinary charisma, it was Campbell who became the movement's principal spokesman.[54] His book, published under the unsurprising title, *The New*

---

[49] *Rhondda Leader*, 23 January 1909, p.5.

[50] W. M. Davies, conversation.

[51] See R. J. Campbell, *The New Theology* (London, 1907), pp.13–14; K. W. Clements, *Lovers of Discord: Twentieth Century Theological Controversies* (London, 1988), pp.37–8.

[52] For Thomas Rhondda Williams (1860–1945), see his autobiography, *How I Found My Faith* (London, 1938); *Bywg.*, p.62.

[53] For R. J. Campbell (1867–1956), see Clements, *Lovers of Discord*, pp.19–48; Keith Robbins, 'The spiritual pilgrimage of the Rev. R. J. Campbell', *Journal of Ecclesiastical History*, XX/2 (1979), 261–76.

[54] See Clements, *Lovers of Discord*, p.27; Williams, *How I Found My Faith*, pp.92, 96.

Theology, appeared in 1907 and plunged Campbell deeper into a controversy surrounding his alleged heretical interpretation of the Christian faith. Campbell's book intentionally demonstrated the attraction of his ideas for Socialists. His New Theology claimed that 'the religion of Jesus is primarily a gospel for this life and only secondarily for the life to come' (p.256). For Campbell, God was the source of life and sin was selfishness. Accordingly, atonement was interpreted as man's recognition of his oneness with God and the consequent encouragement to self-sacrifice for the good of the whole (p.177). All this undoubtedly appealed to some theorists in the Socialist movement who sought a connection with organized Christianity. In Wales, and to working-class audiences, it was the more populist stance which was required in order to influence men. Campbell condemned modern society unequivocally. Its slums and sweat-dens were un-Christian, while it was pervaded with the anti-social ideals of selfishness, cruelty and injustice (pp.251–2). The social system had to be destroyed and replaced with a better one (p.253). Campbell had claimed that his theology was 'the religious articulation of the social movement' (p.14), and he offered a vocal and enthusiastic support of Socialism which would inevitably get him noticed.

It would be a mistake, however, to view the New Theology as a Socialist message in religious garb. It was a redefinition of Christian religion according to the tenets of Hegelian philosophy, emphasizing the immanence of God in the creation, a recognition of the moral value of Jesus as the perfect man, and the evolutionary process of history culminating in the perfecting and ultimate unity of the whole creation. The stress on morality and on unity would lead naturally into a discussion of society and a condemnation of the economic and industrial system along with the injustice and division which had arrived in its wake. Both Campbell and Williams had adopted Idealistic Monism as the philosophical basis of their world-view. This was accompanied by the popular assumption that orthodox Christian doctrine offended the intellect of modern man (p.9). The League for Progressive Thought and Social Service was established in June 1908 for 'people who desired to unite for spiritual fellowship on Liberal Religious lines and to help in the bringing about of a better social order'. R. J. Campbell was elected

President.[55] Some branches were set up in Wales[56] and there is evidence of theological differences causing divisions and even splits in some chapels at this time.[57] The Progressive Theology Leagues seem to have had a short life-span, however, and although their arrival was heralded with some publicity, their attraction quickly waned. This points to the fact that Campbell won very few supporters for his theology in Wales.[58] Even at the height of his popularity it seems that most of his meetings were not particularly well attended.[59] Those Nonconformist ministers who were sympathetic to his views tended either to support the need for the chapel to be involved in leading the labour movement, or concurred with the call for a wholesale reinterpretation of theology on liberal lines. T. E. Nicholas, Glais, and Herbert Morgan, London, were of the first opinion and John Morgan Jones, later Principal of the Bala-Bangor Theological College, of the latter. Few, if any, swallowed his ideas wholesale. Some critics resorted to personal vilification and called for his excommunication as a heretic.[60] The wider implications of Campbell's theology were rightly identified as a challenge to orthodoxy.[61] His system robbed God of personality, making him a divine presence within creation. Christ lost his divinity, becoming simply the man who had lived the perfectly moral and consequently divine life, demonstrating 'what we can potentially be'.[62] Sin seemed to lose its eternal and terrible significance, being reduced to mere selfishness; indeed, it was even transmuted into 'a quest for God, although a blundering one'.[63] Ironically, Campbell's popularity stemmed from his association with the ILP and the call for social reform, but

---

[55] *Llais Llafur*, 20 February 1909, p.7.

[56] There were branches at Gwauncaegurwen, *Llais Llafur*, 10 July 1909, p.4; Swansea, Cardiff, Treorchy and Tonypandy, *Glamorgan Free Press*, 29 January 1909, p.5; Colwyn Bay, *Glamorgan Free Press*, 13 August 1909, p.2.

[57] *Aberdare Leader*, 7 November 1908, p.4; *Glamorgan Free Press*, 22 January 1909, p.5.

[58] *Llais Llafur*, 14 May 1910, p.1; *Glamorgan Free Press*, 22 January 1909, p.2; *Y Goleuad*, 17 April 1907, p.4; 1 April 1908, p.4.

[59] *Y Goleuad*, 1 April 1908, p.4; 23 September 1908, p.5; 23 December 1908, p.4; 7 April 1909, p.4.

[60] 'Adolygiad y mis: y Dduwinyddiaeth Newydd', *Y Greal* (1907), 54; D. Powell, 'Duw y Dduwinyddiaeth Newydd', *Y Greal* (1908), 57; 'O.E.', 'Nodiadau misol: Mr Campbell a'i feirniaid', *Y Dysgedydd* (1907), 234.

[61] J. Lewis Williams, 'Diffygion y Ddiwinyddiaeth Newydd', *Y Geninen* (1908), 145; Hugh Jones, 'Y Ddiwinyddiaeth Newydd', *Yr Eurgrawn* (1907), 112–13.

[62] Campbell, *New Theology*, p.93.

[63] Ibid., p.161.

Nonconformist criticism was exclusively doctrinal rather than politically motivated.

Although it appears that Campbell did influence some individuals significantly,[64] this was more the result of his friendship with Keir Hardie and his identification with the labour movement than any deep resonance with his theological stance. It was his belief in Socialism as the 'practical application of the Sermon on the Mount'[65] rather than his more developed theology which caught the attention of some Welshmen. James Griffiths, later MP for Llanelli, recalled that his own conversion to Socialism occurred at a meeting in Pant-teg chapel, Ystalyfera, addressed by Campbell.[66] Tickets had been advertised in *Llais Llafur* several weeks before this meeting and were sold out within days. Campbell had thus achieved sufficient popularity, or probably notoriety, to fill Pant-teg chapel with people eager to hear first-hand his 'New Theology' and his message for contemporary society. The labour press tended to emphasize Campbell's successes and this meeting received considerable coverage in the *Llais*. Denominational papers, on the other hand, were keen to denigrate Campbell's ideas and recorded meetings at which the attendance had been low. In both cases it is difficult to draw any firm conclusions about the extent of Campbell's influence at this time. Griffiths was certainly persuaded in part by Campbell's extraordinary appearance, which gave the impression that the youthful minister was a 'seer'. But it was Campbell's Socialist message which he recalled and not his theology. In his address, 'The Socialist's Ideal', Campbell had claimed that Jesus definitely taught Socialism and that consequently contemporary Socialists sought the same goal as the religion of Christ, namely to establish the Kingdom of God on earth.[67] Campbell called on Nonconformity to 'cut itself loose' from the Liberal Party and apply Christian ethics to the social order, or else lose contact with the working class.[68] For the rest of his life, Griffiths claimed to

---

[64] W. C. Thomas, Gwaelod y Garth, conversation with David Egan, 9 July 1973, SWML; W. M. Davies, conversation; Huw Walters, *Canu'r Pwll a'r Pulpud* (Denbigh, 1987), pp.233ff.

[65] *Llais Llafur*, 30 August 1907, p.4; 30 March 1907, p.4; 10 August 1907, p.3.

[66] Ibid., 2 May 1908, p.5.

[67] Ibid., 16 May 1908, pp.2, 4.

[68] Griffiths, *Pages*, p.14.

adhere to the tenets of the New Theology, though in reality his was a vague, social religion, which fell far short of an espousal of Campbell's philosophical doctrines. Griffiths viewed Campbell solely as a preparation for Hardie.

Another Socialist pioneer, S. O. Davies, initially intended to train for the Congregational ministry. He defined the religion of Christ in terms similar to those of Campbell, and on being called by the council of the Memorial College, Brecon, to give an account of his beliefs, it transpired that he had adopted the tenets of class warfare. It was not so much the heresies of Campbell as Davies's preaching of violent revolution from the pulpits of south Wales chapels which led to his expulsion from the College.[69]

Despite receiving much attention in the national and local press at the time, it seems that Campbell's significance in the development of Socialism lay in his support of the labour movement, giving it a spiritual gloss. He should be seen as the exponent of the most recent philosophical developments, taking them to their logical conclusion. Some individuals were probably able to remain within the chapels because of his teaching, only to find their social vision encouraged and renewed in the labour movement. But in emphasizing both Monism and the need for social reform, Campbell eased the way for men to leave the chapel completely as they increasingly regarded it as an irrelevance to their lives. Campbell had always claimed that the labour movement needed a spiritual element[70] but what he and others like him had actually achieved was to allow men to find that element within a secular movement, to think of themselves as Christians without having to be chapel-goers.[71] At the same time, his espousal of heterodox theology militated against the nascent labour movement's winning wide support from the ranks of Nonconformist ministers in Wales. Socialism's call for social justice and better conditions for ordinary people was undoubtedly popular, but the New Theology was never recognized as being its necessary partner. It seems that R. J. Campbell and the New Theology played only a minor role in the history of the labour movement in south Wales.

[69] Robert Griffiths, *S. O. Davies: A Socialist Faith* (Llandysul, 1983), p.29.

[70] Campbell, *New Theology*, p.14.

[71] Edgar Evans, conversation with Dai Smith and Hywel Francis, 14 July 1973, SWML; also *Glamorgan Free Press*, 2 April 1909, p.3; *Llais Llafur*, 11 July 1908, p.6.

Rhondda Williams was more important than R. J. Campbell in the initial promotion of Socialism in Wales. He regularly visited south Wales in 1907–8, although his direct influence was also probably minimal. Regarded as a 'local boy made good', he was the minister of a thriving Yorkshire congregation, author of several books, and well known within his denomination as well as beyond it. Wales could be proud of him, even if his theology was heterodox.[72]

Williams had progressed from orthodox evangelical theology towards the 'New Theology' independently of, and earlier than, R. J. Campbell. Though not as intellectually astute as Campbell, he was an emotive preacher whose pulpit style could catch his congregation's imagination. This is evident from the report of a meeting which he addressed in 1907.

> . . . the time had passed when the Church of Christ should rely solely upon conversion. (hear hear). It was not sufficient to 'pluck the brand from the burning;' they wanted to put out the fire. (Loud applause). It was not sufficient to act the Good Samaritan; it was their duty to catch the robbers, otherwise the wounded men would speedily increase. (hear hear). The best type of Socialists were religious. The main note of the Socialistic movement today was an ethical note. (hear hear).[73]

Williams had been a minister in Dowlais and Neath before moving to Bradford in 1888. It was there that his 'social conscience' had been truly awakened. Hitherto, religion for him had been 'a personal, individual thing concerned only with saving the soul', which meant life after death, but thereafter he came to see individual salvation as being impossible without social salvation.[74] The worst sins of his day he deemed to be socialized sins, and it was only on social lines that the gospel would reach the masses.[75]

Before entering the ministry, Williams had been a miner and was naturally drawn to the labour movement,[76] and although never a member he took an interest in the ILP from its inception.

---

[72] *Y Goleuad*, 10 March 1909, p.4; *Seren Cymru*, 6 March 1908, p.4.
[73] *Llais Llafur*, 23 March 1907, p.5.
[74] Williams, *How I Found My Faith*, pp.23, 29.
[75] *Llais Llafur*, 23 March 1907, p.5; 7 November 1906, p.7.
[76] Williams, *How I Found My Faith*, p.8.

During his visits to south Wales he addressed meetings under the auspices of the local ILP but, unlike Campbell, he was also invited to address church gatherings of local Congregationalists. His message was always the same. Socialism and Christianity were similar in ideal and outlook. Socialism was not irreligious as its aim was the establishment of a brotherhood in which private property was replaced with collective ownership. Co-operation would replace competition, as competition was inimical to the spirit of brotherhood. Thus, although Socialism as an economic doctrine could not be found in the New Testament, there could be no doubt that Christianity led to Socialism as the establishment of universal brotherhood was an inevitable consequence of following Jesus's example.[77] Economic Socialism was, for Williams, the 'proper embodiment of the Christian moral and spiritual ideal'.[78] As a Hegelian, Williams believed that the eventual establishment of a new society was the assured result of inevitable progress. As the world was evolving towards perfection, revolution was unnecessary. It was also dangerous as it tampered with the eternal order. The church's role in this scheme was one of service, as a firm moral and spiritual force in society. Credal systems were unnecessary and unimportant for 'doing the truth ensures the best doctrine of the truth'. The church's mission was to lead individuals towards the 'spiritual life', but also to oppose all environmental factors which hindered its achievement. The spirit of Christ should be embodied in society, enabling men to attain 'the best of which they are capable'.[79] In order to achieve this, individuals still needed to be converted from selfishness to selflessness,[80] which would result in the social embodiment of the spirit of brotherhood. Quite what would provide the dynamic for such a conversion is unclear, although it would seem reasonable to suppose that it would be evoked by his own version of Socialist Christianity. The church's role was not to be overtly political but to be a moral one. It should attempt to produce 'energetic workers for social justice'.[81] But social reconstruction would require state intervention and

[77] *Llais Llafur*, 23 March 1907, p.5; 20 June 1908, pp.2, 5, 8; 27 June 1908, p.6.
[78] *Merthyr Express*, 9 January 1909, p.5.
[79] *Llais Llafur*, 31 October 1908, p.8.
[80] *Aberdare Leader*, 9 January 1909, p.6.
[81] *Llais Llafur*, 27 June 1908, p.6.

not merely individual regeneration.[82] As the Socialist agenda alone promoted this, Williams hoped that even if the churches found themselves in disagreement they would not oppose it.

The greatest criticism of both Williams and Campbell is that although they appealed to the right of the individual conscience, they were unable to see that other individual consciences could come to conclusions vastly different from their own. Their warning that Socialism was becoming too popular to resist was valid. However, their total acceptance of both philosophical Idealism and Socialism had led them into a naïve belief that evolutionary improvement was integral to the structure of the universe; that, in turn, brought them into conflict with those whose consciences were free from dependence on the current philosophical trends. Williams, like Campbell, met with some opposition which centred on his theological heterodoxy and on his vocal and energetic support of Socialism, which was widely regarded at the time to be materialistic and anti-Christian in tendency. He was, on occasion, refused permission to use chapels for his meetings, while the attendance at many of them was not particularly high.[83]

Williams was undoubtedly a 'New Theologian' in the sense that God's immanence, man's moral duty and ever-onward progress towards perfection were central to his thinking. Yet his addresses at this time virtually always concerned the propagation of Socialism and social reform. Although he encouraged Christians to support Socialism, very rarely did he encourage Socialists to support Christianity. He affirmed Christianity's commitment to social reform, but did so in order to promote the ideals of Socialism *per se* rather than to formulate a distinct social Christianity. Socialism coexisted with Liberal Theology, as both stemmed from the most modern developments in social, political and religious thought, but they did not necessarily lead to each other, certainly not in the common mind. Nevertheless, the close association of Socialism with New Theologians undoubtedly prevented its more general acceptance amongst ministers at this time. Campbell and Williams were extremists and as such were

[82] Ibid., 23 March 1907, p.5.
[83] For problems experienced at Gwauncaegurwen, Garnant and Ammanford, *Llais Llafur*, 12 June 1908, p.8; for problems at Ferndale, *Glamorgan Free Press*, 22 January 1909, p.5.

probably stumbling-blocks for more orthodox Nonconformists. Their theology was never popular and their significance, such as it was, lay in the fact that, as ministers, they were willing to support the Socialist cause. Their 'social Christianity' was merely a Socialist message clothed in philosophical and religious garb. For them Socialism and Christianity had become synonymous. As a result they had little to offer from a specifically Christian standpoint.

4. CHRISTIANITY, SOCIALISM AND THE 'GWERIN'

One of the problems thus far was that, despite its apparent popularity, particularly in the south Wales coalfield, and despite the validating air of religiosity which surrounded it, Socialism could still be seen as a foreign import, something which was not Welsh and did not belong to Wales.[84] Hardie was deemed dubious by some because he was Scottish.[85] Campbell and his New Theology may have been appropriate to London, but they were out of touch with Welsh traditions and culture.[86] Rhondda Williams was criticized even by his supporters for failing to address them in their native tongue.[87] Even the Welsh word most commonly used, *Sosialaeth*, was generally considered a corruption derived from the English. *Cymdeithasiaeth*[88] had been attempted and occasionally *Cymundebaeth* or *Cymrodiaeth*[89] were used, but they never found popular favour.[90]

To combat this attitude, it was considered imperative by some Welsh Socialists that they make the movement instinctively and historically Welsh. A Socialist thread was claimed to run through Welsh history, its ideals supported by famous Welshmen whose memory was held dear by Nonconformists and the *gwerin*.[91] That this argument often went too far is evident from one claim that

---

[84] 'Dewi', 'Socialism—Can it succeed in south Wales?', *The Monthly Democrat* (1912), 45.
[85] W. F. Phillips, 'Y Ddraig Goch ynte'r Faner Goch? Sosialaeth a Chenedlaetholdeb', *Y Geninen* (1911), 254–5; *Aberdare Leader*, 8 September 1906, p.4.
[86] *Rhondda Leader*, 25 April 1908, p.7; 3 October 1908, p.2; Edward Foulkes, 'Sosialaeth', *Y Geninen* (1908), 21–5, *passim*.
[87] *Llais Llafur*, 20 June 1908, p.5.
[88] E.g. ibid., 29 September 1906, p.1; 15 December 1906, p.7.
[89] E.g. *Y Goleuad*, 23 August 1911, p.10.
[90] Foulkes, 'Sosialaeth', p.21; Kenneth O. Morgan, *Wales in British Politics 1868–1922* (Cardiff, 1991), p.212.
[91] E.g. *Labour Leader*, 12 September 1912, p.594.

Lloyd George himself was a Socialist, a claim sure to be rejected by professing Socialists and Liberals alike. More likely candidates were Henry Richard, Samuel Roberts, 'Gwilym Hiraethog' and Michael D. Jones, all of whom were called on from time to time to show how the Welsh spirit had been evolving in a Socialist direction. Although Robert Owen and Robert Jones Derfel had remained on the periphery of Welsh Nonconformist culture, their ideas were often presented to demonstrate that, far from being a foreign import, Socialism was a home-grown product.[92] It was the nationalist R. J. Derfel[93] who had published the first Socialist articles in Welsh. These appeared in *Y Cymro* and *Llais Llafur* between 1892 and 1903, while the *Merthyr Pioneer* later published articles assessing his contribution.[94] Although his argument was principally economic, seeking a just distribution of wealth according both to the need and contribution of each person, he also spoke of Socialist goals in moral and emotive terms. 'In short', he wrote, 'Socialism is freedom, equality and brotherhood; labour, wealth, bliss; cooperation, annexation (*cyfeddiant*), common pleasure (*cydfwynhad*), love, service, sacrifice, justice.'[95]

Although Derfel had at one time been an assistant preacher with the Baptist denomination, his initial attempts to synthesize his Christianity with Socialism proved fruitless, and he consequently abandoned religious practice altogether. This only exacerbated the concern of the chapels that Socialism led inevitably to irreligion. Wales needed someone who could root Socialism firmly in the radical traditions of a specifically Welsh Nonconformity.

[92] J. Lewis Williams, 'Y Sosialist Cymreig', *Y Dysgedydd* (1912), 258.
[93] For R. J. Derfel (1824–1905), see *DWB*, p.168; T. E. Nicholas, 'Beirdd Cymru beth am danynt?', *Y Geninen* (1913), 242; idem, 'R. J. Derfel', *Y Geninen Gŵyl Dewi* (1912), 23–4; idem, 'R. J. Derfel: y Gwrthryfelwr Cymreig', *Y Geninen Gŵyl Dewi* (1914), 59–62; Islwyn ap Nicholas, *R. J. Derfel* (London, 1945); D. James Jones (Gwenallt) (ed.), *Detholiad o Ryddiaith Gymraeg R. J. Derfel* (Denbigh, 1945); idem (ed.), *Detholiad o Ryddiaith Gymraeg R. J. Derfel*, II (Llandysul, 1945).
[94] E.g. *Merthyr Pioneer*, 7 October 1911, p.3; 14 October 1911, p.7; 21 October 1911, p.3; 9 December 1911, p.3; 16 December 1911, p.3.
[95] *Merthyr Pioneer*, 9 December 1911, p.3.

5. DAVID THOMAS

It was David Thomas of Talysarn, Gwynedd,[96] who came closest
during these years to achieving the required synthesis between
Socialism and the Welsh spirit. He was probably the most
important Welsh Socialist interpreter and activist of his generation. Although Socialism had not gained as much ground in
north Wales as it had in the south, of the nine ILP branches that
existed in 1910 six had been founded by Thomas.[97] Like Hardie,
his religious affiliation had been tenuous for many years. Despite
having been raised a Wesleyan and having commenced circuit
preaching, he increasingly found that the credal basis of his
church was incompatible with scientific and philosophical
advances. This led him to resign his membership and thereafter
his attendance at worship was at best infrequent. He only
resumed attendance when it became clear that orthodoxy would
no longer be measured in terms of creed but of actions. His
reason for seeking readmission to membership was that 'the
Church is the most suitable society for me to circulate my
principles'. Those principles were undeniably those of the Socialist movement. Despite this, the moral dimension of his Socialism
cannot be denied and the Welsh Radical Nonconformist heritage
is plain to see. Thomas fervently believed that Socialism not only
needed to express itself in Welsh but also needed to be 'saturated
with the history and traditions of the Welsh democracy'. His
contribution became especially effective with the publication of
the most clear and thorough appraisal of Socialism in Welsh to
date, *Y Werin a'i Theyrnas* (The *Gwerin* and its Kingdom) in 1910.[98]
  The book is divided into three sections. The first, 'Tywyllwch
ein Teyrnas' (The Darkness of our Kingdom), described the
economic and social conditions of the day and advocated
Socialism as the solution to the country's ills. It included a
graphic account of overcrowding and slum life (pp.15–31)[99] and
blamed poverty on the unfair distribution of wealth (p.71).

[96] For David Thomas, see his autobiography *Diolch am Gael Byw: Rhai o f'Atgofion*
(Liverpool, 1968); Ben Bowen Thomas (ed.), *Lleufer y Werin: Cyfrol Deyrnged i David Thomas
M.A.* (Caernarfon, 1965).
[97] Cf. Deian Hopkin, 'Y werin a'i theyrnas—ymateb Sosialaeth i Genedlaetholdeb
1880–1920', in Geraint H. Jenkins (ed.), *Cof Cenedl VI* (Llandysul, 1989), p.172.
[98] Caernarfon, 1910.
[99] Cf. David Thomas, 'Hawliau Sosialaeth ar grefyddwyr', *Yr Eurgrawn* (1911), 262–3.

Thomas claimed that labour, as the producer of wealth, was the most vital part of the economic system. The working class consequently deserved a fairer share of the fruits of their efforts (pp.57–8). Thomas advocated the formation of unions amongst the workers in order to combat the strength of the capitalists and their combines (pp.11–12). Virtually half the book described the current situation in which the government was at fault for keeping the masses in thraldom and poverty. The influence of both capitalism and privilege had enslaved the workers to money ('Y Llo Aur') and, as a result, the masses ought to control the government and institute reform. Change, however, should only be sought through education and effort and not by revolution (p.126).

The second section, 'Goleuni yn y Tywyllwch' (Light in the Darkness), discussed some organizations established to promote a better, more just society, 'inspiring men to work towards the dawn of that better age which can be discerned by the eyes of faith alone' (p.156). While isolated measures had already emerged, Thomas argued that a new system based on the higher ideals of justice, fairness, co-operation and brotherhood was needed (p.172). He advocated nationalization of the land and of major industries, including coalmining and slate-quarrying, and also nationalization of the railways (pp.238–44). The net result would be of benefit not to individuals but to society as a whole (p.245).[100] It becomes apparent in this section that Thomas's Socialism was not merely economic: it had a moral aspect (p.87). He believed that it was valid to judge every social movement by the kind of people it produced; thus Socialism's purpose was 'to produce as many men and women as possible of full stature, shining eyes and happy heart' (p.260).

The final section, 'Toriad y Wawr' (The Break of the Dawn), was a presentation of theoretical Socialism and an appeal to readers to join the ILP. Thomas claimed that the nationalization of the Post Office was merely the first step on the road to fuller socialization (p.320). He had previously used religious imagery in support of economic change, but here he began to refer to Socialism itself in specifically religious terms. Even his choice of titles indicated his belief that Socialism was something more than

[100] Cf. ibid., p.263.

an economic policy. The apocalyptic battle is echoed in the use of the terms 'darkness' and 'light', while the eschatological hope is reflected in the phrase 'break of the dawn'. In this final section he referred to Socialism as the 'total devotion to some cause greater than ourselves whose aim is to drive the human race upwards' (p.333). It was to be born in men's hearts, 'The Kingdom of Socialism is within you' (p.340). The purpose of Socialism was to breed and nourish 'the principles of brotherly love and sociability'. It seems to take the form of a primordial plan which has a place for all men and all creeds. For Thomas, Christianity should be considered as a movement within Socialism working for Socialist ends. Religion, if not productive of Socialism, becomes almost superfluous, a nice addition to life but otherwise irrelevant. Although the teaching of Jesus had instilled in many the desire to see a fair society in which peace and co-operation were maintained, Christianity could never in itself be enough. It could only work in a perfect system which Socialism alone was able to create.

Like the other Socialist agitators, Thomas aimed at least some of his remarks at those who professed religion. He believed that Socialism and religion were patently compatible, despite some misunderstandings among certain religious leaders. Although they were separate movements, operating within different spheres of life, they shared the common aim of 'promoting and improving mankind'. Their difference was more one of method than of substance.[101] For him, the churches had been neglecting their responsibilities. Believing that they had fulfilled their responsibility towards the poor, they had restricted their contribution to distributing charity. But Christianity demanded more than that. It involved the creation of a society in which charity would become superfluous, and the building of which would call for a great sacrifice (pp.9–10).

Because of this similarity of purpose, Socialism could justly be described in religious terms through the use of biblical phrases and imagery. Socialism averred that society as a whole was responsible for every individual within it, a principle taught by the Apostle Paul who claimed that we are all 'members of one

---

[101] Ibid., p.262.

another'.[102] The establishment of Socialism would herald a golden age, even a new heaven and a new earth. In that day, he claimed, violence and destruction would be things of the past:

nation will not lift sword against nation, and they will learn war no more. 'For as the earth makes its grass grow and as a garden makes its seeds take root, so the Lord will make justice and praise issue forth from all the nations.'[103]

It was the moral argument more than any other that linked Socialism and Christianity. Thomas called on all who professed Christianity to study social problems and to give a fair hearing to any plan which sought their removal. Socialism, however, had a greater hold on Christianity than on any other political or economic movement because it promoted fairness and justice.

I believe that it is Christian work to abolish a system which teaches people to measure the value of a man according to the total of his wealth, and compels men to be merciless towards each other instead of inculcating in them mutual and fraternal cooperation.[104]

Thomas argued that both Jesus and the Old Testament prophets had preached some of the principles of Socialism. The prophets had condemned social sins while Jesus had shown that men should be judged by the quality of their service and not their riches, for the Kingdom of God would be established through mutual love. The communalism of the Book of Acts, which had been accepted as valid for the life of the early church, went much further than the Socialist programme of nationalization.[105] However, it was the church itself which had so often betrayed Christianity. Instead of trying to ensure decent housing for the poor, a living wage for the worker and every man's right to work, the churches were concentrating far too much on such inconsequential matters as disestablishment and Sabbath observance.[106]

---

[102] Ibid., p.263. See Ephesians 4: 25.
[103] *Y Werin a'i Theyrnas*, p.143.
[104] 'Hawliau Sosialaeth ar grefyddwyr', p.265.
[105] Acts 2: 44; 4: 32; see David Thomas, 'A yw crefyddwyr yn Wrth-Sosialaidd?', *Yr Eurgrawn* (1912), 15.
[106] Ibid., p.18.

David Thomas's contribution to the propagation of Socialism is particularly important as his main aim was to make Socialism Welsh and therefore acceptable especially to the Welsh-speaking population of his native Gwynedd. To this end, he called a meeting at the National Eisteddfod in Carmarthen in 1911 to discuss the possibility of forming a Welsh Labour Party.[107] Those who attended included ministers such as T. E. Nicholas, Herbert Morgan, D. D. Walters and W. D. Roderick, while Gwilym Davies, J. Edryd Jones, John Jenkins (Gwili), W. Rowland Jones and R. Silyn Roberts expressed an interest but were unable to attend.[108] Although convened during the progressively bitter industrial unrest ripping through south Wales at the time and in spite of the level of interest which it engendered, the meeting achieved virtually nothing. Socialism was to be associated increasingly with progress and the English language whilst the Welsh language, especially in the valleys of the industrial south, became identified with the Nonconformist and Liberal past.

6. CONCLUSIONS

Although these men were not the sole contemporary protagonists of Socialism, there being no lack of more materialistic propaganda, it was their emphasis on its moral nature that made their contribution vital to the conversion of Welsh Liberal Nonconformist working men. Their affirmation that Socialism's duty was the formation of the brotherhood of man led to the belief amongst the working class that the adoption of Socialism would lead to a transformation in both society and personal relationships. Socialism's goal was not merely to improve social conditions but to offer the gift of life 'in all its fulness'. In the language which they used, Socialist apologists tried to demonstrate a basic similarity between their message and the Christian gospel. This ultimately posed a threat to the institutional church for it was a secular organization, the labour movement, which was promoted as the chief means to fulfilling Jesus's commands.

The direct effect which these agitators had on their audiences differed markedly. Hardie certainly wielded a great influence

---

[107] Cf. Deian Hopkin, 'Y Werin', pp.165–6.
[108] *Labour Leader*, 18 August 1911, p.522.

and his specifically moral interpretation of the Socialist message was echoed time and again, by no one more enthusiastically than David Thomas. It is unlikely that their intention was to see the labour movement replace organized religion entirely, though for some this was the logical conclusion of accepting the 'religion of Socialism' interpreted more as a moral creed than as an economic doctrine. The consequent ambiguity surrounding Socialism's relationship to organized religion certainly did not help the church to come to any firm conclusions about the nascent labour movement. Socialism was held to embody the spirit of religion both in its divine commission and in its ethical and practical aims. It gave expression to the highest morality and ideals. Yet it was claimed that Socialism was greater than individual religions. It was an all-embracing spirit which transcended human divisions, appealing alike to men of any religion and to men of none. Its moralistic content led agitators to contend that Socialist policy had a particular hold on the Christian religion and this led many into challenging professing Christians over the social implications of their faith. Keir Hardie, the Wilsons, R. J. Campbell, Rhondda Williams and David Thomas all used this challenge in their speeches. In the case of Hardie and Thomas, this was done in the context of an indistinct religious allegiance and certainly irregular appearances at Sunday worship.

As it was presented to the people of south Wales, Socialism promoted the elevation of man to a central position, with little or no place for the divine. Man could control his own destiny and thus was able to achieve the perfect state through the evolutionary process. Socialists were heard to mutter, 'God helps those who help themselves', and that, in grasping its opportunity, labour would work 'in accordance with God's wishes for man's evolution to a higher plane'.[109] Through the efforts of Keir Hardie and the Socialist ministers, the cause of the ordinary Welsh working man was inextricably linked to an understanding of Socialism. Such an understanding was invariably vague, relying to a greater extent on emotional response than on rational argument, but it appealed to many who sought a religious authority for their political beliefs and social aspirations.

[109] *Merthyr Pioneer*, 21 October 1911, p.7.

II

THE NONCONFORMIST RESPONSE TO SOCIALISM, 1906–1914

The presentation of Socialism as a semi-religious creed, through the ILP and the efforts of Keir Hardie and others, posed the main threat to organized religion in early twentieth-century Wales. While the response of Welsh Nonconformist ministers to Socialism ranged from the enthusiastic to the openly antagonistic, contemporary evidence indicates that confusion characterized the discussion about the nature, role and implications of the new political creed. Although Keir Hardie, R. J. Campbell, Rhondda Williams and, to an extent, David Thomas had all advocated its principal economic tenet, namely nationalization, their emphasis had been on its ethical nature: that Socialism would establish justice and righteousness. As a result, Socialism was understood by many as merely an ill-defined force for social reform, devoid of specific policies and quite in keeping with the prevailing ideas of Liberalism. Its challenge to current social thinking was perceived to be more moralistic than economic.

The Nonconformist response to Socialism was characterized by two main features. First, Nonconformists emphasized the supremacy of the spiritual over the material. They tended to support Socialism's call for greater justice and equality as representative of the eternal order, but were wary of its political and materialistic implications. Given this dual tendency, it was natural that Nonconformists sought to demonstrate Christianity's superiority over Socialism and to affirm that the latter could never succeed without the unique message and dynamism of the former. Secondly, they interpreted social reform as being Socialism's prime concern. This resulted in the widespread use of the word 'Socialism' to describe Christianity's supposed ability to build a better society. Nonconformists at this time were virtually unanimous in recognizing the need to remove social evils. Disagreement came over the best methods to achieve reform.[1]

[1] E.g. *Y Goleuad*, 26 August 1908, p.9; 9 September 1908, p.10; 7 October 1908, p.6.

The result was confusion over the content of the Socialist message and the correct Christian response to its claims. In an attempt to clarify the situation, *Yr Eurgrawn Wesleaidd* published articles in January and February 1910 under the title 'Paham yr wyf yn Sosialydd' (Why I am a Socialist) and then 'Paham nad wyf yn Sosialydd' (Why I am not a Socialist) in March. These articles demonstrate the difficulties of definition encountered at the time. The authors, both Nonconformist ministers, wanted to emphasize the need for social reform as well as the superiority of spiritual values over material comfort. Yet they came to vastly different conclusions over the content of Socialism and its compatibility or otherwise with the Christian faith.

According to the 'Socialist' H. Maldwyn Hughes, Socialism was the 'spirit . . . which can be used gradually to establish a co-operative commonwealth instead of the present system which is based on self-benefit'. It was because society did not embody the principle of 'love thy neighbour', rather than for specifically economic reasons, that the Christian gospel would condemn the social system. As a result, the solution to society's problems lay not in economics but in Jesus Christ, who had espoused the general brotherhood of man 'which stems from the general Fatherhood of God'. The important thing was for the 'principle of brotherly love' to govern society.[2] This was not Socialism but Liberal Theology, particularly as interpreted by Adolf Harnack, one of the leading theologians of the day. Although Maldwyn Hughes was vehement in his criticisms of society, his critique was based on his belief that current social practice promoted not brotherly love but cunning, ruthlessness and self-satisfaction. Hughes was a Socialist only according to the most superficial understanding of the word. He believed Christianity to have a social message and vitality and therefore referred to himself as a Socialist. He was, in fact, simply a Christian with a social conscience. Socialism may 'give expression to the moral and central truths of the Gospel', but 'apart from the divine grace which is able to change the hearts of men, Socialism is totally pointless'.

---

[2] H. Maldwyn Hughes, 'Paham yr wyf yn Sosialydd', *Yr Eurgrawn* (1910), 15–18, 59–62, *passim*.

In his responding article, Owen Evans drew attention to the lack of clear definition of the word Socialism. Some Socialists believed in armed struggle, others were religious believers, while yet others denied both these things. His main criticism was that Socialism wrongly affirmed that environmental improvement would automatically encourage human improvement. It was materialistic and ignored man's spiritual and moral needs. Evans stated that 'every outward improvement must run alongside a moral effort'. The present system encouraged moral effort through requiring that a man work in order to live and support his family. Socialism sought to remove this condition, supply all human need from a common store and expect work to be offered as a 'service'. As long as sin existed, such a scheme would be 'a futile dream'. Thus, Socialism could never be as effective as Christianity. Socialism also offended Evans's Nonconformist sensibilities because it destroyed freedom, placing all decision-making in the hands of the state, even in personal affairs.[3]

These articles hardly clarified matters. Indeed, it is difficult to see where Maldwyn Hughes would have disagreed with Owen Evans's objections. Despite this, the debate did point to the basic difficulties which were continually expressed before 1914 as Nonconformists tried to come to terms with the Socialist challenge. The conclusion to be drawn is that many Non-conformist ministers recognized the need for social reform and that reform required the character-transforming Christian dynamic. They disagreed over the use of the title Socialist. Socialism was considered to entail the end of personal freedom through state control. As Nonconformists had spent the previous two centuries and more trying to win that freedom, it is hardly surprising that some were highly suspicious of the Socialist agitators.

It is worth noting that Owen Evans's criticism of Socialism was not economic but moral. Although he recognized its fundamentally political nature, Evans had criticized and ultimately rejected Socialism on purely religious grounds. Those who opposed Socialism often used the argument that it made no attempt to meet the moral or spiritual requirement that men and women be 'born again'. Similar criteria were never applied to

---

[3] Owen Evans, 'Paham nad wyf yn Sosialydd', *Yr Eurgrawn* (1910), 104–7, *passim*.

Liberalism or Toryism, but as Socialism had been presented as a moral cause, it was valid to ask how it would affect the moral nature of the individual. For those whose Socialism merely entailed support for social reform, the task of personal regeneration would be fulfilled by the church. For those in opposition, the church became the protector of freedom and morality and thus the chief means of preventing Socialism from achieving political supremacy. Whether hostile to or supportive of the new movement, all Nonconformists were aware of the ideological tension which existed between the gospel and Socialism. It hinged on the question of whether material improvement could bring about individual moral regeneration. The suspicion that this was not the case would prevent many Nonconformist ministers from wholehearted acceptance of Socialism, while it led others into bitter and vitriolic criticism of the new movement.

During the correspondence which followed the publication of these articles, it is significant that only one letter was received which opposed the Socialist ideal. W. O. Williams, Bangor, based his opposition on the apparent failure of state control in every department including the Army, the Navy, the Post Office and even the established church.[4] However, the general feeling of most correspondents was that Socialism alone was insufficient as a creed for it could not transform the individual person into a social being. The Revd W. O. Evans admitted that the waste and injustice of capitalism had made him a Socialist, but Socialism, he claimed, needed Jesus Christ: 'With Christianity embodied in society there will be a better hope that the Kingdom of God be established in the world, and the will of our Father will be done on earth as in heaven.'[5]

The last word in the debate went to Owen Evans, who showed a distinct inability to read the signs of the times. 'We certainly believe', he wrote, 'that the Socialist wave will disappear from our land very soon.'[6] For Owen Evans, and probably for Maldwyn Hughes too, Socialism stood for no more than social reform by political means. The traditional Nonconformist stress on individual responsibility, as well as mankind's need of

---

[4] 'Y ddadl ar Sosialaeth', *Yr Eurgrawn* (1910), 178.
[5] Ibid., 153.
[6] Owen Evans, ibid., 226.

redemption uniquely provided by Christ, made this difficult for them to accept without some degree of criticism.

A number of Nonconformist ministers certainly considered Socialism to be an important addition to their faith and commensurate with a practical application of Christian ideals. One such minister, the Revd D. D. Walters, Newcastle Emlyn ('Gwallter Ddu'), consistently voiced this opinion in regular articles in *Llais Llafur*.

> Socialism taught men how to live correctly. So does the Bible. The Bible's principal teaching concerns Freedom and Justice. That also is the Socialist's cry—that the *gwerin* and the masses be freed from the slavery of oppressive capitalist forces . . . The freedom Jesus preached will not be enjoyed until individualism has been destroyed and Socialism has come to rule in its place.[7]

Through his emphasis on the moral effect of Socialism, Walters echoed Hardie's message that, until Socialism was established, Christianity was unworkable. He called on the church to move 'from creeds to works'[8] to ensure the required social reform. In his opinion, Jesus was a Socialist, and Socialism was 'synonymous with a perfect description of a new world: "a new heaven and a new earth"'.[9] 'Works' had been left to those outside the church and within the Socialist movement. Walters warned that it was through works and not prayer that men and women would find their way to heaven.

Men like 'Gwallter Ddu' could have argued that as the ideals of Socialism were incorporated in Christianity a distinctly social version of Christianity would bring the desired reform and thereby stem the flow of men from the chapels. Instead, Walters argued that 'that which is good in Socialism makes me a Socialist and makes Christ a Socialist too'. This simply exacerbated Nonconformity's problems. Socialism was perceived to be a distinctly practical creed and as such deserved the support of the working class. Instead of making the church 'practical', they advocated, whether implicitly or explicitly, that people leave the church and support the labour movement as a practical

---

[7] *Llais Llafur*, 6 June 1908, p.4.
[8] Ibid., 9 February 1907, p.1.
[9] Ibid., 29 September 1906, p.1.

application of Christian principles. The Christian gospel may have provided a vision and an ideal of a better society, but Socialism was the means to bring it about. Tension existed at the time between Socialist supporters and Nonconformist ministers concerning the means to achieve a better society. When traditional theology considered the environment at all it had stated that the depravity of humankind was responsible for conditions in the world. Socialists challenged this by contending that environment formed human personality and that social improvement would encourage individual regeneration. This was why Socialism as a theory for social improvement was advocated as the strategy to make Christianity, the dynamic for individual regeneration, effective. But many within the church, particularly those who represented evangelical Nonconformity, saw this as an impossibility. The priority had to be a change in the individual. Even those who were sympathetic to the Socialist ideal felt compelled to draw the line here.

Ministers such as the Baptists, the Revd James Nicholas, Tonypandy, and the Revd W. Rowland Jones, Merthyr, achieved a level of recognition as Socialist supporters. Rowland Jones in fact was sufficiently attracted to the labour movement to preach a sermon to the ILP conference when it visited Merthyr in 1912.[10] Both men had recognized an economic and political aspect to Socialist teaching,[11] but they refused to call themselves Socialists on the grounds that they did not belong to the ILP or any other Socialist body.[12] Furthermore, they believed that any political or economic theory was inadequate for full social reform. True reform had to take account of the spiritual in life.[13] Even the Revd George Neighbour, another Baptist minister whose enthusiasm for the Socialist cause led him into conflict with the deacons of his church at Miskin, Pontyclun, recognized that Socialism would never meet all his needs. Socialism, for him, represented the nearest political programme to the principles of Christ. It represented a moral challenge, but its ascendancy would be temporary, for the evolution of humankind and of society would result in something 'higher and more

---

[10] For his speech to the ILP conference, see *Merthyr Pioneer*, 15 June 1912, p.2.
[11] Cf. *Llais Llafur*, 25 July 1908, p.8.
[12] W. Rowland Jones, 'Yr Eglwys a Sosialaeth', *Seren Gomer* (1910), 86.
[13] *Rhondda Leader*, 18 May 1907, p.3; W. R. Jones, 'Yr Eglwys', 92, 93.

advanced'. Even when Socialism supplied all it could, he would still seek more. 'There is still that within which cries for something more', he said. 'My heart must still cry out for the living God.'[14] While J. R. Jones, in the only Fabian Tract to be written in Welsh, *Sosialaeth yng Ngoleuni'r Beibl* (Socialism in the Light of the Bible),[15] had recognized the seminal place of economics, he held that economic solutions were not the most expedient in ensuring social reform. The strenuous efforts for co-operation between the churches and the labour movement, on the grounds that both sought to establish the perfect society, neglected the dissimilarity of their claims and methods. Socialism desired an earthly utopia while Christianity dealt with a 'higher Kingdom than [that which] Socialism longs for' (p.3). For Jones, Socialism was an economic theory that sought to redistribute wealth, giving a fairer share to the working class through nationalization (p.6). As fine as such a theory was, he suggested that God's dealing with the Israelites, reaching its climax in Jesus Christ, provided a better plan, one which would 'defeat the world through friendship' (p.12). This, he claimed, was superior to the theory provided by the Socialists. In establishing the Kingdom of Heaven on earth, a 'paradise far beyond the hopes of the Socialists of our time', Jesus had established that towards which the Socialists had set their faces (pp.12–14). Christianity therefore surpassed Socialism both in its theory and in its efficacy for reform.

There were, however, ministers whose support for the labour movement was unequivocal. In many respects, such supporters as the Revd R. Silyn Roberts, Calvinistic Methodist minister at Tanygrisiau, Blaenau Ffestiniog, John 'Gwili' Jenkins, for much of this period a tutor at the Gwynfryn Academy, Ammanford, and the Revd T. E. Nicholas, Congregationalist minister at Glais in the Swansea valley, were more important than James Nicholas, W. Rowland Jones and J. R. Jones. Through their enthusiastic support for the ILP and for Socialism, these three ministers helped the nascent labour movement to gain grass-roots popularity.

---

[14] *Llais Llafur*, 1 October 1910, p.3.
[15] Fabian Tract no. 143 (London, 1909).

1. ROBERT SILYN ROBERTS

R. Silyn Roberts[16] was already a national figure in Wales, having been the crowned bard at the 1902 National Eisteddfod. He had established the ILP branch in Blaenau Ffestiniog in 1908 and sat as a Labour member of the Meirionnydd District Council. In his pamphlet, *Y Blaid Lafur Annibynnol: Ei Hanes a'i Hamcan* (The Independent Labour Party: Its History and its Aim),[17] he demonstrated the communality of fervour and zeal between religious activists and Socialists. It was no surprise that he considered that most members of the ILP believed Socialism to be a religion: 'To some Socialism is an intellectual conviction: to others it is a political or economic belief: but to ninety-nine per cent of membership of the I.L.P. Socialism possesses the living power of a great religious truth' (p.5). Because it was primarily a 'great religious truth', Socialism's 'economic side' could be summarized as the nationalization of land and industry in order to benefit all (p.6). Mostly, however, it meant freedom: freedom for the working class from the 'bounds of thankless labour and bruising poverty'; freedom for the middle class from the 'oppression of the market'; and for the rich it replaced 'the burden and chains of wealth' by 'true happiness' (p.7). Even to advocate Socialism as the harbinger of 'freedom' was to raise it above the role of ordinary political theory and recognize its ethical value and moral effect on society. Socialism could not be forced upon an unwilling people, however. The ILP required both organization and education in order for the *gwerin* to work out their own salvation industrially, politically and economically (p.12).

As far as Silyn Roberts was concerned, religion was a personal matter in which the individual had to be free to follow his own conscience. Once Socialism had been accepted, it was still the case that religious affiliation and belief remained matters for the individual conscience. Given this, and the fact that he did not make specific claims in this pamphlet concerning Socialism's relationship to Christianity, it is significant that it was his

---

[16] For R. Silyn Roberts (1871–1930), see *DWB*, pp.878–9; David Thomas, *Silyn* (Liverpool, 1956); T. Huws Davies, 'Silyn', *The Welsh Outlook* (1930), 291–2; John Morris, 'Yr Arloeswyr 6, Robert Silyn Roberts', *Lleufer* (1952), 75–7.

[17] Blaenau Ffestiniog, 1908.

religious views and status that appear to have made the most lasting impression on both his readers and his listeners. Following an address which he gave at Aber-craf, *Llais Llafur*'s reporter recorded that, while he spoke 'masterly on nationalizing the land and the railways', it was Silyn's explicitly Christian message which was most appreciated.

> He showed that Christianity deals with God while Socialism only deals with man. That Christianity deals with the life of man in its divine source and eternal fate, while Socialism only deals with the life of man in the small part of it which is contained between the crib and the grave. The Socialist's realm is only time, but religion's field includes time and eternity (*Amser yw gwladwriaeth Cymdeithasiaeth ond amser a thragwyddoldeb yw maes crefydd*).[18]

It was precisely the fact that he was an ordained minister, and therefore practical proof of the ability of the new to live alongside the old, which established Silyn's popularity as a spokesman for both Socialism and the ILP. The publication of his pamphlet and innumerable ensuing invitations to address ILP gatherings in south Wales secured Silyn's national reputation as a Socialist.[19] James Griffiths recalled that it was he more than anyone else who helped young men to reconcile politics with faith.

> He preached God and Evolution. He was a minister and a Socialist . . . he became our inspirer and our justification. To be able to tell our parents, who feared this new gospel we talked of, 'Ond mae Silyn Roberts yn credu fel y ni' [But Silyn Roberts believes the same as us]. How many devout fathers became reconciled to Socialist sons by that assurance? He linked the South Wales of Evan Roberts to the South Wales of Keir Hardie.[20]

For Silyn, the adoption of Socialism had coincided with an espousal of recent biblical scholarship, resulting in his feeling a 'certain unease' in the pulpit.[21] He considered many of the traditional doctrines to be untenable in the light of modern scholarship. This may have contributed to his resignation from

[18] *Llais Llafur*, 13 March 1909, p.2.
[19] Thomas, *Silyn*, pp.76–7.
[20] Ibid., p.77; cf. Jim Griffiths, 'Silyn Roberts a recollection', MS 18979, David Thomas Papers, Bangor General Collection, UW Bangor; this is also found in MS 17197, the R. Silyn Roberts Papers, UW Bangor.
[21] Thomas, *Silyn*, p.57; Huws Davies, 'Silyn', p.292.

the ministry in 1912, and serves to demonstrate the link between the new Socialist ideas and modern tendencies in theology. After this, Silyn became less important for the labour movement. His interests would eventually take him into educational movements, lecturing for the Department of Extra-Mural Studies in Bangor (from 1922) and organizing the Workers' Educational Association (WEA) in north Wales (from 1923). The sum total of Christianity, he claimed, was based on Jesus's words to the rich young ruler, that love of God and of neighbour were more important than creeds, and if Christianity had been preached in its purity then the religion of the Carpenter would also have had a social dimension. Undoubtedly, however, he was attracted to Socialism by the romantic ideal that a better world could be established through individual effort and dedication.

2. JOHN 'GWILI' JENKINS

From the very beginning of his public ministry, it was clear that 'Gwili'[22] belonged to the ranks of the liberal theologians. Whereas Nonconformity had previously perceived its mission in 'other-worldly' terms, namely in the presentation of eternal life after death as the sole goal and purpose of life on earth, Gwili discerned a message in the Christian gospel which was directed at this life *per se*. This theological opposition came to light in the years 1895–6. Gwili was moved to respond to articles by J. Gwynedd Jones, Penrhyndeudraeth, published in *Seren Cymru*. Jones had written 'Seven Letters to the Next World' under the pseudonym 'One on his Way There'. Gwili replied to these in a series entitled 'Seven Letters to This World' under the pseudonym 'One who is in It'.[23] This clash between a representative of the older orthodoxy and a Modernist theologian demonstrated the revolution in interpretation, purpose and orientation which had occurred through the effect of theological liberalism. For Gwili, when the pulpit failed in its duty to speak against oppression and injustice in this world, it

---

[22] For John 'Gwili' Jenkins (1872–1936), see *DWB*, pp.435–6; J. Beverley Smith, 'John Gwili Jenkins 1872–1936', *Transactions of the Honourable Society of Cymmrodorion* (1974–5), 191–214; E. Cefni Jones, *Gwili: Cofiant a Phregethau* (Llandysul, 1937).
[23] Cf. Cefni Jones, *Gwili*, p.62; *Seren Cymru*, 21 June 1895 to 28 February 1896.

was unfaithful to its heavenly vision.[24] Through advocating what he considered to be the social basis of Christianity, expressed in God's Fatherhood and the universal brotherhood of man, Gwili claimed that all Christians should be Socialists and all Socialists should be Christians. The church had been disobedient to its social calling and as a result the labour movement had awakened it to a clearer understanding of New Testament religion.[25]

The radical tenor of his preaching before 1914 earned him a reputation as a heretic and a rebel. His 1908 commentary on portions of the Book of Isaiah which he co-authored with Herbert Morgan, and his subsequent volume on aspects of the history of Israel, *Llin ar Lin* (1909), illustrate how deeply he had drunk of the wells of 'higher criticism'. For Gwili, modern scholarship went hand in hand with political radicalism. Preaching at Cwmaman in 1910, he 'surprised some of his congregation' by advocating support of Keir Hardie and attacking the landlords, 'who had appropriated the land which had been given to the people'.[26] His sermon, 'The two gospels', first preached in October 1908, explained how the Socialist movement was insisting that the churches should exchange their 'devotional dreaming' for condemnation of social inequality. They were to 'give some help to the world'.[27] This help would come from the 'gospel of these things' which sought to form a brotherhood of the workers in the world: 'It includes more than daily bread. It includes a desire for greater freedom, for wider culture, for peace in the world, for fuller life to every man regardless of his birth right or other.'[28] But this 'gospel', almost certainly a reference to the labour movement's message, was still deficient. It made no provision for the individual men who formed society. Jesus himself had sought to improve society through individual moral regeneration. As a result, the 'gospel of these things' needed the 'gospel of the Kingdom' to be more effective.[29] Thus, the true place for the social reformer was

[24] Gwili [Jenkins], 'Iawnderau Dyn', *Y Geninen* (1914), 62–3; cf. *idem*, 'Cyfiawnder yn Nysgeidiaeth Iesu', *Seren Gomer* (1906), 236.
[25] Gwili [Jenkins], *Y Ddwy Efengyl* (Carmarthen, 1915), p.63.
[26] *Aberdare Leader*, 22 January 1910, p.6.
[27] *Y Ddwy Efengyl*, p.9.
[28] Ibid., p.17.
[29] Ibid., pp.22–3.

within the church, where he could express his vision in the spirit of Jesus.[30]

There can be little doubt that Gwili was a radical who achieved a certain popularity among the ranks of the ILP in the years before the Great War. James Griffiths recognized a debt to both Gwili and R. Silyn Roberts for ensuring that the ILP in Wales would have a Welsh dimension.[31] But Gwili always maintained that the labour movement alone was insufficient to meet society's needs. Labour needed the church: 'I spoke with the ILP, not as a member, but as one who wished to keep Welsh workers in their place. It would be a shame for them to break away from the churches.'[32]

Like so many others, Gwili's prominence as a Socialist evaporated after the Great War. During the 1920s, certainly from his appointment to the chair of New Testament Studies at the North Wales Baptist College in 1923, he concentrated almost exclusively on theological study. A highly intelligent, well-read man, Gwili's greatest desire was to make the latest developments in scholarship accessible to ordinary chapel-goers, not in order to disprove the traditional doctrines but to help them deepen their Christian life. His support for Socialism was due to his belief that it would improve the lot of the *gwerin*. But they would still need the spiritual teaching and salvation of Christ.

3. THOMAS EVAN NICHOLAS

The Revd T. E. Nicholas[33] came to Glais when the fires of the revival were at their hottest in 1904, and was known as 'Niclas y Glais' throughout the rest of his life. During the succeeding ten years he became famous for his support of the ILP and Socialism, not least through his poetry. D. Tecwyn Lloyd has shown how his conversion to Socialism, sometime after the revival, was reflected in his poetry. Initially, he welcomed the

[30] Ibid., pp.27–8.
[31] J. Beverley Smith, 'John Gwili Jenkins', p.207.
[32] Quoted in E. Cefni Jones, 'Gwili a'i waith', competition essay, Machynlleth Eisteddfod, 1937, p.190 (NLW).
[33] For T. E. Nicholas (1879–1971), see J. Roose Williams (ed.), *T. E. Nicholas: Proffwyd Sosialaeth a Bardd Gwrthryfel* (Bangor, 1971); T. J. Morgan, 'Niclas y Glais', *Y Genhinen* (1971), 141–7; James Nicholas, *Pan Oeddwn Grwt Diniwed yn y Wlad* (Llandysul, 1979); Siân Howys, 'Bywyd a Gwaith T. E. Nicholas' (MA thesis, University of Wales, 1985); David Howell, *Nicholas of Glais: The People's Champion* (Clydach, 1991).

religious revival without qualification. By 1908 the unique blend of Christianity and Socialism which would characterize all his subsequent work had been achieved.[34] In 1906 he helped to found a branch of the ILP in Glais and worked assiduously for the party in the Swansea valley.[35] Following the publication of knowledgeable, cogent and passionately argued articles in *Y Geninen* between 1912 and 1914, he became a national figure in Wales, and was invited to address meetings in the north as well as the south.

Nicholas is a vitally important character in the development of Socialism in Wales before the Great War. He not only had a firm grasp of Socialist essentials but had a sense of Welsh identity which had, for the most part, been lacking in labour circles. He claimed that of all the political theories, Socialism alone was truly nationalistic because one of its principal tenets was nationalization of the land. This would return the land to the hands of the people to be used for the benefit of all.[36] For Nicholas, Socialism and Christianity were inextricably linked; both shared the ideals of Jesus's teaching but Socialism provided a 'practical expression' of those ideals.[37] It was thus the way to 'assist in enthroning Christ in the life of the nation'.[38] To do the work of Socialism was to do 'God's work in the world'[39] and demonstrated mankind's high calling and responsibility. It stood for social and commercial morality and had emerged as a protest against materialism.[40] He would change his allegiance to any party which was shown to be nearer the Christian ideal.[41]

Despite his importance as a Socialist spokesman, Nicholas did not advocate Marxism or economic Socialism. He was a prophetic visionary who initially joined the early ILP and then

[34] D. Tecwyn Lloyd, 'T. E. Nicholas', in Aneirin Talfan Davies (ed.), *Gwŷr Llên* (London, 1948), pp.148–9.
[35] Howell, *Nicholas of Glais*, pp.13–14.
[36] T. E. Nicholas, 'Y Ddraig Goch a'r Faner Goch: Cenedlaetholdeb a Sosialaeth', *Y Geninen* (1912), 15.
[37] Ibid., p.14; cf. T. E. Nicholas, 'Yr Eglwysi a phynciau cymdeithasol', *Y Geninen* (1914), 23.
[38] 'Y Ddraig Goch', p.15.
[39] T. E. Nicholas, 'R. J. Derfel: y Gwrthryfelwr Cymreig', *Y Geninen Gŵyl Dewi* (1914), 61.
[40] 'Y Ddraig Goch', p.265.
[41] 'Yr Eglwysi', p.25.

switched his allegiance to the Communist Party because he thought that it would best fulfil his dream.[42]

> We are waiting and working for a better day; a day of peace between the nations of the world; a day when the earth is handed over to the people; a day when the workers receive the whole product of their labour; a day when soldiers will be driven to more useful work; a day when the kings and idlers of the world are overthrown. I hear someone whisper that things like these are dreams. I would rather dream of peace than be silent in the midst of cannons. I would rather dream of social justice than be quiet in the midst of all the injustice which is in the land today.[43]

For Nicholas, Socialism did not represent a new religion to replace Christianity but a purifying force to change a degenerate Christianity which had been silent in the face of cruel social and industrial conditions.[44] Socialism would fulfil the Christian social vision through providing not merely fair wages but the means to provide 'life' for working people. 'He [the working man] will be paid in a healthy life, in free education, in warm clothes, in a spacious and beautiful home (*cartref eang a phrydferth*), in leisure time, in less hours of work. In a word, he will be paid with life.'[45] This would, however, require a moral effort and commitment to self-sacrificing service. Like Ben and Stitt Wilson, Nicholas used the cross to represent such an effort.[46] It was not the cross of Calvary which would save the world, but the cross of suffering and self-sacrifice which each person had to carry.[47]

For Nicholas, the church was failing both its Lord and its members because it had not taken up the cause of the working class. The labour movement required not the church's co-operation but its leadership, for politics and education alone could never save the world. A spiritual element would always be required. But the church's very existence depended on its response to the social problem.[48] The church therefore needed to

---

[42] W. T. Pennar Davies, 'T. E. Nicholas bardd o ddyneiddiwr', in Roose Williams (ed.), *T. E. Nicholas*, p.35.
[43] T. E. Nicholas, 'Gornest Cyfalaf a Llafur', *Y Geninen* (1912), 127.
[44] *Merthyr Pioneer*, 8 April 1911, p.3.
[45] T. E. Nicholas, 'Cyflog byw', *Y Geninen* (1913), 25.
[46] Cf. *Llais Llafur*, 9 January 1909, p.8.
[47] *Merthyr Pioneer*, 10 February 1912, p.8.
[48] 'Yr Eglwysi', pp.21–2.

stop emphasizing the 'other-worldly' element of the gospel and respond to the needs of this world.[49] In Nicholas's opinion the adoption of two principles would facilitate a working relationship between the church and the labour movement. The first was a recognition that the ideals of Socialism were virtually those of Jesus and that therefore Socialism deserved the support of the church. Secondly, Socialism had to allow each individual his or her freedom of conscience concerning religious creed.[50] This merely demonstrates the inherent contradictions of Nicholas's message. Socialism needed only to be void of antagonism towards the church, while the church was to put all its energy and influence behind Socialism, never vice versa. Freedom of conscience was only to be practised in connection with religious matters. Religious people were not afforded the same luxury over issues of politics or economics.

Inasmuch as he espoused any coherent theology at all, Nicholas's doctrine, like that of so many younger Welsh Nonconformists at the time, was moral, liberal and largely anthropocentric. Concepts such as peace and justice figured large in his thinking, while the doctrine of man, understood in terms of his evolution towards perfection, was of central importance. 'True Christianity', he claimed, 'recognizes the divinity of man . . . not as a fallen being but one who is continually advancing to higher levels, and who is endowed with unlimited possibilities.'[51] Central to Nicholas's thinking is the man who lived and worked for others. This was connected to his belief in human ability to influence the future, both in political matters and in personal morality. In short, Nicholas believed that human beings could control their own destinies. He had no patience with the working man who refused to turn to Labour despite knowing that Labour would bring him the most benefits.[52] Until the working classes learned to make their own decisions, they would always live in poverty and under the social and political oppression of the capitalists. This also applied to the specific social problem.

[49] T. E. Nicholas, 'R. J. Derfel', *Y Geninen Gŵyl Dewi* (1912), 23.
[50] 'Yr Eglwysi', p.22.
[51] Quoted in Howell, *Nicholas of Glais*, p.29.
[52] Cf. *Y Geninen* (1912), 127, 158, 265.

The 'slums' are the work of Man, the wasteful lives seen along our streets are the work of Man, the work of Man was to take the land from the people. The taverns are the work of Man; and we believe that Man alone can save society from these things.[53]

Society would only be saved through human effort, and Nicholas believed that the doctrine of the incarnation pointed to that fact. Although all people still required salvation, Nicholas, like Hardie, averred that social organization damned the individual as soon as the church had saved him. Man was the product of his environment and, therefore, society itself must be saved before there could be any possibility of permanent salvation for the individual.[54] Socialism, once again, could be invoked to make Christianity more effective. Of the social elements that damned human beings, poverty was the worst. Contrary to popular opinion, Nicholas believed that 'bad health', 'drunkenness', 'unemployment', 'scarcity of the land's produce' and 'waste', far from causing poverty, were the result of poverty.[55] The *gwerin* were poor because of the unfair and unequal distribution of wealth: the scandal being that it was the *gwerin* who produced the wealth.[56] These points are characteristic not merely of Nicholas's understanding of Socialism but also of his understanding of Christianity. Both Christianity and Socialism at this time recognized the important role that human beings were to play in the creation of a better world and in their own salvation. Socialism could thus be a policy for Christians.

Hardie's influence on Nicholas is clear and undeniable. Nicholas and Hardie had become firm friends, and Nicholas concurred with the Scotsman not only in his attempt to present Socialism as a moral ideal and prerequisite for a truly Christian society, but also in his uncompromising pacifism. Despite some obvious similarities between his ideas and those of R. J. Campbell, it is unlikely that he was directly influenced by the London minister; his own thought seems to have developed simultaneously with that of Campbell. Nicholas's concern stemmed from witnessing the injustices of industrial society.

[53] 'Y Ddraig Goch', p.14.
[54] 'Yr Eglwysi', pp.25–6.
[55] T. E. Nicholas, 'Paham y mae'r werin yn dlawd', *Y Geninen* (1912), 150–8, *passim*.
[56] 'Y Glofeydd', p.263.

. . . we saw men being exploited by the unprincipled bosses, and there was enough of that in the Swansea valley at that time. And as a minister of the gospel I had to do something. My protest came about as I held the injustices side by side to the New Testament.[57]

One of Nicholas's poems, 'Eglwysyddiaeth' (Churchianity), did appear alongside Campbell's famous adage 'Churchianity is not Christianity'.[58] This only proves Nicholas's general agreement with Campbell's point, however, and not the direct influence of the New Theology. The only real piece of autobiography which we possess seems to suggest that Nicholas's ideas about God, man and theology stemmed from his own thinking about his upbringing and the people he knew.[59] In his youth, chapel attendance had been the sole measure of human goodness. It was as he came to know men who never attended chapel but in whom he saw 'as good a representative of God as anyone' that he dispensed with this naïve view. These autobiographical articles were, of course, written towards the end of his life and possibly present an idealized rather than a real view of his past,[60] but he certainly became convinced that goodness could only be judged by the extent of a man's self-sacrifice for the good of the community.

In the period before the Great War, Nicholas advocated the contribution of religion as crucial to the success of the social movement. After 1918, though, he seems to have lost all such faith in the church,[61] despite persisting in outward religious observances for the rest of his life. Nicholas is typical of the crusading, evangelistic Socialist agitators of the period, offering the people a moral vision and stirring up discontent against an unjust social order. He could use emotive and emotional language, calling the workers to run to the 'Shadow of the Red Flag'.[62] Virtually his sole political policy was nationalization: that the land, industry and capital should be run for the benefit of all

---

[57] 'W. J. Edwards yn holi Niclas y Glais', *Y Cardi Gŵyl Dewi* (1970), 7.

[58] T. E. Nicholas, *Cerddi Gwerin* (Caernarfon, 1912), pp.23–6.

[59] MS 23359, T. E. Nicholas Papers, Bangor General Collection, UW Bangor.

[60] *Y Cymro*, 18 February 1965, p.12.

[61] Ibid., 25 February 1965, p.12.

[62] 'Werin Cymru! I gysgod y Faner Goch!', cf. *Y Geninen* (1912), 158, 265; *Y Geninen* (1913), 26.

and not merely for the profit of the capitalists.[63] His Socialism provided a beleaguered working class with the possibility of a better future, even if that future was never really defined.

These early religious apologists for the ILP were twentieth-century representatives of the radical Welsh Nonconformity of a century before. They sought to use the political means at their disposal to ensure that their social vision would become a reality. That those political means were Socialist matters little; that they were prepared to use politics at all places them firmly in the political tradition of the nineteenth century when Non-conformists had identified themselves with Radical politics in order to secure the recognition of their rights. In propagating Socialism as the only means to restore basic rights to the working class, T. E. Nicholas and others simply continued the struggle and gave it a more contemporary twist. But the danger of his argument is clear. Christianity becomes little more than a religion of works-righteousness in which justification before God depends on self-sacrifice and humanitarian actions. This being so, many believed that the labour movement offered a better opportunity to live that life than did the church. Nicholas himself would ultimately become a kind of victim of this when he left the ministry in 1918 to become a dentist. Because of this, and also because of his later zeal for Communism, Nicholas tends to be dismissed as an eccentric. In the period before 1914, however, he proved a welcome asset for the labour movement because in him it had a popular, able and effective spokesman.

Rowland Jones, James Nicholas, R. Silyn Roberts, 'Gwili' and T. E. Nicholas had all appeared on 'labour' platforms and their support for Keir Hardie and the ILP was beyond dispute.[64] However, they were not absolutely convinced that Socialism had any necessary connection with the Christian faith. T. E. Nicholas more than the others seemed to have welcomed the advent of Socialism as a true application of Christianity, but even he sought a more active involvement by the church during this period. Rowland Jones certainly believed that, despite the common principles and the excellence of its aims, Socialism would work in a different sphere from Christianity. Socialism would always need

---

[63] 'Yr Eglwysi', p.23.
[64] Cf. e.g. *Merthyr Pioneer*, 6 May 1911; *Aberdare Leader*, 22 January 1910, p.6; *Llais Llafur*, 4 December 1909, p.7.

a religion which 'saved souls' from sin, and as a result there would always be the need for a Christian church.[65] Socialism could work in government and in society but only Christianity could work in men's hearts. This is hardly surprising. Whatever Socialism could offer, it could only provide for the external welfare of men; it was concerned only with material comfort and not with the orientation of the individual. Two other Nonconformist ministers came to similar conclusions, two whose political affiliation was not as overt as that of those named above, namely John Morgan Jones, Merthyr, and D. Tudwal Evans.

4. JOHN MORGAN JONES (MERTHYR)

John Morgan Jones[66] had come to Merthyr Tydfil as the minister of Hope English Calvinistic Methodist chapel in 1898. Apart from a short stay in Bangor in 1902, he remained there until his death in 1935. His concern for the welfare of the local people, his sympathetic interest in social conditions as well as his uncompromising pacifist stance during the Great War, earned him the respect, admiration and affection of generations of working men. His genuine humanity enabled him to mix with all kinds of men, the poor and working classes, students and scholars, and also with industrialists and capitalists, and led him on occasion to mediate between workers and employers and then to practise his belief in reconciliation.[67] The question of Socialism, particularly in its relationship with organized religion, was deemed sufficiently important for him to have lectured extensively on the subject, eventually publishing his views in a pamphlet entitled *Religion and Socialism*.[68] The booklet was welcomed by those who felt Socialism and Christianity should co-operate,[69] despite its containing a far from uncritical acceptance of the Socialist creed.

Jones's lectures are carefully argued, sympathetically written but not propagandist accounts of the relationship between

[65] Cf. W. Rowland Jones, 'Yr Eglwys', 92–3.
[66] For John Morgan Jones, Merthyr (1861–1935), see *DWB*, pp.486–7; *Blwyddiadur y Methodistiaid Calfinaidd* (1936), 204–5; G. M. Ll. Davies, 'Rev. John Morgan Jones M.A.', *The Treasury* (1935), 138–9; M. R. Mainwaring, 'John Morgan Jones', in D. B. Rees (ed.), *Hero'r Byd* (Liverpool, 1980), pp.63–9.
[67] G. M. Ll. Davies, *Cenhadon Hedd*, Pamffledi Heddychwyr Cymru, 2nd ser., no. 8 (Denbigh, 1943), p.7; cf. *Merthyr Pioneer*, 5 April 1913, p.2.
[68] Merthyr Tydfil, 1910.
[69] *Y Goleuad*, 20 July 1910, p.4.

Socialism and certain aspects of Christianity. Their aim was to be a 'Word of Reconciliation' between Socialism and the church, both of which were in danger of being undermined, on the one hand, by the large numbers of men forsaking the churches in order to embrace Socialism, and due to the church's mounting hostility towards Socialism, on the other (pp.5–6). He believed that synthesis and reconciliation were possible, but that first of all a clarification of terms was required. In his view, religious objections to political and economic theories were invalid (p.7). This also meant that religious arguments could not be used to support Socialism. Many Socialists had made the mistake of appealing to the Sermon on the Mount and the Lord's Prayer to maintain that 'their Socialism is only the exposition of the teaching of Jesus' (p.8). Jones's plea was for a better understanding of the claims of Socialism and Christianity alike. In his own mind the distinctions were clear. Jesus was no Socialist and as his own political and social context was totally different from that of industrial society, it was difficult to determine what his message would have been for the twentieth-century world (pp.24–6). To claim that Socialism could be found in the gospel was to harm the cause of religion. Christians who did so only offered the false hope of discovering in religion that which religion could not give. Disillusionment would follow and religion would inevitably be cast aside as something useless. All Christianity could offer the social reformer was the 'inspiration of social reform', namely the principle of man's eternal value irrespective of his circumstances (pp.48–9). The motive of Jesus's ministry was religious and moral, not social and political (p.28).

> His mission to the poor and the oppressed of His time was to reveal to them a Father in Heaven and to lift them out of their apathy and despair into the blessings of Faith in that Heavenly Father and the Love which springs from that Faith. (p.29)

Christ's gospel did not give the poor a better social system but a spirit which would triumph over the environment and gradually create a new one. This pointed ultimately to the importance of the individual. The sole purpose of Jesus's mission was to seek and save individual men and women and restore their fellowship with God. For Jones, 'the social problem to.the mind of Jesus is that of producing a good man, a virtuous character, a moral personality' (p.33). The purpose of Jesus's mission was to create men and women in whom the 'anti-social principle' of selfishness was overcome by the 'social principle' of love, whose life was dedicated to the service of God and of humanity. There was no contradiction in his mind between the Christian message and theoretical Socialism (p.34). The Socialism which was currently being preached in Merthyr, however, was in danger of promoting individual and sectarian interest under the guise of social concern. 'A Trade Unionist who is only careful about the interests of his own Union', he said, 'is only a little less selfish than the man who is only careful about his own interest.'

The aim of both Christianity and theoretical Socialism was to awaken the social conscience which would result in the condemnation of the current social order. Jones recognized that such reform required a 'deliberate, concerted action of the community' and could not be satisfied with 'individual, capricious acts of charity' (p.44). Jesus had presented the only feasible course of action, namely to 'leaven' society with the principles of the Kingdom of Heaven. This was the responsibility of the church (p.46). They would not find direction in the words of Jesus but in the 'divinely appointed discipline' of 'reason and conscience' (p.47). This required religious believers to practise their Christianity (p.11). The practice of Christian principles would not only ensure the conversion of democracy but also the solution of the social problem (pp.16, 18). Jones appears to have believed in the individual's ability to control his or her own destiny, or to have believed in it at least as much as the Socialists did. Human beings had created the injustice and inequality in the world and it was therefore they alone who could change it. The challenge was for them to work out how this change could be brought about (pp.43–4, 47, 49).

John Morgan Jones's particular expertise was in the field of Old Testament studies.[70] He considered that the discovery of the social function of the Old Testament prophets was the greatest achievement of biblical scholarship to date. His familiarity with

---

[70] *DWB*, pp.486–7; also his book *Y Datguddiad o Dduw yn yr Hen Destament* (Caernarfon, 1936).

biblical scholarship, and his insistence that Jesus's message could not immediately be applied to the contemporary situation due to the vast differences in social context, shows that he accepted the fundamental precepts of his academic discipline. However, he was not a 'new theologian' in the same sense as R. J. Campbell. Although he supported individual rights, demonstrated by his approval of the Methodist rebel, Tom Nefyn Williams, his theological stance was basically conservative. There is no evidence that he deviated at all from the orthodox understanding of man's need for salvation which was met in the atoning sacrifice of Jesus Christ, the Son of God.[71] His strong personality, idealism and his human sympathy made him, in the words of the rector of Merthyr at his funeral service, 'the greatest moral force in the town'.[72] He was primarily a sympathetic Christian pastor with a desire to see society reformed, rather than a Socialist in any economic sense. Were it to achieve these humanitarian aims, Socialism, he believed, was worthy of adoption. Ultimately, though, true salvation for the world would be found in Christianity alone. His presence and ministry in Merthyr doubtless kept some within the bounds of the church, but for those who simply sought a rubber-stamp for Socialist policies he was a disappointment.[73]

5. D. TUDWAL EVANS

Amongst the Welsh Baptists it was D. Tudwal Evans of Newport, Monmouthshire, who made the most serious attempt to explain the theory and ideal of Socialism both in his articles in *Seren Cymru* (from February 1909 onwards) and then in his book, *Sosialaeth*.[74] He claimed to have seen enough in a week in Newport to become thereafter a 'most fanatical and extreme' Socialist (p.107). Socialism, in his view, was worthy of support as it would make life worth living for so many ordinary people. He hoped that his book would demonstrate two things: that Socialism was not antipathetic to Christianity and that Christ alone was the saviour of the world (p.11).

[71] G. M. Ll. Davies, *Cenhadon Hedd*, p.10.
[72] Ibid., p.14.
[73] Ibid., p.7.
[74] Barmouth, 1911.

Evans had a very high opinion of Socialism. It had preached Christianity's sermon of universal brotherhood, although it had stopped short of revealing the Father as Lord (p.117). There was a prima-facie difference between Socialism and Christianity. Christianity's ethical requirement was 'Do not live for self, but for God'. Socialism's imperative, on the other hand, was slightly different, commanding that its adherents 'Do not live for self, but for society'. Evans claimed, however, that what had appeared to be a difference was in fact no such thing. Jesus had said that the way to live for God was through self-sacrificial service, which in practice meant to live for society (pp.133–4).

Evans's interpretation of Socialism was exclusively moral. It stood for the recognition of the general brotherhood of man and held that, consequently, relationships should be formed on that basis. As a result, every man's responsibility was to deny his own will and live according to the will of society (p.131). Sacrificial service of God and of others was, he claimed, the crux of Jesus's teaching (p.133), and the similarity of the two creeds was thus proven. Because his understanding of Socialism was moralistic, Evans could claim that Jesus himself was a Socialist, his Socialism being found in the principles which he espoused rather than directly in his words. Jesus's teaching would promote the changing of society along lines of co-operation and recognition of mutual dependence.

> Jesus could not be the Saviour of the World without being a Socialist because the world was imprisoned in the clutches of SELF. But Jesus came into the world to save it. He taught man the way to come out of the clutches of self. He taught him self-denial. He taught him to lose his life through living for others, and through living for others to save his life. If we follow Jesus faithfully we can be nothing less than Socialists. (p.138)

Evans's message was that Socialism was undeniably located in the Bible and that Christ aimed at the temporal as well as spiritual salvation of humankind. Therefore, it was the duty of his followers to do the same (p.139). Socialism had developed because religious believers had abrogated their social responsibility and the church needed to be warned that 'there is too much of life and of God in it to defeat it now'. Thus, for him Socialism was divinely appointed to make up for religion's failure to accomplish its social task. To fight against Socialism now would be to fight against God. However, Socialism needed Christ and Christianity to transform individuals, or else their paradise might not be an abiding one (p.143). Christ therefore was the friend of Socialism, and Socialists should seek to work with and not against him.

6. CHRISTIAN SOCIALISM

The perceived parity between Socialism and Christianity led to the advent of Christian Socialism, which aspired to differentiate the moral and spiritual aspects in contemporary social thought from the material and physical. There is little evidence of the existence of Christian Socialism in Wales, such as had developed in England from the mid-nineteenth century through F. D. Maurice, Stewart Headlam, Conrad Noel and movements such as the Guild of St Matthew, the Christian Social Union or the Church Socialist League.[75] The reason for this is unclear. Christian Socialism in England had been associated with High-Churchmanship within the established church. Despite the Nonconformist culture which was well established by the turn of the century, there had been strong traditions of Anglo-Catholicism in certain Welsh parishes[76] and Canon J. D. Jenkins of Aberdare, for example, was a highly vocal supporter of labour.[77] Possibly the reason for the lack of theoretical Christian Socialism was that Nonconformity, still a greater religious force than Anglicanism in Wales, did not offer either a strong theology of incarnation, or an adequate doctrine of the church as the society of the redeemed, two doctrines which the English Anglo-Catholics deemed essential. At first glance, the social aspect inherent in the gospel would make the term Christian Socialism unnecessary. In adopting such a title, all the 'Christian Socialists' could hope to achieve was to turn the minds of religious men

[75] See Peter d'A. Jones, *The Christian Socialist Revival 1877–1914* (Princeton, 1968); Charles E. Raven, *Christian Socialism 1848–1854* (London, 1920; new edn. 1968); K. S. Inglis, *Churches and the Working Classes in Victorian England* (London, 1963); Reg Groves, *Conrad Noel and the Thaxted Movement* (New York, 1968).

[76] See A. Tudno Williams, *Mudiad Rhydychen a Chymru* (Denbigh, 1983).

[77] Christopher B. Turner, 'Ritualism, railwaymen and the poor: the ministry of Canon J. D. Jenkins, Vicar of Aberdare, 1870–1876', in Geraint H. Jenkins and J. Beverley Smith (eds.), *Politics and Society in Wales, 1840–1922: Essays in Honour of Ieuan Gwynedd Jones* (Cardiff, 1988), pp.61–79.

away from individualism in order to redress society's problems, while at the same time attracting those drawn to the Socialist movement.

Those who claimed the title 'Christian Socialist' believed that 'true Christianity was impossible' without Socialism. Yet the Revd J. Lewis Williams still considered it necessary to demonstrate that Socialism was quite insufficient for it was only concerned with the life of man on earth.[78] The Revd Bedford Roberts, Neath Abbey, had accepted Socialism after reading Robert Blatchford's book, *Merrie England*. He believed that there was no 'clash' between Socialism and Christianity. They both condemned 'individual ownership [and taught that] man is to be the steward and not the owner of things'. Justice and freedom were at the heart of Christianity and Socialism alike, and Socialism's ideal was the same as that of the Kingdom of God. For him, 'Socialism is the hope of the present and the aim of the future.'[79] The Revd J. H. Howard had discovered his social conscience while serving as a minister in Cwmafan[80] and would eventually switch his allegiance from the Liberal Party to Labour. He was amongst the first authors to offer an exposition of Christianity's social teaching in the Welsh language and considered the topic at length in his book, *Cristionogaeth a Chymdeithas* (Christianity and Society).[81] He insisted that the term 'Christian Socialism' was valid because there were different types of Socialism, differentiated by 'their spirit and the media used by them to reach their goal' (p.57). Although there were similarities between Socialism and Christianity, Christ was certainly no Socialist as he had espoused no economic system. Howard did not believe Christianity and Socialism to be synonymous. Christianity had given the governing principles to Socialism and therefore the essence of Socialism was in Christianity (p.58). The difference between Christian Socialism and other forms of Socialism centred on the fact that the former could never promote 'class consciousness' and 'class warfare'. Howard believed that it was the message of Christian brotherhood that had raised mankind in the past. This message, which

[78] J. Lewis Williams, 'Sosialaeth Gristionogol', *Y Geninen* (1908), 107.
[79] *Llais Llafur*, 11 January 1908, p.7.
[80] J. H.Howard, *Winding Lanes* (Caernarfon, 1938), pp.116–19.
[81] Liverpool, 1914.

transcended class allegiance and social and financial status, was at the heart of Christian Socialism.

> Is it not this wide and religious idea of Brotherhood which until now has raised man? Class Consciousness did not save the child in the factory, free the slave, clean the prisons in Europe, extend annuity to the elderly, and save the beggar from the gutter! No, but a brotherhood which knows no bounds, except for the relation of a Divine Father. And this is the power that will put an end for ever to social, political and national battles. (p.60)

However, Howard, like these other 'Christian Socialists', seems to have been promoting social Christianity or Christianity as an impetus for social reform (p.69). Christianity was basically a religion of certain moral principles, namely the absolute value of human life and the ethical requirement of service. The sum total of Christian Socialism was that the religion of Jesus was practical for the present. Thus the Revd J. Tywi Jones, a lifelong supporter of the Liberal Party, could also claim that he was a 'Christian Socialist' who learned his Socialism from the New Testament.[82]

Without a doubt the confusion once again arose from the imprecise use of the word 'Socialism'. Most ministers would have agreed about Christianity's efficacy in social matters but they would have questioned the need to call it Socialism. The Revd W. F. Phillips opposed the title 'Christian Socialist' on the grounds that it denied the wholeness of Christian salvation, which was effective for society as well as the individual.[83] But the title was also opposed by Socialists because it failed to do justice to Socialism. The Lord Mayor of Cardiff, Morgan Thomas, and David Williams, the Mayor of Swansea, clashed over the term during a debate at Swansea in April 1913. Thomas believed Williams to be a Christian Socialist, which was 'alright'. For Williams, however, Socialism was 'an economic doctrine' and had nothing to do with religion.[84] The claim that the term 'Christian Socialism' was irrelevant gained support from a manifesto signed by a group of Socialist ministers and published

---

[82] *Llais Llafur*, 22 December 1906, p.7.
[83] W. F. Phillips, 'Sosialaeth a Christionogaeth', *Y Geninen* (1911), 83.
[84] *Llais Llafur*, 26 April 1913, p.1.

in *Llais Llafur*. They claimed that there was only one Socialism, involving 'public ownership and management of the means of production, distribution and exchange'.

> The central teaching of Socialism is a matter of economics and may therefore be advocated by all men, whether they be Christians or unbelievers; yet we feel as ministers of the Christian faith that this economic doctrine is in perfect harmony with our faith, and we believe that its advocacy is sanctioned and indeed required of us, by the implications of our religion.[85]

Despite the efforts of some, the term Christian Socialism never really became popular in Wales.

For these ministers popularity within the labour movement was to be measured according to their use of the term 'Socialism'. Their support of labour from the pulpit and, certainly before the Great War, the political platform assured them of favourable treatment in the labour press. A closer look at their work reveals that their 'Socialism' was highly moralistic and hardly economic at all. Thus, they all recognized the need for Socialism to be moderated by the message of Jesus Christ, who was the great moral teacher in history if not the saviour of the world. The labour movement had found genuine allies in the sense that they all believed in the need for social reform and most also believed the working man to be under-represented in Parliament. But the labour movement and press were often too quick to welcome such support. Their lack of discernment is best revealed in their treatment of the Revd John Williams, Brynsiencyn.

John Williams was hailed as an 'enlightened and powerful' minister in the early years of the century, mainly for asking why Nonconformist ministers were concentrating far more on fighting Keir Hardie than on their true vocation of fighting the devil.[86] He was considered 'broad-minded and progressive' for having dealt with social problems such as a living wage and decent dwellings in his retiring address as moderator of the Calvinistic Methodist assembly in 1914.[87] Williams's view was

---

[85] Ibid., 25 January 1908, p.6.
[86] Ibid., 13 September 1913, p.3.
[87] Ibid., 30 May 1914, p.4.

that these were moral questions in so far as they affected the nation's conscience, and as moral questions they directly concerned the church and the Christian religion. But Williams was certainly no Socialist. He lived in greater luxury than most Nonconformist ministers and virtually assumed the role of local squire in Brynsiencyn, where he indulged in the aristocratic pleasures of fishing and hunting.[88] Furthermore, he would prove to be a faithful and zealous Liberal during the war, when he acted as a recruiting agent. That even he had mentioned social problems demonstrates how important they had become by 1914, but the labour press's attempt to hail him as an ally demonstrates its shallowness in misunderstanding the political, economic and even theological position of Nonconformist ministers. The press tried to win support by naming a group of ministers whose position was vaguely compatible with its own.

Williams would ultimately fall out of favour with the labour press when he objected to the Calvinistic Methodist Reconstruction Commission's report on social affairs in 1921, on the grounds that a religious body should not decide which kind of industrial system would be the most just. By then Williams had adopted the position that religious bodies should not overtly support any single political system on the grounds that differing opinions existed amongst all men of goodwill within the denominations.[89] A denominational line would thus threaten to split churches. Unfortunately, his claim inevitably appeared hollow in view of his own unshakeable allegiance to the Liberal Party.

7. NONCONFORMIST OPPOSITION

Hitherto, two main attitudes have been identified among Nonconformists. First, the idea that Socialism could be adopted as a practical application of Christian principles. Those who agreed with this varied in the importance they gave to the nascent movement. Their attitude differed as to what they considered their primary concern: either social or individual

[88] R. Tudur Jones, *Ffydd ac Argyfwng Cenedl*, I, *Prysurdeb a Phryder* (Swansea, 1981), p.211; II, *Dryswch a Diwygiad* (Swansea, 1982), p.229; R. R. Hughes, *John Williams Brynsiencyn* (Caernarfon, 1929), pp.188–9, 190–1.
[89] *Y Goleuad*, 9 February 1921, p.5; *Y Darian*, 3 March 1921, p.1.

salvation. It should be obvious by now that although attitudes towards Socialism could be conciliatory, they were based on ethical considerations and did not necessarily result in particular support for the labour movement. Secondly, there was pressure on the church to find its own unique answer to the social problem, an attitude which was not necessarily hostile towards the labour movement but which recognized the uniqueness of the Christian message. Christ alone was necessary for the world's salvation and thus any call to work alongside secular movements would compromise his sovereignty and efficacy in all matters human. Many Nonconformists sought to preserve this aspect of the gospel, though they mostly failed to discern an adequate social theology. However, there was a third group of Nonconformists who, for ideological reasons, political as well as theological, opposed Socialism and sometimes sought to discredit its followers.

Despite the support of some Nonconformist ministers, the church was generally considered to be hostile to Socialism and the ILP. There were incidents when Socialism was singled out to be opposed[90] and there were occasions when chapel vestries were refused to labour and Socialist organizations but open to Liberal groups, even when resolutions forbidding the use of vestries by political parties had been passed.[91] This hostility came from elders and deacons as well as from ministers. Some ministers actually suffered because of the political allegiance of their deacons. The Revd George Neighbour encountered opposition from his deacons because of Socialist propaganda work he was undertaking. He resigned as pastor of the English Baptist church in Miskin, Pontyclun, and formed a short-lived 'Labour Church'.[92] The Revd Daniel Hughes of Crane Street Baptist church, Pontypool, was locked out of his chapel by the deacons on the pretence that 'illegal baptisms' were to occur. It is almost certain that his Socialism caused this reaction. He later stood as a Labour candidate for the local council, defeating the sitting Liberal member who was also one of the deacons at Crane Street.[93]

[90] E.g. *Llais Llafur*, 18 April 1908, p.6; 12 June 1908, p.8; 27 June 1908, p.4; 5 December 1908, pp.1, 5; 9 September 1911, p.4; 4 May 1912, p.4.
[91] *Merthyr Pioneer*, 10 February 1912, p.6; cf. *Llais Llafur*, 22 April 1913, p.4.
[92] *Llais Llafur*, 19 October 1907, p.8; 26 October 1907, p.6.
[93] Cf. ibid., 16 January 1909, p.1; 4 December 1912, p.2; 18 January 1913, p.1; 8 March 1913, p.1; 29 March 1913, p.3.

The pulpit was also pressed into service against Socialism. Occasional insults were hurled at undignified 'street-corner' Socialism.[94] According to the Revd W. Saunders, speaking during the annual conference of the Baptist Union at Holyhead in 1908, Socialism was a 'virus'.[95] It was claimed that Socialism made 'spiritual impression' impossible in Bargoed,[96] while the Revd George Freeman advertised the launch of a new fund for 'The Anti-Socialist Campaign in Wales'.[97] The Revd J. T. Davies, Nantymoel, had been accused of vilifying members of the ILP, whom he had referred to as 'infidels'. He responded that he would stop this practice when members of the ILP ceased criticizing the church.[98] Even as late as 1920 ministers were still pointing to the anti-religious elements in the labour movement. E. D. Lewis was keen to show that the Socialist emphasis on the coming of the Kingdom obscured man's need of forgiveness and reconciliation to God.[99] Nonconformists often complained that the ILP held its meetings on Sundays,[100] though few churches went as far as Bodringallt Welsh Independent chapel, Ystrad, Rhondda, which threatened excommunication for any member who attended a political meeting on the Sabbath.[101] This was the reaction of a Nonconformity anxious to retain its social status and preserve its interests in the face of attack. Those who wished to prolong the Liberal hegemony sought to ostracize chapel adherents who belonged to the new Socialist movements. But it was also a real attempt to answer the perceived threat of an atheistic political movement, and to retain the need for the specifics of the Christian gospel.

Questions were asked as to whether Christians could be Socialists at all. Those who listened to the anti-religious propaganda of the atheistic elements in European Socialism claimed that Socialism was incompatible with Christianity. Thus, *Yr Efengylydd* presented H. Musgrave Reade as a former Socialist

[94] Ibid., 9 November 1912, p.8.
[95] Ibid., 3 October 1908, p.6.
[96] *Merthyr Pioneer*, 18 November 1911, p.7.
[97] *Llais Llafur*, 16 April 1910, p.5; cf. Leonard Smith, *Religion and the Rise of Labour* (Keele, 1993), p.100.
[98] *Llais Llafur*, 19 December 1908, p.7.
[99] *Seren Cymru*, 13 August 1920, p.2.
[100] *Llais Llafur*, 31 July 1909, p.1; 23 October 1909, pp.1, 4. For opposition, see e.g. *Llais Llafur*, 12 June 1909, p.8; 27 June 1908, p.4.
[101] Ibid., 21 May 1910, p.1.

who, following an evangelical conversion, had renounced his political allegiance and dedicated himself to opposing Socialism: 'We might improve the material surroundings, increase the wealth of people, give greater facility for culture and ease to the working classes; but until sin, sorrow and death were abolished, true and lasting happiness was impossible.'[102]

Other Nonconformists were concerned that Socialism appeared to be inherently atheistic or that it caused men to abandon any obvious religious affiliation.[103] *Y Goleuad* published articles on 'Cymrodiaeth a'r Eglwys' (Socialism and the Church) which insisted that many Socialists, though claiming that their principles were those of true religion and of Christ, were in fact atheists: 'So we are bound to believe that a system that is perfectly consistent with faith in God and with the principles of Christianity tends unfortunately and accidentally to produce atheists!'[104] Socialism had caused many to leave the church and turn against it. If Socialists retained their religious affiliations, their tendency was to lose 'sympathy with [the church's] doctrines and its constitution, and soon they become insurgents and a cause of strife'.[105] These articles claimed a sympathy with all attempts to ensure better conditions for the labouring masses, and every effort to give them a higher standard of comfort and happiness. But this was very different from Socialism. Christianity, concluded the articles, includes all this without the wild elements found in political Socialism, and therefore 'contains a full provision for the needs of man and society'.[106] Socialism was not to be confused with mere social improvement and neither were the moral precepts of the Sermon on the Mount to be counted as the sum of Christianity. Christ is the centre of Christianity and 'no man has the right to call himself a Christian solely because he accepts the teachings of the Sermon on the Mount'.[107] The author of these articles was the Revd W. F. Phillips.[108]

---

[102] H. Musgrave Reade, 'Christ or Socialism', *Yr Efengylydd* (1909), 79.
[103] E.g. *Llais Llafur*, 11 July 1908, p.6; 7 November 1908, p.1.
[104] *Y Goleuad*, 6 September 1911, p.9.
[105] Ibid.; cf. R. Tudur Jones, *Hanes Annibynwyr Cymru* (Swansea, 1966), p.275.
[106] *Y Goleuad*, 6 September 1911, p.9.
[107] Ibid., 20 September 1911, p.10.
[108] For W. F. Phillips (1877–1920), see *Blwyddiadur y Methodistiaid Calfinaidd* (1921), 170–1.

8. W. F. PHILLIPS

W. F. Phillips was a native of Penmaen-mawr, Caernarfonshire.
He had studied at Bala, Cardiff, Aberystwyth and Oxford and
tended to flaunt the fact that he had graduated three times. His
penchant for listing his degrees after his name in published
articles earned him the sobriquet 'Alphabet Phillips' for his
pretensions; his political adversaries took inordinate satisfaction in
supplying their own interpretations of BA, BD, namely 'Bili
Anwir' (Billy Liar) and 'Bwli Dialgar' (Vindictive Bully). There is
much confusion over Phillips's early political allegiance. Silyn
Roberts claimed that Phillips was by far the more fiery Socialist of
the pair when they studied together at Bala, while the claim was
also made that during a student pastorate in Newport,
Monmouthshire, Phillips joined the ILP. Be that as it may,
Phillips's opposition to Socialism became belligerent and
vociferous after his defeat by a 'Labour' man in the election of
December 1910 for the Gower constituency.[109] Phillips felt
Socialism had been presented in so many different forms that
clarification was required. He recognized three groups of
Socialists: those who believed Socialism and Christianity to be
totally separate, those who believed them to belong to two
different spheres and those who believed that Socialism was the
practical application of Christian principles. In his judgement, the
first group alone were true Socialists. This was unhelpful to say
the least, as there were significant numbers who saw Socialism as
belonging to one of the other groups.[110] He sought to expose
Socialism as an atheistic system, then to show that sympathy with
labour and social reform was not the same as Socialism.[111] He
chose to clarify it from the works of those who were confessed
atheists, such as Robert Blatchford and E. Belfort Bax, while he
also quoted H. Musgrave Reade and G. H. Bibbings, two former
Socialists who were converted to Christianity and believed that
Socialism was anti-Christian in tendency. Blatchford, he

---

[109] David Cleaver, 'Labour and Liberals in the Gower constituency, 1885–1910',
Welsh History Review, XII/3 (1985), 408.
[110] W. F. Phillips, 'Cymru a Sosialaeth', *Y Geninen* (1911), 17, 83.
[111] *Y Goleuad*, 6 September 1911, p.9; W. F. Phillips, *Y Ddraig Goch ynte'r Faner Goch ac
Ysgrifau Eraill* (Cardiff, 1913), introduction, and p.64; *idem*, 'Religion and labour week at
Cardiff', *The Monthly Democrat* (1912), 106–7.

concluded, 'tells the whole truth about Socialism', while those who see a connection between Socialism and Christianity either 'through ignorance or from choice they hide the truth'.[112]

In fact, Phillips was simply anti-Socialist. Though he did not really explain why, he claimed that the Socialist creed was not only unpatriotic but treacherous and anti-Christian. Socialism, he claimed, rested on materialism, sought social comfort, placed its emphasis on man's environment rather than on his character, and did not take individual rights and responsibilities into consideration.[113] Unfortunately, far from reasonably explaining the implications of the Socialist creed, he tended simply to denounce its plans. This is in great contrast to the careful, though often emotive, explanation given by the Socialists.[114]

Phillips was to an extent supporting the positive claims of Christianity, which sought 'to save man as man and set society on the firm foundation of justice'.[115] Although still a fairly young man, he belonged to an older theological generation and was offended by the increasing attention being given to environment to the detriment of character, and by the implication that man rather than God would be society's saviour.[116] Socialism deprived human beings of ultimate responsibility and accountability for their conduct. Furthermore, Socialism could never improve the individual. Every man and woman is a moral personality and must be morally regenerated as an individual. Only then can all regenerated individuals co-operate in order to form an improved society. Man was a personality and therefore could turn 'unfavourable environment to his advantage in his personal development'.[117] Socialism degraded man to the status of a higher animal whose nature is affected by his environment.[118] Once men could be persuaded to consider their fellow men as 'persons', he believed that would be an end to oppression and selfishness and lead to self-denial on behalf of others. This, for him, was the message of Jesus.[119] Once man was made right,

[112] 'Cymru a Sosialaeth', pp.18–19.
[113] Ibid., p.21; cf. *Llais Llafur*, 1 October 1910, p.3.
[114] Cf. *Llais Llafur*, 24 June 1911, p.5; also T. E. Nicholas's articles in *Y Geninen* (1912–14).
[115] 'Sosialaeth a Christionogaeth', p.83.
[116] 'Y Ddraig Goch ynte'r Faner Goch: Sosialaeth a Chenedlaetholdeb', pp.255–8, *passim*.
[117] W. F. Phillips, 'Crist a Chymdeithas', *Y Traethodydd* (1913), 26.
[118] Ibid., p.25.
[119] Ibid., pp.29–30.

his surroundings would easily be improved: 'The Church's work is not to try directly to solve social problems, but to show what the relationship is between the essential, unchanging and eternal principles of our religion with the changing surroundings of man and society.'[120] Christianity alone offered the solution to the social problem through emphasizing individual personality and status within the context of one family. While Socialism claimed to inaugurate a brotherhood, it offered no reason why all men were brothers. Only in Christianity could such a reason be found, namely that God was Father.[121] Both Phillips and most of the 'Socialist' ministers believed that it was the status and importance which Christianity gave to humankind that clinched their vastly differing arguments.

Phillips wanted to see the church involved in solving the social problem.[122] He suggested that the Calvinistic Methodists establish a committee so that the church could be better informed on the social question.[123] Although Christianity should not be made synonymous with social service, he recognized that it had a vital contribution to make. 'Christ', he wrote, 'is the only medicine which can improve mankind, social service is that which attempts to bring this medicine to the grasp of those who are unhealthy in society.'[124]

Because of his pugnacious and truculent style, Phillips had the ability to generate vastly different reactions, depending on the nature of his readers' attitude towards Socialism. Thus, supporters criticized him severely[125] while those who feared the supposed atheism and immorality of the Socialist message hailed him as 'one of the nation's talented young men'[126] who was 'attempting to raise this land through enlightening its inhabitants'.[127] His articles and speeches were often over-concerned with 'irrelevant flippancies and grandiloquent generalities',[128] giving the impression of a confidence and even an arrogance that he could ill afford. Thus,

---

[120] *Y Ddraig Goch ynte'r Faner Goch ac Ysgrifau Eraill*, p.76.
[121] Ibid., p.74.
[122] *Y Goleuad*, 7 December 1912, p.10.
[123] Ibid., 28 February 1912, p.6.
[124] Ibid., 7 February 1912, p.10.
[125] *Llais Llafur*, 10 December 1910, p.1; 22 April 1911, p.1; 3 June 1911, p.3; *Merthyr Pioneer*, 13 April 1912, p.3.
[126] *Y Goleuad*, 9 August 1911, p.4.
[127] Ibid., 25 October 1911, p.4.
[128] *Llais Llafur*, 24 June 1911, p.5.

he justified to T. E. Nicholas the writing of an 'open letter' to Keir Hardie in Welsh by claiming 'you should thank me for giving you the opportunity to show kindness to your hero through translating my letter for his benefit'.[129] This was unfortunate, as the fears that some had concerning Socialism were real enough and Phillips could on occasion express them well. All too often, however, they were expressed without any desire to see the difficulties and fears removed. Furthermore, his enthusiastic activity on behalf of the Young Liberals leaves the suspicion that all Phillips's complaints, even his religious ones, arose because he was trying to ensure support for the Liberal Party. Many could reconcile their Christianity with economic Socialism, and economic Socialism was not necessarily atheistic. Phillips's failure to treat this as not only a serious but a plausible option only compounds the suspicion of political opportunism.

Phillips represents a period which was drawing to a close. The Nonconformist minister was slowly but surely losing his status, and people were less prepared to take his word as final. While other young ministers were looking more to the labour movement, Phillips remained an enthusiastic Liberal, and whereas his theology remained conservative, other young ministers were drawn to the 'higher criticism' and new movements in theology. His sudden death, aged forty-two, in 1920 signalled the end of an era when the strength of Nonconformity was assured, when the minister was the recognized leader of the local community and when the Liberal Party represented the political and social hopes of the majority of Welshmen. More than anyone else in his generation, Phillips characterized this former era. It was appropriate that his death coincided with its demise.

9. OTHER NONCONFORMIST OPPONENTS

For many Nonconformists, opposition to Socialism was made inevitable by the unique nature of the Christian message, which needed no additional political group to fulfil its vision. Christianity's mission was held to be both social and individualist. It therefore stood alone, not needing Socialism's validation.

---

[129] *Tarian y Gweithiwr*, 8 February 1912: for the letter, see *Tarian y Gweithiwr*, 17 August 1911 to 7 September 1911.

> The main work of the preacher is to proclaim the gospel of reconciliation
> between God and man in the person and name of Jesus Christ. But
> preachers know full well that it is impossible for this gospel to do its work
> thoroughly without influencing society. Every Christian should be a
> missionary for Christ in the social world . . . The Church's job is not to
> make Socialists or Liberals or Conservatives, but to make Christians. In
> making them true followers of Christ the Church will become the strongest
> force in existence to reform society, not from the standpoint of party
> politics but from the standpoint of Christian citizenship.[130]

The main opposition to Socialism arose from its emphasis on
material improvement and its faith in the redemptive effect of
environmental change. Its danger was to forget the 'internal
moral and spiritual conditions which make for all true social
elevation'.[131] T. E. Jones was concerned that the Kingdom of
God, popular in Socialist imagery, had been stripped of its true
meaning. 'The Kingdom of God', he affirmed 'is not in
surroundings (*mewn amgylchiadau*) but in spirit and character.'[132]

Professor Thomas Levi, Aberystwyth, echoed this opposition.
He had forsaken his once enthusiastic adherence to Socialism in
favour of evangelical Christianity because Christianity included
all that Socialism could offer, and much more, by establishing
the Kingdom of God in every man's heart. He drew criticism,
however, for his anti-Socialist stance when he advised the
Eastern Valley Free Church Council that it was not Socialism
they required but practising Christians and that they should
inaugurate a 'pure Christian Club' to ensure that Christians were
produced. The labour press rightly recognized that this
suggestion implied a condemnation of a failed church.[133]

It was the presentation of Socialism, which was after all a
secular agency, as the source of mankind's redemption which
offended some. Richard Morgan drew attention to this in his
orthodox, though in its context provocatively entitled, book,
Cristionogaeth yn Iachawdwriaeth Dynoliaeth (Christianity is Mankind's Salvation).[134] Morgan drew attention to three significant

---

[130] *Tarian y Gweithiwr*, 28 September 1911, p.1.
[131] J. Lewis Williams, 'Y Sosialist Cymreig', *Y Dysgedydd* (1912), 316; cf. *Y Goleuad*, 23
August 1911, p.11.
[132] T. E. Jones, 'Y pulpud a chwestiwn Llafur', *Y Drysorfa* (1913), 10.
[133] *Llais Llafur*, 3 April 1909, p.5; *Y Goleuad*, 17 February 1909, p.6.
[134] Bangor, 1912.

differences between Socialism and Christianity. They differed in nature, Socialism being inherently materialistic while Christianity was 'an internal spiritual system'. They differed in method, Socialism using external compulsion through the dictates of the state government, while Christianity used 'moral influence', the enlightenment of the mind and the 'rebirth of the soul'. They also differed in aim. Socialism sought to change man's relationship with the world while Christianity transformed man's relationship with God, which would automatically reform man's relationship with the world. Because Christianity sought to meet a spiritual need, it would still be required long after the material need had been met (pp.39–41). Sin was man's greatest enemy and one for which Socialism had no answer. Injustice would never be eradicated unless sin was destroyed and this would occur not through a change in laws and statutes but through the rebirth of the soul. Once the soul had been reborn, laws to ensure justice and a fair distribution would not be necessary. But man must first be affected in order to affect the world (pp.44–5).

For all these men it was the existence of sin, embedded in the heart of human nature, which rendered futile any attempts at social reform without individual regeneration. None of them had any concept of structural sin. All evil in the world could be traced back to the depravity of individual men. Significantly, many of the 'Socialist' ministers also tended to emphasize society's need of Christianity to effect individual moral transformation as a prerequisite for social reform.

10. CONCLUSIONS

The problem of Socialism for Nonconformists was not an easy one to solve. Nonconformity had traditionally stood for the rights of the individual, whether to follow the dictates of conscience, to make personal gain or to cherish private property. Notwithstanding the variations which it encompassed, Socialism appeared to threaten each of these long-held ideals. The advent of Socialism certainly coincided with a general agreement that social reform should be a priority in the modern world. Thus, anyone who showed a desire to reform and rebuild society along fairer lines, and sought to ameliorate the living and working conditions of ordinary men and women, could claim the title of Socialist. The question is: did Socialism lead ministers to that conclusion? Some claimed the title Socialist on the grounds that they sought social reform, but few appear to have had a grasp of economic Socialism. Instead, they spoke of it in moral terms as the establishment of a 'brotherhood of man' in which justice and righteousness reigned supreme. It is hardly surprising that so many ministers claimed to be Socialists but were in politics supporters of the Liberal Party. The Revd Rhys J. Huws, for example, recommended that voters in Carmarthenshire support the Liberal candidate, the Revd J. Towyn Jones, rather than the Labour candidate, despite his own membership of the ILP. The Revd John Morgan Jones, then of Aberdare but later of Bangor, claimed much sympathy for the Socialist cause but sat as a Liberal councillor in Aberdare. The propaganda of Keir Hardie and the ILP had in some ways encouraged this view. Hardie's message was that Socialism would enable men to practise Christianity. It was his accusation that the church had not been faithful to the gospel message which was echoed, in varying degrees, by the 'Socialist' ministers. But these ideas developed from a further, equally potent, source. Those who claimed the title Socialist had adopted the modern developments within theology and biblical studies. Two German theologians are of particular importance. Albrecht Ritschl's emphasis on the moral responsibility of mankind in establishing the Kingdom of God on earth, alongside Adolf Harnack's teaching of mankind's brotherhood under God's Fatherhood, corresponds with this ethical Socialism. It stressed the spiritual and moral as well as the responsibility of the individual and thus retained the concern for individual souls which was so important to traditional Nonconformity.

Ironically, it was the ascendancy of the spiritual and the moral in the theological context of the time which resulted in some Nonconformist ministers being attracted to Socialism and provided the basis for the opposition of others. They acquiesced in Socialist thought to the extent that it represented a higher ethical ideal than that which was embedded in the industrial system. All in all it appears that Nonconformists were attracted to Socialism only to the extent that it concurred with the findings of other modern disciplines. The ascendancy of the spiritual in current thought ensured that Socialism's economic claims never attracted any widespread support, or at least were adopted only with the qualification that man still needed a saviour and that saviour was Jesus Christ.

The majority of Nonconformist ministers, even those who were sympathetic to Socialism and the labour movement, were still trying to demonstrate the unique and vital mission of Christianity which Socialism could not fulfil. There were exceptions such as T. E. Nicholas and 'Gwallter Ddu', but on the whole 'Socialist' ministers maintained the traditional view that salvation could only be accepted individually and not *en masse*, a view which showed how far removed they were from truly socialistic ideas. Furthermore, they could see no moral benefit for the individual following social improvement. For the latter to be achieved there had to be an emphasis on the former. Redeemed and regenerated individuals alone could create a better society. Men like Rowland Jones, James Nicholas, R. Silyn Roberts and T. E. Nicholas helped to give the impression that Socialism belonged to the progressive Welsh tradition of radical politics, and this undoubtedly made more impact on the working class than did their protestations that material improvement could never be enough. This was the fundamental difference between the Nonconformist ministers and the Socialist agitators. The ministers believed almost to a man that Christianity involved the making of Christians; the Socialist agitators propagated the view that it involved the creation of a perfect state. Both groups believed that ultimately their work was the creation of the Kingdom of God and that their way alone could be effective.

Nonconformity itself was undergoing a transformation in this period as ministers were becoming ever more aware of the temporal needs of their congregations. Before 1914 there was no generally accepted religious solution to the social problem, apart from that which was implicit in the traditional individualist approach. Thereafter, ministers began to invoke specifically social interpretations embodied in the tenets of Liberal Theology. In the mean time, Nonconformists, allied to the Liberal Party and radical politics since the middle of the previous century, were slowly retreating from the political arena. In some respects the advent of Socialism caused this retreat. When there were just two political possibilities, with both clearly representing the interests of particular sections in society, the allegiance of Nonconformity was never in question. The advent of the labour movement split congregations politically and would soon put an end to the Nonconformist Liberal hegemony. In such an environment it seemed unwise to appear partisan. As Socialists sought support for an explicitly political programme, it is inconceivable that Nonconformists could ever have co-operated with them in an organized way. Instead of adopting Socialism, Nonconformists had to try to contribute something of their own to the social debate. This they were beginning to do, their task made the more necessary following the advent of a strong, confident and highly critical Socialist movement and the catastrophe of the Great War.

Kenneth Morgan claims that up to 1914, apart from in the Rhondda and Aberdare, Socialism was 'at best static if not in decline'. That may have been the case. But it is during that period alone that the issues of Socialism and Christianity, Socialism and religion, and Socialism and the chapel were important. Following the Great War these issues simply disappeared as political groups grasped the unique opportunity to rebuild society as best they could. They also realized that local concerns had given way to international ones.[135] Before Nonconformity's response to this widening of the social problem can be investigated, it is appropriate to consider the evidence for the virtual sea-change which occurred in working-class political thought and allegiance at this time. In so doing, the problems which faced Nonconformists will become clearer.

---

[135] Kenneth O. Morgan, *Wales in British Politics, 1868–1922* (Cardiff, 1991), pp.254–5.

III

LABOUR, SOCIALISM AND NONCONFORMITY

Early twentieth-century Wales was dominated by the advent of Socialism. Keir Hardie's call for working-class parliamentary representation, preached with a profoundly religious zeal, became increasingly popular, particularly following the bitter disputes which plagued industrial Wales at the turn of the century. The six-month lock-out of 1898 in the south Wales coalfield and the Penrhyn quarrymen's dispute in Gwynedd between 1900 and 1903 struck at the heart of the established social system. They marked a turning-point in the history of the Welsh working class, challenging the established authority of the coalfield capitalists on the one hand and the feudal Lord Penrhyn on the other to impose settlements on their workforce. Despite the defeat sustained by both the miners and the quarrymen, this marked the beginning of the end of the prevailing system. The dissemination of Socialism through the South Wales Miners' Federation (SWMF), formed at the end of the 1898 dispute, and through the ILP increased rapidly. As a result of Keir Hardie's tour of the coalfield in 1898 the number of ILP branches increased from four to thirty-one.[1] Eighty-four branches employing five full-time propagandists were reported to have been established in south Wales by 1908, while a further eight had been formed in the north.[2] The years following the 1904 religious revival would see the working class reach new heights of violent militancy. The rioting of November 1910 in Tonypandy and the use of troops in Llanelli during the railway dispute of 1911 are well documented. Industrial action meant conflict with the forces of authority, and a steady flow of men came through the police courts during the troubled and worrying days of economic depression in the 1920s and 1930s. What

[1] Noted in Dylan Morris, 'Sosialaeth i'r Cymry, trafodaeth yr I.L.P.', *Llafur*, IV/2 (1985), 51.
[2] Peter Stead, 'Establishing a heartland: the first Labour Party in Wales', in K. Brown (ed.), *The First Labour Party* (London, 1985), p.73.

percentage of men involved in these disputes merely belonged to
the criminal element is difficult to judge. What is certain is that
many respectable and ordinarily law-abiding citizens were
involved, fired by the depravities of poverty and a sense of
injustice with the capitalist system. There were chapel men
among their number, some of whom would ultimately spend
time in prison.[3] What part the ILP played in this development of
militancy is unclear and its penetration into the Welsh industrial
communities is 'difficult to determine'.[4] But it is undeniable that
by 1918 Labour had virtually replaced the Liberal Party as the
most potent and popular political force in Wales. Despite Lloyd
George's personal triumph in overseeing the end of hostilities,
talk of the Liberal Party being morally and politically bankrupt
pervaded political discussion throughout the 1918 election
campaign. Lifelong Liberals were forsaking their commitment to
a party which had seemingly abandoned all its principles in order
to win the war.[5] In an amazingly short period the Labour Party
became the main alternative to the Conservatives throughout
Britain, and the Liberals, their strength dissipated, were left in
the political wilderness. The breakthrough was made in the early
1920s. The 1923 general election put Labour ahead of the
Liberals with 191 seats compared to 158. By the election of May
1929 the change in political attitudes which had swept through
the country had reached its height. Labour gained 287 seats to
the Conservative 260 and the Liberal 59. If anything, the
transference of political allegiance was more marked in Wales
than anywhere. The election of July 1892 had seen all but three
of the thirty-four constituencies return a Liberal MP.
Remarkably, Liberal influence appeared to increase even from
that triumph and in the landslide election victory of 1906 the
only non-Liberal returned was Keir Hardie, and he was elected
only as the second member for Merthyr.[6] As remarkable as this
ascendancy was the almost total eclipse of the Liberal Party after
the Great War. The Labour Party was gradually increasing its
influence in the strongholds of the industrial south and although

---

[3] See e.g. Hywel Francis and David Smith, *The Fed* (London, 1980), p.67; Cliff
Prothero, *Recount* (Ormskirk, 1982), p.16.
[4] Kenneth O. Morgan, *Wales in British Politics 1868–1922* (Cardiff, 1991), p.95.
[5] Thomas Rees, 'The crisis of Welsh Nonconformity', *The Welsh Outlook* (1920), 58.
[6] See Kenneth O. Morgan, *Rebirth of a Nation: Wales 1880–1980* (Oxford, 1981),
pp.30–1.

it suffered a set-back in Wales as elsewhere with the fall of the first Labour government in 1924, by the end of the decade the pattern of electoral results which would be repeated time and again throughout the twentieth century was already in place. In the 1929 election, one Conservative, ten Liberal and twenty-five Labour members were returned for Welsh constituencies.[7]

While a transference of allegiance from the Liberal to the Labour Party was demonstrated by the results of general elections, the political and religious attitudes of the working class are more difficult to determine. The evidence which exists suggests a highly complex social structure in Welsh communities in which political and religious beliefs could be reconciled, albeit to the occasional detriment of chapel attendance. While some men did leave the chapel at this time, a fact demonstrated more clearly by Nonconformist concern at dwindling congregations than by direct working-class evidence,[8] it is also clear that many did not. Their womenfolk, for the most part, remained solidly within the chapels. No definite pattern can be discerned and no single reason for the decline of organized religion can be given. A perusal of what evidence does exist, however, indicates some of the difficulties which the working class faced in formulating their religious beliefs.

1. THE EVIDENCE

The popular local press is one source for our knowledge of the religious and political beliefs of the working class. Although there were four weekly newspapers published in Wales at different times during the period 1906 to 1939, one cannot be sure whether or not their editorial policy represented the ideas of ordinary working men. Neither were they necessarily Socialist. *Tarian y Gweithiwr* (*Y Darian* from 1914) maintained a radical edge from its inception in 1875 until its demise in 1934. It consciously remained a Welsh-language newspaper throughout its life. Although its support for 'labour' causes was assured, it had never been a Socialist newspaper, tending rather to represent the 'Lib-Lab' position.

---

[7] See Gwyn A. Williams, *When Was Wales?* (London, 1985), p.250.

[8] For concern over decline, *Llais Llafur*, 11 January 1913, p.1; *Labour Voice*, 18 September 1920, p.2; 2 December 1922, p.7; *Y Tyst*, 11 August 1915, p.8; *Y Dinesydd*, 20 June 1923, p.8.

Llais Llafur, established during the fateful year 1898 by the radical progressive Ebenezer Rees, succumbed to Anglicizing influences, changed its name to *Labour Voice* from January 1915 and to the *South Wales Voice* from July 1927. Over the years it lost its radicalism completely, and by the 1920s published virtually no articles of a political or propagatory nature. Religious meetings were reported superficially and the *Llais* became little more than a local newspaper rather than a means for the transmission of either Socialism or progressive thought. Its political content was gradually replaced by reports of local sporting activities and the programmes of Swansea valley picture-houses.

The most Socialist paper of them all was the *Merthyr Pioneer,* which included regular articles by both Keir Hardie and the Revd T. E. Nicholas. Its columns almost invariably included some religious content, usually of an unorthodox and anti-establishment nature. Hardie used the paper to challenge local ministers to practise the social implications of their Christianity,[9] while T. E. Nicholas incurred the wrath of the Methodist minister W. F. Phillips and others by ridiculing the Welsh Nonconformist allegiance to Liberalism and orthodox Christianity's fascination with creeds when more important issues were at stake.[10] The *Pioneer* maintained a Socialist stance, encouraging the working class to retain its union membership and work for fair representation in Parliament. This was combined during the Great War with an uncompromising pacifism. It finally ceased circulation in 1922.[11]

Y Dinesydd Cymreig first appeared in May 1912 and ran until July 1929. It remained a Welsh-language newspaper and officially represented the North Wales Quarrymen's Union and the Caernarfonshire Labour Council.[12] Although it, too, carried much local news, its sympathies were with labour. Its conservatism in both religious and political matters, together with its retention of the Welsh language, reflected the character of north Wales society.

[9] E.g. *Merthyr Pioneer,* 13 May 1911, p.6; 17 June 1911, p.1.

[10] Ibid., 23 October 1911, p.3. For Phillips's response, see 'Y perygl oddiwrth Sosialaeth yng Nghymru', *Y Geninen* (1911), 9; *Tarian y Gweithiwr,* 21 January 1912, p.5.

[11] For *Merthyr Pioneer,* see Deian Hopkin, 'The Merthyr Pioneer, 1911–1922', *Llafur,* II/4 (1979), 54–64.

[12] R. Harrison *et al.* (eds.), *The Warwick Guide to British Labour Periodicals, 1790–1970* (Hassocks, Sussex, 1977), p.134.

Evidence of working-class attitudes to religion and politics is attested by contemporary press reports, biographical accounts and personal reminiscences, and by the oral testimony gathered as part of the South Wales Coalfield Project between 1972 and 1974. Each of these sources presents its own problems. There is a danger of anachronism, a reading back of subsequent attitudes into earlier events, while biographical accounts often reflect the historical and sometimes political preconceptions of the author. The miners' views on the relationship between religion and the labour movement were only incidental to the main interests of the coalfield project. If mentioned at all, religion and chapel-going were usually glossed over superficially and few men gave clear accounts either of why they had forsaken formal religion or else how they succeeded in uniting politics and faith. Their self-expression was often limited and consequently a clear picture is difficult to form. None of this is meant to imply that the politics of the coalfield were not radical, or that these sources are totally unreliable. It is virtually impossible, however, to construct a detailed and systematic account of anything other than individual lives. What was left unmentioned, or simply hinted at, is often as important as what was said.[13]

There is clearly a distinction to be made between the communities of the north and those of the south. North Wales had proved to be far less receptive of militant working-class politics than had the valley communities in the south. Cyril Parry has shown that labour leaders in the north were more concerned with the 'immediate problems of poverty and unemployment' than with ideology.[14] Nonconformity had instilled in the people of north Wales a sense of individual responsibility in morality, industry and, of course, salvation. This was supported by the sense of community in the slate-quarrying districts which was far different from that of the narrow conurbations hastily thrown up in the wake of the industrial revolution in the south. According to Dr Parry, the pattern of the quarryman's life 'emphasized individual effort', with a day's work in the quarry followed by 'an

---

[13] For a positive assessment of the value of oral evidence, see Hywel Francis, 'The secret world of the south Wales miner: the relevance of oral history', in David Smith (ed.), *A People and a Proletariat: Essays in the History of Wales* (London, 1980), pp.166–80.

[14] Cyril Parry, 'Gwynedd politics 1900–1920: the rise of a Labour Party', *Welsh History Review*, VI/3 (1973), 326.

evening's work in scattered smallholdings'.[15] As well as this, the quarrymen had, by and large, enjoyed a relatively high standard of living which made them less prone to militancy than the miners of the south, certainly before the disastrous Penrhyn lockout of 1900–3. Strangely, however, their struggles against a tyrannical employer and virtually feudal landlord would surely have been the ideal context in which the theory of class war could flourish. That it did not is testimony to the strength of the pervading individualist, Liberal, radical and Nonconformist culture. Social, political and religious parameters were generally better defined in the north. The union became the focus for industrial and political activities while the chapel retained its primacy as a religious and social centre. This separation was sufficiently well delineated for north Walians working in the coalfields of the south to complain about the politicization of the chapels there.[16]

This conservatism was reflected in the columns of *Y Dinesydd*, which continually used religious imagery in calling on the church to practise its social responsibility. The church's role was to condemn the atheistic tendencies of the age embodied in the social system.[17] 'Chapel religion is worth nothing if it does not promote a spirit which will leaven society and promote humanity.'[18] Articles in *Y Dinesydd* regularly called on men to use the principles of the Sermon on the Mount and the Kingdom of God as a basis for social reconstruction. Fundamentally, though, the rebuilding required, particularly after the Great War, was moral and could not therefore be achieved through the proliferation of material welfare.[19] The need was for the creation of true brotherhood which would in turn solve all the social problems of the age. This would lead men into self-sacrifice and service, two basic tenets of Jesus's teaching.[20] All this was presented in the context of a general optimism which believed, particularly after 1918, that the world stood at a crossroads. The establishment of a new world was assured if men would dedicate

[15] Cyril Parry, *The Radical Tradition in Welsh Politics: A Study of Liberal and Labour Politics in Gwynedd* (Hull, 1970), p.5.

[16] See Dafydd Roberts, *Y Chwarelwyr a'r Sowth* (Caernarfon, 1982), p.15.

[17] *Y Dinesydd*, 23 May 1923, p.7.

[18] Ibid., 30 May 1923, p.3.

[19] Ibid., 27 July 1921, p.7.

[20] Ibid., 9 January 1924, p.7.

their lives to its construction.[21] But this opinion implied that Nonconformity had lost its 'vision', having refused to listen to the Socialist 'prophets' whom God had raised in the land.[22]

For the working families of north Wales the chapel provided both a collective identity and a base for social activities; indeed they 'dominated behaviour outside of the mere act of worship in the same way as their gaunt shapes overshadowed the terraced streets'.[23] The chapels in the south, with their numerous social activities, had also provided a particular identity for their community, but in the valleys of Glamorgan and Monmouth, far more than in the north, there were other organizations competing for the allegiance of the working men. Consequently, most of this chapter will concentrate on the conditions and attitudes of south Wales society. In so doing it will become clear that religious and political differences existed between the homogeneity of the largely Welsh-speaking western coalfield and the more cosmopolitan eastern districts, which had seen a greater influx of people in the wake of industrialization.

2. The Ascendancy of Socialism

The factor which caused Nonconformists most concern during this period was their apparent helplessness in the face of the multiple challenges to their former hegemony in Welsh society.[24] Nonconformity had been perhaps the greatest single influence on Welsh life for at least half a century. The legacy of the industrial revolution was, for many communities, the constant threat to life and the stark reality of economic hardship. As countless thousands left the country to converge on the developing industrial districts, religion provided them with comfort and hope in the most insecure of situations, as well as an invaluable link with their roots. It had largely educated the working class and instilled in the popular mind the importance of education and democracy. Vital to Nonconformist churchmanship was the responsibility exercised by ordinary members through lay

[21] Ibid., 22 October 1924, p.5.
[22] Ibid., 8 July 1925, p.3.
[23] R. Merfyn Jones, *The North Wales Quarrymen, 1874–1922* (Cardiff, 1981), p.43.
[24] R. Tudur Jones, *Ffydd ac Argyfwng Cenedl*, I and II (Swansea 1981–2).

preaching or election to the diaconate.[25] Nonconformity had enforced standards of morality, recognized individual responsibility and provided hope for a better life, albeit beyond the grave. Nonconformist zeal for temperance fostered 'the great trinity of religion, education and good living',[26] and thus afforded the working class the opportunity and the training to develop the necessary skills for public life. Nonconformist influence extended beyond the spiritual needs of its members and adherents into social and political leadership in the mining, quarrying and agricultural communities. The chapel even affected the lives of those who never attended any of its activities.[27] Walter Haydn Davies remembered this period of his youth as the time when 'the flower of Welsh non-conformity with its petals of so many hues reflecting the sunlight of a special Welsh way of life, came into full bloom'.[28] Nonconformity's greatest weakness, though, was its apparent neglect of the temporal needs of its adherents.

> The religious atmosphere was one in which any form of recreational activity which lacked a spiritual background was viewed with dire suspicion. According to certain people, religion did not appear to take into account the needs of the common man in his desire to provide, here and now, a fuller life for himself and his children and not wait patiently for the hereafter.[29]

Here we see the transition in expectations which occurred at the turn of the century. While previously content with a religion that gave stability and hope in an unstable and precarious environment, the working class now sought a religion which would change their environment.[30] Hardie and others had convinced them that religion should indeed do this. But the end result was that his use of religious language persuaded men to join a secular movement. Labour leaders, many of whom had been nurtured in the chapels, increasingly found themselves having to choose

---

[25] D. M. Griffith, *Nationality in the Sunday School Movement* (Bangor, 1925), p.153.

[26] Walter Haydn Davies, *The Right Place, the Right Time: Memories of Boyhood Days in a Welsh Mining Community* (Llandybïe, 1972), p.60; cf. George Ewart Evans, *From Mouths of Men* (London, 1976), pp.155–6.

[27] Merfyn Jones, *North Wales Quarrymen*, p.43; *Merthyr Pioneer*, 7 October 1911, p.3.

[28] Haydn Davies, *Right Place*, p.67.

[29] Ibid., p.208.

[30] See D. R. Davies, *In Search of Myself* (London, 1961), pp.15–17; J. Vyrnwy Morgan, *The Welsh Mind in Evolution* (London, 1925), pp.157, 175.

between their political commitment and their religious faith. Some, while remaining within the chapel, took an active role in public life more through a sense of civic responsibility than from any firm desire to spread Socialist beliefs. Amongst this group were men like James Griffiths, later MP for Llanelli, and Cliff Prothero, a prominent local official in the labour movement. Others, like Frank Hodges, one-time secretary of the Miners' Federation of Great Britain (MFGB), and S. O. Davies, later MP for Merthyr, would hold the chapel separate from the labour movement, sometimes considering the one to be the theoretical side and the other the practical side of the same thing.[31] Others, such as A. J. Cook, who was Frank Hodges's predecessor, and Arthur Horner, who rose to prominence in the National Union of Mineworkers, would ultimately leave the chapel altogether in order to concentrate wholly on the labour movement.[32] But for many, whatever route they took, theirs was an unsophisticated Socialism based on vague ideas of 'fair play', justice and equality and accompanied by an apocalyptic ideal and sense of destiny. This, of course, is how they had been encouraged to respond to the movement's call. The labour movement was a religion which demanded the utmost loyalty of its followers.[33] Working men would later recall that the labour movement, particularly in the years before 1914, had provided them with a 'great spiritual awakening'.[34] Those who joined the ILP recognized that:

> It was a crusade demanding all the devotion of a religion. It was less a political philosophy than a deeply spiritual cult. I had seen men and women gladly giving up their hours of leisure to further the cause. Some of the men, far gone with consumption, with death not far around the corner, would stand in the snow and rain giving out leaflets and thus hastening an end which, indeed, they met without complaint. Others, because of their work in the I.L.P. branch, lost their jobs.[35]

---

[31] John Evans, Maerdy, conversation with Hywel Francis, 16 June 1973, SWML.

[32] Dai Dan Evans, conversation with Hywel Francis and Dai Smith, 7 August 1973; John Davies, Gwauncaegurwen, conversation with Hywel Francis, 26 July 1973, SWML.

[33] *Llais Llafur*, 14 November 1908, p.7; 1 February 1913, p.4; *Labour Leader*, 15 April 1910, p.225; Walter Haydn Davies, *Ups and Downs* (Swansea, 1975), p.157.

[34] T. Brennan, E. W. Cooney and H. Pollins, *Social Change in South West Wales* (London, 1954), p.149n.

[35] W. J. Edwards, *From the Valley I Came* (London, 1956), pp.103–4.

The increase in working-class political awareness led to strained relations between organized labour and the conventional religion of the day. Before the Great War the growing rift between labour and the churches was condemned as unnecessary. Some within the labour movement expressed the desire to see the churches giving a lead,[36] and early in 1906 *Llais Llafur* could confidently proclaim that Nonconformity and labour, as 'plant y werin' (children of the *gwerin*), were practically identical both in ideals and outlook and could easily unite and co-operate.[37] But although Nonconformity, more than any other religious body, was prepared to meet 'the needs of the age',[38] it was soon clear that something fundamental was amiss. The church was being increasingly criticized as ineffective. It had succeeded in building great temples, in providing men and women with hope of eternal happiness as well as educating ordinary working people. On the other hand, it had done nothing for those in dire material need, and had failed to improve living and working conditions and provide happiness and security on earth. By failing in its social task the church had cast doubt on the integrity of religion itself, though not on the idealism and example of Jesus as expressed in his 'lessons of love' (*gwersi cariad yr Iesu*).[39]

Given the implicit, and often explicit, criticism of the church, it was inevitable that some converts to Socialism and the labour movement would claim that they had turned their backs not on Christ but on his prodigal church. B. L. Coombes, a native of Herefordshire who came to south Wales to work in the mines, recalled that his experiences had simply convinced him of the injustices of the industrial system. His conclusion was that the last two thousand years had proved the failure of Christianity as a religious creed due to its inability to produce a righteous social system.

> I believe in my heart that it would not have failed if we had more sincere advocates, men who practise what they so loudly preach. I have seen so

[36] 'Gwerinwr', 'Eglwysi Cymru a Phlaid Llafur', *Y Geninen* (1910), 260.
[37] *Llais Llafur*, 3 February 1906, p.2.
[38] Ibid., 10 March 1906, p.1.
[39] Ibid., 27 March 1909, p.8; 3 April 1909, p.4; 24 June 1911, p.5.

many men who use religion as a cloak that I have become suspicious ⸢ religionists—though not of the religion.[40]

Coombes's statement shows that chapel religion and the culture that it supported were in serious danger. The Socialist creed had deemed individual rebirth to be insufficient: religion was now expected to produce a better society. Coombes claimed that he had not abandoned personal faith, merely that he had come to distrust any outward practice of religion. Ironically, his need to see a practical result of Christian faith embodied in the social system resulted in a far more individualistic religion than mainstream Nonconformity had ever advocated. The danger was that he would become his own infallible religious authority, lacking any point of reference outside himself, devoid of any recognizable devotional discipline or corporate body with which to ally himself.

Sacrificial service outside the auspices of the chapels was deemed closer to the ideal of Jesus by many Socialists than conventional Christianity had ever been. Thus, the labour movement attracted working men dissatisfied with conventional chapel religion by the claim to encapsulate a genuinely Christian message. The Jesus of Socialism was invariably understood in ethical rather than metaphysical terms. Hence, 'Socialists who deny Christ as Saviour recognize the goodness of his teachings which are practically identical with the underlying ethics of the Socialist movement.'[41] Christ, they claimed, was a Socialist, 'the lowly carpenter who chastised the rich and championed the poor', and so the expectation was for the church to 'work out and strive for those Socialist ideals to be taught'. But Socialists did not merely claim a parity of ethical ideal with Christianity and its vision of the Kingdom of Heaven. Many believed, like Hardie, that Socialism had to be 'a living, governing principle' in people's lives and thus Socialism could actualize Christianity in the lives of ordinary people,[42] and that Socialism had to be 'a living, governing principle' in people's hearts.[43] Conversely, the church's prodigal Christianity had concentrated too much on the

[40] B.L.Coombes, *These Poor Hands* (London, 1939), pp.135, 224–5.
[41] *Llais Llafur*, 11 July 1908, p.6.
[42] E.g. ibid., 10 April 1909, p.4; 24 April 1909, p.3.
[43] Ibid., 4 December 1907, p.1.

issues of heaven and hell hereafter, and completely failed to recognize the hell on earth. The church had failed. Had it fulfilled its proper task then, it was claimed, the current state of society would have been avoided.[44] The Marxian criticism that religion had been no more than 'opium' for the people, preached to 'charm men to sleep and forget their troubles', was propounded regularly. Chapel-goers needed to relocate their spiritual efforts in the present and therefore co-operate with all movements which had 'man's welfare' as their aim. Jesus had, after all, instructed his followers to feed the crowds that had gathered about him.[45] The charge was not simply that Nonconformity was insufficiently practical,[46] rather that it had departed from the precepts of a Christ who had proclaimed the 'Gospel of humanity'.[47] According to one correspondent in *Llais Llafur*, 'there is more religion and more Christianity belonging to the workers' party than to denominationalism and the Church'.[48]

Despite its apparently sincere claim to be faithful to Christ's teaching, in fact the labour movement sought a reinterpretation of religion according to its own theories and ideals. The church was to be brought into line with its own views, in which contempt for existing religious forms was *de rigueur*. The idea that conventional religion was necessarily contrary to true Christianity was rapidly attaining the status of a Socialist maxim. Christianity, it was claimed, was wholly concerned with how life was lived and how man treated his neighbour. As the church had made it difficult for people to be Christians, practical Christianity was now to be found in the labour movement in general and Socialism in particular. Christianity thus remained merely a laudable theory until such conditions prevailed in which men could live in brotherhood and where justice reigned supreme.[49] Socialism alone could create the necessary conditions to achieve this goal by pursuing the necessary policies to establish 'truth, justice and love' in the social system. The press

[44] Ibid., 2 July 1906, p.1; 11 July 1908, p.6; *Glamorgan Free Press*, 2 April 1909, p.3.
[45] Cf. *Merthyr Pioneer*, 13 April 1912, p.3: Mark 6: 37 etc.; also *Llais Llafur*, 11 July 1908, p.6.
[46] *Llais Llafur*, 11 July 1908, p.6; cf. *Y Dinesydd*, 27 July 1921, p.7.
[47] *Llais Llafur*, 13 January 1912, p.7.
[48] Ibid., 2 July 1906, p.1.
[49] *Rhondda Socialist*, 5 (December 1911), 4; *Llais Llafur*, 16 August 1913, p.1; 13 September 1913, p.3.

representatives of organized labour were constantly warnin,
churches that only a change in outlook concerning sc
problems could save them from impending failure.[50] Their l:
of social concern had lost them many adherents among the
young who could only be recovered with a rediscovery of the
Christian ideal of society, considered to be the central element in
Jesus's teaching. Following this, the church had to take practical
steps to ensure the establishment of that society in the world.[51] In
the contemporary context, and in the labour movement's
terminology, the church had to reinterpret its message along
practical lines and have the courage to condemn social injustice.
In order to see this new society become a reality, the church was
required to rediscover the teaching of Jesus which concerned the
building of the Kingdom of God on earth.[52] Individual salvation
needed to be seen in the context of social salvation, with one
impossible without the other.[53] This, labour apologists averred,
would be a return to Christian principles rather than merely an
adoption of Socialism.[54] Christian principles, when faithfully
adhered to, would inspire the church to become a means for
social change, while compassion dictated that slum-life, endured
by so many church members, would be condemned. The labour
movement maintained that if 'the churches wake up to and
thoroughly realise their position and duty towards the social
problem . . . one of sheer religious conviction and enthusiasm',
not only would the church have recovered its divine mission but
it would attract those men who had transferred their allegiance
to the labour movement.

> The churches will then be real, living bodies, pregnant with life and
> vitality, abounding in all the attributes of grace and having an irresistible
> attraction for the legions who are now without their doors, and to whom
> their appeal is now cold, bloodless and of no avail.[55]

All this points to the fact that before the war the labour
movement provided a challenge to religious expectation and

[50] *Llais Llafur*, 1 May 1909, p.7; 19 July 1913, p.1.
[51] Ibid., 9 September 1911, p.4; 13 January 1912, p.7; 25 April 1914, p.5.
[52] *Glamorgan Free Press*, 2 April 1909, p.3; *Llais Llafur*, 3 January 1914, p.3.
[53] *Merthyr Pioneer*, 4 July 1914, p.5.
[54] *Y Dinesydd Cymreig*, 5 March 1913, p.7; *Rhondda Socialist*, 5 (December 1911), 4.
[55] *Merthyr Pioneer*, 18 January 1913, p.7.

interpretation. 'The basis of the Christian faith', claimed *Llais Llafur*, should be 'decent living conditions of life and labour here on earth' in order to enable men and women to live their lives as Christians.[56] Christianity had more to do with 'the elevation of the standard of living, the obliteration of class privileges and the gospel of charity' than with 'the institution of bishops in one communion and deacons in the other'.[57]

The problem of labour's withdrawal from traditional religious forms, however, was no simple one to solve. Keir Hardie and others in the labour movement had often made the claim that it would be easier to follow Christ outside the churches,[58] a claim which had also been endorsed by Nonconformist ministers such as Rhondda Williams.[59] It was posited that many, 'though dimly and unconsciously', had perceived 'a higher ideal of Christianity' than that found in organized religion. As they had discovered this 'higher ideal' in the labour movement, friction was inevitable.[60] The result, though, was that the movement became for some the true expression of Christianity, as Hardie had in fact claimed it to be. Henry Lewis of Aber-craf remembered being taught by his staunchly Liberal and chapel-going father that Christianity had to be taken out to the people. Whereas his father had done this through the chapel, he saw more opportunity for doing so through the Labour Party, 'because I always thought that the Labour Party was next to Christianity'.[61] This reflected the general confidence of pre-war labour agitators that it was they, rather than the church, who faithfully represented Christ, as revealed in their increasingly vocal criticism of organized religion. Certainly by 1912 this included the claim that labour's own sphere of responsibility was wider than that of the church and even of Christianity. As a result labour's position should be alongside, if not above, that of organized religion. The call was not for the church to influence

[56] *Llais Llafur*, 16 August 1913, p.1.

[57] Ibid., 3 January 1914, p.3.

[58] Keir Hardie, Address on Labour and Christianity, 5 May 1910, National Library of Scotland Department 176, Box 25 File 6: quoted in Caroline Benn, *Keir Hardie* (London, 1992), p.261.

[59] Edgar Evans, conversation with Dai Smith and Hywel Francis, 14 July 1973, SWML.

[60] *Llais Llafur*, 3 January 1914, p.3; 3 April 1909, p.4; 24 June 1911, p.5; 22 March 1913, p.4.

[61] Henry Lewis, Aber-craf, conversation with David Egan, 4 December 1972, SWML.

and lead it, but to join with the labour movement in creating a 'force for social betterment against which no vested interest could stand':[62] 'We believe the I.L.P. needs that spiritual vision which can come alone from the Churches. We believe the Churches need the zeal for social justice which animates the I.L.P.'[63]

But religion for the labour movement was to be fundamentally social and practical rather than narrowly individual and credal.[64] Worship was virtually ignored except for that implied in good works. Chapel attendance was regarded as of little consequence so long as people helped the needy, the old and the sick. This, claimed the early Socialists, was the sum of Christianity.[65] By 1920 the labour press was insistent that religion should not be expressed in complex theology and dogmatic creeds but in the effect which it had on men's lives.[66] 'Religion is not summed up in the differences of the two and seventy sparring sects. It is a vital and positive matter believing in the conduct of the individual in relation to the other members of society with whom he is connected.'[67] This meant that true religion, being inherently political, had no choice but to renounce capitalism, whose 'animating motive' was selfishness, and to adopt collectivism, 'which is inspired by the motive of serving others'. Such claims reflected the way in which the labour movement increasingly felt it could dictate to the chapels how Christians should respond to political issues of the day. Much to the chagrin of the Socialist agitators, however, Nonconformists in general were not prepared to adopt specific political programmes at this time.

3. HOSTILITY

There was an insidious undercurrent of hostility towards the churches, and in some cases towards the Christian faith itself, throughout the period before the Great War. While claiming to seek co-operation with the churches, Socialist speeches contained

[62] *Y Dinesydd Cymreig*, 5 March 1913, p.7.
[63] *Llais Llafur*, 22 March 1913, p.4.
[64] Ibid., 11 July 1908, p.6.
[65] Henry Lewis, conversation.
[66] *Y Dinesydd*, 6 September 1922, p.8; 8 July 1925, p.3.
[67] *Labour Voice*, 6 March 1920, p.3.

not merely implicit criticisms of their ineffectiveness in social reform but also occasionally an explicit dismissal of religion as being either worthless or false.

Socialist atheism which sought to denigrate Christianity outright was illustrated by 'Port Talbot', the pseudonym of a correspondent to *Llais Llafur*. What is especially remarkable is that 'Port Talbot' couched his biting critique in strong and idiomatic Welsh. Those who appealed to the New Testament for their Socialism did so, he claimed, by depending on the 'most foggy idea'. Christ's teaching was 'too childish, too impractical' to merit any consideration. His concern was with a different existence, possibly imaginary, called the 'Kingdom of Heaven'. This could offer no assistance to the current state of things. Jesus's advice in the Sermon on the Mount that men and women should worry as much about tomorrow as the flowers worried about their clothes and the birds about their food was totally impractical.

> The gospel of laziness, the gospel of poverty, the gospel of apathy, the gospel of a blind reckless faith, the gospel of everything but common sense, as common sense is understood by the vast majority of civilized inhabitants of the world, that, in real terms, is the gospel of those verses [Matthew 7: 25–33]. It is as far from the gospel of Socialism as the East is from the West, the South Pole from the North Pole!

> Efengyl diogi, efengyl tlodi, efengyl difaterwch, efengyl ffydd ddall anystyriol, efengyl pobpeth ond synwyr cyffredin, fel y mae synwyr cyffredin yn cael ei ddeall gan fwyafrif anferth trigolion gwareiddiedig y byd, dyna, mewn ystyr fydol, yw efengyl yr adnodau yna. Ac y mae cyn belled oddi wrth efengyl Cymdeithasiaeth ag yw y Dwyrain oddiwrth y Gorllewin, Pegwn y De oddiwrth Begwn y Gogledd![68]

For 'Port Talbot', Christ's teachings were the ramblings of a religious fanatic which could never be practically applied to the sophisticated industrial society of the twentieth century. There was no evidence that Jesus ever condemned the social order in which he lived. The best he could offer was charity. 'Go and sell that thou hast, and give to the poor, and thou shalt have treasure in heaven' (Matthew 19: 21). Hardly conscious of the self-

[68] *Llais Llafur*, 3 August 1907, p.1.

contradiction, 'Port Talbot' admitted, however, that 'the moral teaching of Christ's Gospel is practically identical with Socialism'. Unfortunately, most professing Christians did not walk in Christ's way.[69]

Another correspondent to *Llais Llafur*, 'Galileo', claimed that Socialists who sought to link their Socialism with Christianity actually aspired to attain the respectability which church life at the time offered them. He echoed the concern of 'Port Talbot' that Christianity was little more than an impractical creed.

> The truth is, Christianity has nothing to do with this world at all. 'My Kingdom is not of this world' said its founder. And who would know better? What is taught today by teachers of Christianity from the pulpit? Only the Being of God—his attributes—the Trinity—God's plan—the Fall—Justification, etc., etc.? Will social salvation come through believing those things? The wretched of the world answer—it will never come!

> Y gwir yw, nid oes a fyno Cristionogaeth â'r byd hwn o gwbl. 'Fy nheyrnas I nid yw o'r byd hwn' meddai ei sylfaenydd ei hun. A phwy a wyddai'n well? Beth ddysgir heddyw gan ddysgawdwyr Cristionogaeth o'r pwlpud? Ond am y Bod o Dduw—Ei briodoleddau—Y Drindod—Arfaeth—Cwymp—Cyfiawnhad, etc. etc.? A ddaw iachawdwriaeth gymdeithasol trwy gredu pethau'r fath yna? Trueni'r byd a etyb—na ddaw byth![70]

However, 'Galileo' and 'Port Talbot' were really only exceptions to the rule. On the whole, Socialism tended to be delineated as ethically identical with Christian principles, while the main Socialist agitators of the time actively encouraged the harmony of interest which they perceived between Socialism and Christianity. The *Merthyr Pioneer* even listed biblical passages which, it was claimed, proved that Christians must be Socialists.[71]

Having said that, even the conciliatory remarks of staunch Socialists involved an accusation, not always explicit, that the organized religion of the period was inadequate, impractical and an aberration from the religion of Jesus. It was claimed that the

---

[69] Ibid., 12 September 1908, p.1.
[70] Ibid., 9 November 1907, p.1.
[71] *Merthyr Pioneer*, 17 February 1912, p.7. The verses were Exodus 23: 25, Leviticus 25: 35–7, Deuteronomy 23: 19–20, Nehemiah 5: 7, Psalm 15: 5, Ezekiel 18: 8, 17, Proverbs 28: 8, Luke 6: 34–5.

workers of the present could find little similarity between the Christ of the gospels and the Christ of the church. This was the reason for their having forsaken conventional Christianity.[72] It was claimed that only the Socialist party 'is capable of being the political exponent of Christian democracy . . . let any really "converted" man who doubts this examine for himself the tenets of Socialism and he will recognize the identity of the teaching with the wise and ennobling teaching of Jesus'.[73] Consequently, due to the purity of Socialism, it was Socialists alone who were 'keeping the Sabbath'. Many church people criticized the ILP and Socialist groups for holding their meetings on Sunday evenings, partly because they considered material gain an inappropriate topic for such a holy day but also because it prevented some men attending chapel. The response of Socialist supporters was to claim that Socialism alone sought to implement the principles behind the keeping of the Sabbath and thereby make it a reality.[74]

More general hostility surrounded the church's inactivity regarding social reform and the new Socialist message.[75] It was alleged that hostility towards labour on the part of Non-conformist ministers and deacons had resulted in the departure of many working-class men from the chapels.[76] This was partly caused by the historical connection between Nonconformity and the Liberal Party, on the one hand, and the traditional links between the Tory Party and the Anglican Church, on the other. The result of this was that no 'section of organised Christianity . . . forces into prominence the sufferings of the poor, and the need and hardships of Labour'.[77] There were occasions when chapel vestries were refused to Labour representatives while Liberals could use them with impunity, and this even after resolutions were passed forbidding the use of chapel property for political meetings.[78] Not surprisingly some called for Socialists to

[72] Ibid., 4 July 1914, p.5; cf. *Y Dinesydd*, 27 July 1921, p.7.
[73] *Llais Llafur*, 25 April 1908, p.1.
[74] Ibid., 4 July 1914, p.6.
[75] Cf. e.g. ibid., 9 September 1911, p.4; 25 April 1914, p.5.
[76] 'Gwerinwr', 'Eglwysi Cymru', pp.258–60, *passim*; *Merthyr Pioneer*, 28 December 1912, p.1; *Llais Llafur*, 24 December 1910, p.7; 13 January 1912, p.1; 22 March 1913, p.4; 24 May 1913, p.2.
[77] *Llais Llafur*, 1 May 1909, p.7; cf. Morgan Watcyn-Williams, *From Khaki to Cloth* (Caernarfon, 1949), p.39.
[78] Cf. 'Gwerinwr', 'Eglwysi Cymru', p.260.

choose between Socialism and the church.[79] But the implications of this went far deeper, for Welsh Nonconformity had always prided itself on being synonymous with labour. Its traditional links with the Liberal Party, supported by a generation of ministers, was threatening to end the allegiance of a social class previously considered loyal.

This problem was exacerbated by the use of religious arguments in political elections.[80] Perhaps the most celebrated example was that of the Mid Glamorgan constituency and its by-election in March and the general election in December 1910. Vernon Hartshorn stood as the Labour candidate and lost to the Liberal, largely because local Nonconformist ministers vehemently opposed his Socialism. The Liberals distributed a pamphlet linking Socialism with atheism and immorality, revolution and free-love. Despite admitting that 'organisation was sadly lacking',[81] it was the religious slur which he believed caused the party's defeat. The workers, he claimed, would soon realize that the chapels had 'degenerated into spiteful and narrow-minded cliques of Party politicians, run by Liberal ministers and Liberal deacons who exercise more energy in looking after the interests of Liberalism in its fight against Labour than in spiritual work'.[82]

An article in the *Merthyr Pioneer* in 1919 admitted that, while 'the prostitution of Christianity' during the war had led men to leave the church, this process had begun well before 1914 when the churches first refused to recognize the truth of Socialism. Welsh Nonconformity was still pervaded by the spirit of the Liberal Party and thus would invariably condemn Socialism and its adherents as immoral. It is not to be wondered at, therefore, that many left religion far behind. Nonconformist support for the Liberal Party was no longer overt, however, because of the rise of Socialism.

> The spirit is still ready, but the intellect cannot cope with this dreadful new thing which has so insistently and forcibly insinuated itself into the very marrow of political life. Dolorous groans and sometimes vituperative

[79] *Llais Llafur*, 1 May 1909, p.3.
[80] Ibid., 6 April 1912, p.4; cf. Peter Stead, 'Vernon Hartshorn: miner's agent and Cabinet Minister', in S. Williams (ed.), *Glamorgan Historian*, VI (Cowbridge, 1969), pp.83–94.
[81] *Labour Leader*, 8 April 1910, p.212.
[82] Ibid., 27 October 1911, p.674.

shrieks are heard from deacon and priest but the basis of brazen trumpets have no power to withstand the flowing power of truth.[83]

Nonconformity, in the view of the labour movement, needed to be modernized. It had failed to evolve alongside the achievements and discoveries of science and philosophy, while it 'practises observances which are at variance with the needs and aspirations of the toilers'. It was time to recognize that Socialism was now strong and had replaced a Liberalism 'hoary with age' which should be allowed a 'peaceful demise'. Those who had adopted Socialism should be allowed freedom of conscience and the ability to interpret religious, social and political need in the 'new light radiating in his [or her] mind'. Socialism was the modern movement fighting an antiquated religion that should either modernize itself or simply forsake modernity totally. The spectacular growth in labour confidence in the first decade or so of the century had become overt by the end of the war. Its criticisms of the churches were as vocal as before; what had changed was its advocacy of co-operation. Calls for the church to join forces with the labour movement became markedly less frequent. Co-operation was not ruled out, but the church's help was no longer sought or required.

Accusations of impracticality and irrelevance continued even as late as 1935. In a time of economic depression it once again became popular to challenge preachers not to dissociate themselves from the material condition of their congregations but to endeavour to embody their religious ideals in society. Ministers of religion should assist the working class 'to transform their idealism into realism'.[84] Religion was to affect politics and national policy. 'The life of Jesus got [sic] a wonderful teaching for politicians if they look at it', claimed T. Nicholas of Neath. According to him, the chapels seemed to be emphasizing the miraculous and the extraordinary in Jesus's teaching when they should have been emphasizing 'the economic side'.[85]

According to this interpretation of religion, the individual, towards whom all Nonconformist theology had been aimed, now became merely a victim of social forces which needed to be

---

[83] *Merthyr Pioneer*, 19 April 1919, p.1.
[84] *Labour Voice*, 29 January 1935, p.6; 6 July 1935, p.6.
[85] T. Nicholas, Neath, conversation, 16 March 1974, SWML.

addressed. The church perceived sin in individualistic terms, emphasizing personal morality, whereas the labour movement was pointing to structural sin, embedded in the industrial system which made injustice and inequality inevitable. The labour movement and the chapels clashed over the cause of social ills. The question whether man affected his environment or whether he was merely the victim of social forces beyond his control was never satisfactorily resolved.

All this points to the fact that the labour movement was providing a credible challenge to religious expectation and interpretation. If the pages of the labour press are to be considered an accurate reflection of working-class opinion, such a change in expectation was sufficiently widespread to cause many young men to abandon religion entirely. It was claimed that, in order to win them back, the church would have to change its own ideas of religion and enter into partnership with the forces seeking social justice.[86]

4. SOME WORKING-CLASS RESPONSES

There was a uniformity in the ideological and social development of many of the working men who left the chapel in this period. They witnessed to the strength and importance of Nonconformity by recording that their upbringing revolved around devout Sunday observance and the social activities of the chapel. The dissemination of Socialism and of scientific theories of evolution caused them to question orthodox Christian doctrines, and this despite showing a definitely uncritical attitude towards the labour movement. They sometimes gave frankly trivial reasons for leaving the chapel.[87] Even then they would often admit that when they had left the chapel their wives had remained actively involved.[88]

[86] *Llais Llafur*, 1 May 1909, p.7; 9 September 1911, p.4; 13 January 1912, p.7; 19 July 1913, p.1; 25 April 1914, p.5.
[87] See David Brown, Mountain Ash, conversation with Alun Morgan, 2 July 1973; A. J. Martin, Blaengarw, conversation with David Egan, 11 July 1973; Ernest Lewis, conversation with Alun Morgan, October 1972, SWML.
[88] Will Arthur, Glynneath, conversation with David Egan, 24 May 1973, and conversation with David Egan and Alun Morgan, 13 June 1973; Tom Watkins, Ynysybwl, conversation with David Egan, 23 October 1972; Ernest Lewis, conversation, SWML.

It is unclear to what extent chapel attendance was connected with specifically religious faith in the mind of the working class. While the chapel was the centre of social life in the community, many gave the reason for their attendance at services solely in terms of their social need.[89] When there were alternatives ranging from football to the labour movement, they left.[90] It is this issue which marks the difference between north and south Wales most explicitly. The North Wales Quarrymen's Union never achieved the social status that the SWMF achieved in the coalfield. It remained a trade union, while the SWMF virtually replaced the social function of the chapel in many men's lives. This is probably a contributory factor to Nonconformity's greater hold in the north during the period in question. The Federation, on the other hand, was described as serving all the social and personal needs of the men and their families, providing 'an all-round service of advice and assistance to the mining community on most of the problems that could arise between the cradle and the grave'. The local community could approach the leaders of the local miners' lodges to help with all their problems and the status they achieved was commensurate with their social duties. In Will Paynter's words, the leaders were 'the village elders' who were called upon to assist people in all their problems.[91] Although he lived outside the hotbed of radical Socialism which set itself against the chapel-orientated culture in the Rhondda, James Griffiths also recalled that even in the anthracite areas of the Amman and Gwendraeth valleys 'the Fed' did not confine its responsibility to economics and industry alone.

> The Federation was not only a trade union; it was an all embracing institution in the mining community. In the pits it kept daily watch over the conditions of work, protecting the men from the perils of the mine, caring for the maimed and the bereaved, and providing the community with its libraries and bands and hospitals and everything which helped to make life bearable and joyous.[92]

[89] Will Arthur, conversation; W. H. Taylor, Blaenavon, conversation with R. Merfyn Jones, August 1973, SWML.

[90] Will Arthur, conversation; W. H. Taylor, conversation.

[91] Will Paynter, *My Generation* (London, 1972), p.110.

[92] James Griffiths, *Pages from Memory* (London, 1969), p.28.

Griffiths's statement is highly significant, for the change in religious expectation was accompanied by the establishment of an organization whose activities helped 'make life bearable and joyous'. Thus, the threat to the chapel was not merely ideological but also social. The SWMF had provided a counter-culture, an all-pervading influence which discovered its relevance in every aspect of community life and not just in the industrial sphere. Thus, it could not live quietly alongside the chapel or other social organizations; in fact, tension, and even friction, were inevitable. The labour movement, particularly in the south, made provision to meet the intellectual and social needs of the people. There are instances, particularly before the war, of ILP branches fulfilling a more direct religious function, such as the study of scripture or debating the implications of social Christianity.[93] It is impossible to prove that all working men switched their allegiance from the chapel to the union lodge or ILP institute, but the existence of the latter two did provide a powerful rival to the former.

The choices for working men did not surround the labour movement and the chapel alone. Harold Watkins, a tutor for the WEA in the coalfield from 1920, noted that those students who had eschewed religious beliefs had done so in the search for companionship, which they found not in the trade union or labour movement but in the public house.[94] This suggests that the social fabric of Welsh communities, together with the loyalties and ideals held by the working class, is far more complicated than a mere replacement of outward allegiance in the fulfilment of a religious ideal. Not all men involved in the labour movement had left the chapels, while those who had abandoned religion had not always done so in search of a practical embodiment of their spiritual convictions. When Will Arthur, for example, returned to Glynneath after the Great War, he found that those who had always attended chapel continued to be faithful,[95] while those whose allegiance had never been strong would play football or frequent the local public houses. Yet men who had returned to their villages after fighting in the war discovered that it was no easy transition back to their former

[93] *Llais Llafur*, 1 February 1913, p.5; 20 October 1913, p.5.
[94] Harold M. Watkins, *Unusual Students* (Liverpool, 1947), p.12.
[95] Will Arthur, conversation; Tom Watkins, conversation, confirms no great move away from the chapel after the war.

way of life. Some working men pointed to intellectual difficulties as justification for their departure from organized religion, though the plausibility of their arguments varies considerably. Will Arthur himself had religious doubts caused by the war:

> there was then, I say, probably some other ex-servicemen like myself, there was our doubts, that our teaching had reached a kind of chasm . . . We couldn't cross it, on that side we could see what we had been taught and on this side our experience in the army, and of course there was a big gap between the two you see.

His wartime experiences had challenged the teaching which he had received in chapel, and he could not reconcile the two. His wife never experienced such doubts and she continued to be faithful in her chapel attendance and their children were brought up to attend. But Arthur himself confessed that 'it was a long time before I could settle down and agree to . . . a form of religion then'.

The war did not merely cause problems concerning religious teaching but widened the experience of many men who had never previously left the confines of their village. Apart from the horrors of trench warfare, their experiences gave them a new outlook on life and morality. Having won the war, they were encouraged to believe that they stood on the threshold of a new age. All these elements caused genuine problems for some soldiers, and for the religion of the chapels. Walter Haydn Davies recalled that while four years previously many young men had 'responded to the bugle call in the spirit of Gideon's men', they 'returned to civilian life as one of the Devil's own'. Their experiences made them easy prey for Socialist agitators. This was compounded by the discovery that, far from being greeted as heroes, their return was rewarded with unemployment and consequent hardship. Thus, the transition from Christianity to materialistic Socialism had been much easier for many, although Davies appears to suggest that this change was simply automatic. In the case of one,

> He no longer sang with devotion the Welsh hymn 'Pa Dduw sy'n maddeu fel Tydi' (What God savest like Thou), but with head uncovered bawled out 'The People's Flag is Deepest Red,' that stirring line of *The Red Flag*.

Thus, like many previously dutiful Christians who had seen active service, he had returned from the war with his religious beliefs undermined.[96]

For these men the war had revealed problems which had existed beneath the surface in Welsh religion.[97] For others it was the very nature of that religion itself which caused them to question their allegiance to the chapel. Nonconformity had concentrated on the ephemeral to the exclusion of the temporal and disregarded the glaring injustices and depravity of industrial society. Thus, many pioneers of the labour movement reacted strongly against traditional, organized religion. Arthur Cook,[98] for example, had initially welcomed the 1904 religious revival, but he later considered that its emotionalism had diverted attention from the plight of the working man. It offered no solution to the injustices of industrial society.

> Towards the end of the Revival, a certain faculty of scepticism and critical judgement asserted itself in me. I realised that . . . this powerful current of feeling flowing as strong as a tide produced astonishingly little change in the fundamental economic and industrial facts of the miner's life. It did, indeed, divert attention of the miners from these facts. And that, as I was beginning to see, was wrong.[99]

Cook's objection to emotionalism in the face of injustice and hardship in industrial society is understandable. He broke with the chapel after being challenged by his minister to choose between the radical politics in which he was growing daily more involved and his chapel commitment. Paul Davies, Cook's biographer, sees this move out of the chapel as a result of the particular conditions in south Wales at that time. In more prosperous times he believes that Cook would have remained within Nonconformity, his energies directed towards religious revivalism.[100]

---

[96] *Right Place*, p.54.

[97] Cf. e.g. Watcyn-Williams, *Khaki to Cloth*, p.39.

[98] For A. J. Cook (1883–1931), see Paul Davies, *A. J. Cook* (Manchester, 1987); Paul Foot, *'An Agitator of the Worst Kind': A Portrait of Miners' Leader A. J. Cook* (London, 1986); M. Bellamy and J. Saville (eds.), *Dictionary of Labour Biography*, III (London, 1976), pp.38–44.

[99] P. Davies, *Cook*, p.5.

[100] Ibid., p.6.

The charge that chapel religion was merely impractical and therefore of no use to modern man was a common one. However, working-class expression of that impracticality once again raises questions. For Tom Watkins, Ynysybwl, this was because he 'was hearing the same, sometimes I would hear the same sermon two or three times a year you know. Too much theory . . .' He left the chapel and claimed that the availability of social alternatives led to the departure of many others. He did not welcome this, however, for 'once the chapels were getting closed the respectability of Ynysybwl was gone'.[101] It is not obvious why the repetition of sermons alone leads to a charge of impracticality, but there is a hint here of a belief that while the chapel offered a theory which could help build a fairer, more just society, it was only through the labour movement that such a society could be created. The polarizing of theory and practice was common in the words of those who criticized the chapel, but this in itself did not always mean an automatic break with organized religion. John Davies, Gwauncaegurwen, claimed to have been too busy with duties as a local councillor and member of the Labour Party as well as 'secretary of the welfare' to have had much interest in religion. Yet he was a member of Carmel chapel.[102] We never really discover why such men concluded that, despite teaching the correct theory, the chapels were unable to put it into practice. There is a general acceptance that they needed to express their discontent with society and conditions of work and housing, and that the labour movement gave them the opportunity for revolt. Though retaining their connection with the chapel, both Len Jeffreys of Cross Keys and Phil Abrahams believed that Nonconformist religion had bred rebellion in them. Yet they could not express this within the structures of the chapel itself. For that they needed the labour movement and, in Abrahams's case, the Communist Party.[103]

---

[101] Tom Watkins, conversation.

[102] John Davies, conversation; other such men were David Davies, James James and Watkin Phillips, see Dai Smith, 'Leaders and led', in K. S. Hopkins (ed.), *Rhondda Past and Future* (Ferndale, 1975), p.48.

[103] Len Jeffreys, Cross Keys, conversation with David Egan and Hywel Francis, 12 September 1972; Phil Abrahams, conversation with Hywel Francis, 14 January 1974, SWML.

5. THE ROLE OF REASON

The view of Frank Hodges (1887–1947), later to become general secretary of the Miners' Federation of Great Britain (MFGB), and his colleague Arthur Horner (1894–1968), who would subsequently rise to prominence in the National Union of Mineworkers, was that religion was insufficiently practical. Although both had been active chapel members, lay preachers and, in fact, prospective candidates for the ministry, they both recalled a period of intense ideological struggle.

Hodges gave an insight, albeit an anachronistic one, into his religious belief in his autobiography *My Adventures as a Labour Leader*.[104] As he looked back to the turn of the century, which was a seminal period in the development of the labour movement in Wales, Hodges claimed that certainly by 1904 he was in a 'state of downright mental uncertitude' (p.17). He found himself caught up in a 'religious tempest' (p.18) and later confessed that he 'was carried away for the time being by the downright emotionalism of the revival period' (p.20). He concluded that during this period 'the critical faculties had been temporarily taking a nap' (p.18). Christianity had to go beyond mere emotionalism and be translated into social service (p.19). He was turned down for ministerial training, he believed, because of his theologically unorthodox sermons (p.20). He never really explained how he came to his conclusions about Christianity as a social dynamic, neither does he show how Christianity could, or why it could not, be joined to the labour movement to work for social reform. His only explanation is that he felt liberated from the fetters of 'theological formulae or dogmatic creed' in trade-union work, and could then work for 'an improvement in the lot of my fellow men in this very real world' which he considered to be the crux of religion. His conversion was complete: 'For here was the instrument of revolt ready for the using. Here was a means of industrial power. Here was the weapon of the poor and oppressed. I saw a new world of action opening up before my eyes' (p.21). Although irregular in attendance, he still claimed an association with the Methodist Church, and 'its simple religious life and its social aspirations', for the rest of his life (p.20).

---

[104] London, 1925.

Hodges's claim is understandable. Christianity needed to be linked to social service. He found organized Christianity unwilling to consider its social responsibilities, and so he left to put his energy into a movement which conformed to his ideal. Although the validity of the argument can be refuted, the logic is correct. In the case of other men, such as Arthur Horner and Idris Cox, this is not the case. Both appear simply to have rejected the Christian world-view for an alternative, and although they claimed to use 'critical faculties' in this process, they were unwilling to be equally critical of the Socialist ideal.

Arthur Horner's period of intense critical questioning left him not only rejecting the emotionalism of religion but also denying its significance.[105] He recalled being conscious of the social problems caused by rapid industrialization, 'the poverty, the oppression and the injustice', and felt that religion offered 'the hope and the opportunity' to remedy the situation, with the 'ready-made audience in the chapels'. Christianity, however, had to be 'linked with practical measures to relieve all these social evils'.[106] Still retaining a degree of respect for the Christian ethical ideal, he rejected explicit belief in favour of the 'materialistic conception of history', holding the working-class struggle as the only way to emancipation. His early vision of religion as paving the way to a better society led to disillusionment, and he concluded that religion was unable to work practically for such an end. Once he had reached this stage, he drew the conclusion that religion was worthless. He was influenced by Noah Ablett, himself a former boy-preacher who had become a Socialist and left the chapel.[107] This gave Horner the precedent he needed. It was Ablett who took Horner 'fully into the working class struggle', the publication of *The Miners' Next Step* in 1912 providing him with 'something far more practical in terms of helping my fellow men than the religious services I had been taking part in'.[108] Distinctly Syndicalist in policy, the threat of this pamphlet was not its advocacy of an

[105] For Arthur Horner (1894–1968), see his autobiography *Incorrigible Rebel* (London, 1960); Bellamy and Saville, *Labour Biography*, V (London, 1979), pp.112–18.

[106] Horner, *Incorrigible Rebel*, p.14.

[107] For Noah Ablett (1883–1935), see Bellamy and Saville, *Labour Biography*, III (London, 1976), pp.1–3; also David Egan, 'Noah Ablett 1883–1935', *Llafur*, IV/3 (1985), 19–30.

[108] Horner, *Incorrigible Rebel*, p.21.

economic theory but the suggestion of a scheme to implement such views in the working of the SWMF.[109] Ablett had been one of the authors of the pamphlet and it was he who resolved Horner's soul-searching by showing him that 'in this world the most important thing is what you do for your fellow men and not some abstract conception of right and wrong'.[110] However, Horner had at least a degree of apathy towards religion, highlighted by his decision to play football rather than attend his future wife's baptism when it was he who had insisted that she be baptized.[111]

An early member of the Communist Party, Idris Cox lost his interest in the chapel after he began work as a miner and when he became involved in trade-union activity. He recalled reading *Das Kapital* about 1919–20, joined the Labour Party in 1920, and became chairman of his SWMF lodge in 1921. Cox attended the Central Labour College in London during 1923–5, as did many men from the south Wales coalfield, and claimed that it was while he was resident there that he underwent a 'sharp mental battle' trying to justify religion in the face of the Marxist critique. After about two months, he believed he had reasoned religion away as untenable.

> I had to confess that there was no realistic foundation for religion and religious theory, although still believing that most Christians I knew were genuine who were people who would fight for a progressive cause but from the theoretical standpoint religion was no solution to the problems of mankind. The solution lay in the application of the theory.[112]

As he does not explain why the structures of organized religion could not apply the theory, this again appears to be an insufficient reason for abandoning religion. His opinion also appears to be contradictory. If there is no realistic foundation for religious theory, how can it be applied? These men appear initially to believe that religion could be harnessed for social service, only subsequently to forsake religion and enter more

---

[109] R. Merfyn Jones, foreword in reprint of *The Miners' Next Step* (Shoreditch, 1973), p.3.
[110] Arthur Horner, *Incorrigible Rebel*, p.21.
[111] Ibid., p.22.
[112] Idris Cox, conversation with Hywel Francis, 9 June 1972, SWML.

fully into Socialist and Communist ideology, without ever adequately explaining why. This leads us to the conclusion that Horner, Cox, and to an extent Hodges, simply replaced one set of beliefs with another, the latter based on action and economics, and centred on the activity and condition of human beings. Admittedly, they found this ideology and world-view more satisfying, but it was equally as theoretical as the one which they had abandoned. Rather than employing their 'critical faculties', these men tended to accept Socialist dogma *en bloc*, which gave them the opportunity to revolt against the industrial system. Such could have been the experience of many.[113] W. J. Edwards summed up both the need to rebel against existing forms and the total and uncritical acceptance of the new message.

> We swallowed Marx whole and mentally digested him with enthusiasm, and never a sign of indigestion. His dismissal of a Supreme Being was in harmony with what we thought enlightenment in contrast to the grey mixture of stupidity and hypocrisy we believed we saw in and around the chapel.[114]

In similar vein, Trevor Davies of Ferndale noted that many boys left the chapel 'following the fashion of boys' when they started work, very often led by others into a movement they scarcely understood.

> Q: You had that feeling that lots of people were being led that way?
> A: Oh yes, yes I had that feeling, led like sheep. Not because they knew the meaning of communism or anything else, they were just led.[115]

As well as the influence of atheistic Socialism, there are instances of men rejecting orthodox doctrine as the result of avid reading of the scientific and rationalist literature which was prevalent amongst some miners at the time. W. H. Taylor had certainly read Voltaire, and remembered catching out a ministerial candidate preaching in the chapel.

---

[113] W. J. Edwards, *From the Valley*, p.104; Haydn Davies, *Ups and Downs*, p.105; R. J. Barker, *Christ in the Valley of Unemployment* (London, 1936), p.15; W. H. Taylor, conversation.

[114] W. J. Edwards, *From the Valley*, pp.211–12.

[115] Trevor Davies, Ferndale, conversation with Hywel Francis, 3 July 1972, SWML.

I asked this student now a question see, I said 'In the first place God said "let there be light and there was light!" Now,' I said, this is what occurred to me at that age and I was only about fifteen. I said 'I was only reading' I said 'In my science books that all our light comes from the sun! The sun is the source of all life. Now,' I said, 'God didn't make the sun until the third day!' you see. And he said, 'Oh everything is possible to God because', he said, 'He is omnipotent, he can do everything.' 'Well,' I said, 'it is an established principle in science that effect always follows cause. Now,' I said, 'The cause of light is the sun, the effect is the light as we know it. Well,' I said, 'are you telling me that for three days cause followed effect and not effect cause!' He didn't know what to make of it. Well that gradually went around the Chapel workers, all the big ones, they thought I was going to the devil.[116]

Obviously this reveals more of a desire to win the debate than discover the truth. There is an implication that his reaction against religion was more the result of blind acceptance of what he was reading rather than a totally reasoned response to the inequalities of the world. He was willing to believe that science held a monopoly of the truth while that which could not be reconciled to it was, of necessity, superstition. Although he, and others like him, could not see it, Taylor was being as dogmatic as the admittedly unthinking young preacher.

For some men the abandonment of organized religion was symbolic of their independence of mind and of a wider militancy. Thus, when they came of age they made their own decision to leave.[117] Will Paynter admitted that the attraction of so many young men to Socialism in the years after the Great War was in part a natural reaction of the young against the 'established institutions'.[118] He joined the chapel at the age of sixteen, though he later claimed that he lacked any real conviction. He considered that Darwin offered a 'better explanation for man's existence on Earth than the Bible' and recalled the narrowness of the chapel as evidenced by the dismissal of a Socialist teacher in the Sunday School.[119] While his family maintained their respectability by continued chapel attendance, it is obvious that religion meant little to him.

---

[116] W. H. Taylor, conversation.
[117] Bob Morris, Bedlinog, conversation with Alun Morgan, 19 November 1973, SWML.
[118] Will Paynter, *My Generation*, p.7.
[119] Ibid., p.27.

6. LABOUR MOVEMENT AND THE CHAPELS

The inception of the labour movement, and particularly its dissemination in religious terms, had led some to recognize not so much an intellectual battle but a choice of how to channel their energy and hope. The choice which Hodges and Horner made was to forsake their ministerial vocation for a career in the labour movement. Different generations tended to choose different paths. Whereas older Nonconformists took their religious consciences into society and used the labour movement as a convenient means of commitment to social reform, the younger generation was more prepared to dismiss the church's exclusive claim to the divine. Hodges, Horner, Cook and others believed that their political radicalism and their absolute commitment to the labour cause were incompatible with traditional religious practice. This required them to leave the chapel completely.

The choice was not always polarized between the chapel and the labour movement. Some were able to achieve a synthesis, though to varying degrees. Abel Morgan[120] retained religious belief and practice all his life, but whereas his father's zeal had led to the establishment of Welsh Baptist churches in the Rhondda, Abel's religious zeal went into serving the community of Ynysybwl and the wider labour movement. Joseph Branch was a member of the ILP and the chairman of the Briton Ferry Rural District Council. He was a committed member of the local Calvinistic Methodist chapel, although he never served in office. He dedicated his public life to fighting for better housing for the workers.[121] His adoption of Socialism did provoke hostility in some quarters, however.[122]

Like so many other young men, James Griffiths recalled his father's wish that he enter the Congregationalist ministry.[123] A conversion to Socialism through the influence of R. J. Campbell

---

[120] For Abel Morgan (1878–1972), see conversation with David Egan and R. Merfyn Jones, 9 October 1972, SWML; David Egan, 'Abel Morgan, 1878–1972', *Llafur*, I/2 (1973), 29–33.

[121] *Y Goleuad*, 26 May 1909, p.4.

[122] Len Williams, conversation with David Egan and Richard Lewis, 21 May 1974, SWML.

[123] See Griffiths, *Pages from Memory*; J. Beverly Smith (ed.), *James Griffiths and his Times* (Ferndale, 1978).

and Keir Hardie meant that his energies were channelled into the labour movement, though he retained a link with the chapel throughout his life.[124] Under the influence of Campbell and Hardie, Griffiths maintained that Christianity and Socialism were synonymous. Although he recalled a meeting he attended during the revival which was led by Evan Roberts, he spoke sparingly of the religious excitement of that period but most emphatically about his 'conversion' to Socialism. The impression is that, whereas one was transient, the other was something of real and lasting significance. Although he could only recollect the revivalist's message hazily, he could recall perfectly R. J. Campbell's message at Pant-teg chapel, Ystalyfera, and Keir Hardie's speech at Gwauncaegurwen, in 1908. Hardie had appealed to Griffiths where Roberts had failed to do so. Griffiths related these meetings in terms of a conversion experience and he admitted that it profoundly affected the course of his life. He saw Socialism as a fulfilment of his faith.

Cliff Prothero did not view Socialism as a dogmatic creed, nor in reality a vision for society, but as 'a way of life as we strive for brotherhood and friendship knowing that people and their welfare are more important than constitutions'.[125] Although this was not a substitute for his personal religion, there is an implication that Socialism was to be a universal spirit that would encompass all personal beliefs and devotion.[126] Whereas religion was 'a personal matter', the Labour Party embodied a 'brotherhood', which 'inspired its members to be prepared to make sacrifices in order to change the system of capitalism'. If Nonconformity emphasized the value of individual personality, and each person's need of salvation, the labour movement was seen by many as the opportunity for this faith to be socialized. Prothero, like many labour stalwarts, was active in local politics as well as putting his energies into organizations such as the Welsh Tourist Board, the Welsh Joint Education Committee and the Broadcasting Council for Wales. He also remained a lay preacher and lamented the fact that so many men left the chapel after the 1921 lock-out.[127]

---

[124] Cf. Kenneth O. Morgan, *The Red Dragon and the Red Flag: The Case of James Griffiths and Aneurin Bevan* (Aberystwyth, 1989), *passim*.

[125] Cliff Prothero, *Recount* (Ormskirk, 1982), foreword, p.xii.

[126] Ibid., p.6.

[127] Ibid., p.14.

For many of these labour pioneers, Socialism, however they understood it, gave a cause to believe in and, if necessary to die for; their loyalty towards it sometimes bordered on the fanatical. This suggests that the movement was for them some kind of substitute religion,[128] just as Hardie and others had presented it. The cause demanded their total obedience. Its teachings were to permeate their whole lives. They were utterly devoted to its principles while they accepted its dogmas without question. Service of humankind was the fundamental principle in life and the labour movement had presented them with the opportunity to put this principle into practice. When a clash occurred between the chapel and the labour movement, the question of allegiance became acute. Invariably it was the chapel that suffered. When challenged to choose, both Horner and Cook left the church and not the labour movement. For Dai Dan Evans,[129] who was a member of the Communist Party, this was the automatic consequence of a conversion to Socialism. The Socialist movement represented an ideal which gradually replaced the religious ideal in the mind of the people of south Wales. 'And the people now that became socialists in South Wales, became automatically irreligious.'[130] We can hardly be satisfied with Evans's over-simplistic view, however. Nonconformity and the labour movement must have flourished alongside each other at least for a time, and for many they were not mutually exclusive. While the relationship between the chapel, Socialism and the labour movement changed in the inter-war years, the *Labour Voice*'s response to a statement that 'A Socialist cannot be a Christian' in 1923 was:

> It is rather late in the day to utter this nonsense, for there are thousands of Welshmen to-day who can find no inconsistency in singing 'Diolch iddo' and 'Ar ei ben bo'r goron' with the Welsh hwyl at one meeting, and then proceeding to another meeting to sing 'The Red Flag' with the same enthusiasm.[131]

---

[128] James Griffiths, *Pages from Memory*, p.14.
[129] For Dai Dan Evans (1898–1974), see *Llafur*, I/3 (1974), 3–4.
[130] Dai Dan Evans, conversation with Dai Smith and Hywel Francis, 7 August 1973, SWML.
[131] *Labour Voice*, 14 April 1923, p.2.

John Evans, Maerdy, recalled that while he was not involved in chapel life, religion had retained a level of popularity amongst the working class: 'On Sunday when people were walking the roads Chapel was a big thing then. And the Ferndale Workman's Hall during the week was always full.'[132]

T. Ashley, the inspector of mines for the Swansea area, recorded that a short religious service was held every Monday morning by some workmen at the Mynydd Newydd colliery, Swansea, on arrival at the pit bottom.[133] This practice had been observed for some thirty-five years and preceded the 1904 revival. It has remained a vivid part of local folk-lore and it is held today that no accidents ever occurred in the mine. More importantly, it gives valuable information that, although this practice may have been unique, there still existed amongst the miners a group whose religious allegiance, and whose outward practice of that religion, remained in an entirely traditional form. It certainly seems the case that further west in the coalfield in the Tawe, Gwendraeth and Amman valleys where the Welsh language and traditions remained strong, miners continued to attend chapel alongside their interest in union and labour affairs. This is reflected in the pages of the *Labour Voice* (*Llais Llafur*) and *Y Darian* (*Tarian y Gweithiwr*), which were produced in the Swansea valley. A picture of industrial society in Wales is complicated by geographical considerations. The Welsh traditions in language, religious observance and social practices were far stronger in the western coalfield. This did not preclude adherence to labour and Socialist politics but gave it a different character. Thus, Hardie and Campbell were vital for James Griffiths, born and brought up in the Amman valley, while at least some in the Rhondda were drawn towards rationalist and materialist thought. Clearly, the relationship which existed between political and religious belief is complex and thus the claim that the adoption of Socialism, or adherence to the SWMF and its counter-culture, led automatically to the abandonment of religion would appear too simplistic.

Often the men who led in industrial society, the owners and managers as well as representatives of the workers, became

---

[132] John Evans, Ferndale, conversation with Hywel Francis, 13 June 1973, SWML.
[133] *Labour Voice*, 4 October 1930, p.3.

leaders in the chapel and vice versa. It is hardly surprising that managers in the mines often became deacons. Some were remembered for being 'tyrants' in work and 'angels' in the *Sedd Fawr*.[134] There were reports in newspapers sympathetic to the labour cause of injustice and harassment suffered by working people in industrial and rural areas at the hands of apparently religious managers. This was obviously a stumbling-block for some,[135] but as chapels were occasionally connected to particular coalmines men would attend chapel in order to secure a job.[136] This was true particularly in the Swansea valley,[137] but was also true of Glynneath[138] and Cwmcynon.[139]

It is untrue, however, that the *Sedd Fawr* had been taken over by the capitalist classes wholesale. Some of the workers' representatives were also deacons.[140] Hector Bolwell was one of the youngest deacons at Moriah chapel, Bedlinog, and also served on the Council of Action Committee which planned and implemented a remarkable show of defiance and solidarity during the Taff Merthyr dispute in 1934 (see below, pp.113–14).[141] John Williams of Cwmtwrch in the Swansea valley and later manager of the Banwen colliery, recalled that his father had been both chairman of the lodge and secretary of the chapel. Often when he met with the colliery owner during times of industrial dispute, they would begin their meetings with prayer.[142] William Davies recalled that 'the members of the Union were often deacons in the chapel'.[143] And sometimes the deacons were the most politically radical in the community. W. C. Thomas, Gwaelod y Garth,[144] was a founding member of

[131] Cf. John Williams, Cwmtwrch, conversation with Dai Smith and Hywel Francis, 23 July 1974; Henry John, conversation with David Egan, 1 December 1972; Josiah Jones, Cwmllynfell, conversation with Hywel Francis, 23 July 1974, SWML.

[135] *Y Darian*, 17 April 1919, p.4; Henry Lewis, conversation.

[136] George Ewart Evans, *From Mouths of Men*, p.156.

[137] See Dick Cook, Ystradgynlais, conversation with Hywel Francis, 24 January 1974; Penry Davies, conversation, 20 October 1972; Dai Dan Evans, conversation, SWML.

[138] Will Arthur, conversation.

[139] Penry Davies, conversation.

[140] See Dai Smith, 'Leaders and led', p.48; T. M. Bassett, *Bedyddwyr Cymru* (Swansea, 1977), p.368; Michael Lieven, *Senghennydd: The Universal Pit Village* (Llandysul, 1994), p.91; Christopher Mark Williams, 'Democratic Rhondda: politics and society 1885–1951', (Ph.D. thesis, University of Wales, 1991), pp.287n., 505–6n.

[141] Edgar Evans, conversation; cf. John Williams, conversation.

[142] George Ewart Evans, *From Mouths of Men*, p.156.

[143] William Davies, conversation with Hywel Francis, 4 October 1972, SWML.

[144] W. C. Thomas, Gwaelod y Garth, conversation with David Egan, 9 July 1973, SWML.

the SWMF and had been converted to Socialism by Keir Hardie. A doctrinaire Marxist, he remained a deacon at his chapel, though his theology was unorthodox, hailing R. J. Campbell as a mentor. Samuel Davies was a deacon and secretary of the Siloa Congregational church in Maerdy. He was also secretary of the lodge committee of the SWMF and a militant Socialist, a situation considered scandalous by some in the locality.[145] Needless to say, the same was true of many of the labour MPs for south Wales constituencies. Will John, MP for Rhondda West, 1920–50, William Jenkins, MP for Neath, 1922–44, and Charles Edwards, MP for Bedwellty, 1918–50, were all deacons.[146] According to J. Graham Jones, 'it is clear that within the south Wales coalfield at least, pre-Parliamentary service to the community had often embraced membership of the diaconate of the non-conformist chapels'.[147] The correct conclusion is that it was the men who could 'speak publicly' (*siarad dipyn yn gyhoeddus*), whatever social class they belonged to, that would lead in the mines and the works as well as the chapel.

7. LABOUR, RELIGION AND MORALITY

In its early years the labour movement held similar ideals to the chapel on subjects such as temperance and coarse language, ideals which certainly had emanated from the chapel culture.[148] The labour movement had ensured that its moral standards were similar to those of the chapel, thus rendering its existence acceptable to many working men in a culture so influenced and dominated by Nonconformist puritanism.[149] The irony was that, at least for a time in the 1920s, the labour movement was not simply the inheritor of the Nonconformist ethical tradition. It began to challenge the chapels as the safeguard of morality in a district. This was undoubtedly the result of a growing confidence on the part of the labour movement, but also pointed to the fact

[145] Stuart Macintyre, *Little Moscows: Communism and Working Class Militancy in Inter-War Britain* (London, 1980), p.160.

[146] J. Graham Jones, 'Welsh politics between the wars: the personnel of Labour', *Transactions of the Honourable Society of Cymmrodorion* (1983), 179–80.

[147] Ibid., p.178.

[148] Cf. Will Paynter, conversation with Hywel Francis, 6 March 1973; Claude Stanfield, conversation with Alun Morgan, November 1972; Mrs J. Evans, Maerdy, conversation with Hywel Francis, 11 June 1973, SWML.

[149] Claude Stanfield, conversation.

that by and large the labour movement in south Wales had adopted a Socialism that was basically ethical and required a high personal morality from its adherents.

The tension between a confident and vocal labour movement and a Nonconformity attempting to retain its influence and status as moral guardian of the community came to a head when it was proposed that a Workingman's Club be established at Tai'r Gwaith between the Swansea and Amman valleys. According to the Revd T. M. Roderick, Cwmgors, this awakened 'the moral conscience' of the local churches as it was feared that the club would be little more than a drinking institution. This whole incident is interesting for several reasons. Roderick was a labour sympathizer and regularly appeared on labour platforms up to the election of 1918, yet the establishment of a workingman's club brought out in him the crusading and prohibitive moralism of the 'Nonconformist conscience'. A resolution was passed in all of the local churches to pledge to use their power and influence to prevent the club's establishment.[150] The attitude of the *Labour Voice* is also informative. In response it made the point that the labour movement did not welcome such clubs, for while 'it provides a tired man with a warm fire and good company in the evenings' it also sees its 'laudable objects' being displaced by the 'main function [of] the provision of a rendezvous for drinking'. T. M. Roderick had acted to preserve the moral character of the area in the sight of a possible threat of added drunkenness. However, the labour movement was equal to this in that its own ethical code objected to such clubs. The challenge to Nonconformity was consequently twofold. The church was not only losing its sole possession of the message of salvation, the labour movement having preached an alternative social salvation, but it was now losing its unique position as the preserver of moral standards. Furthermore, without any sensationalism or attempt to denigrate the church, the *Labour Voice* demonstrated that such negative crusades were no longer sufficient. The churches had only been moved into action because of the connection between the liquor trade and the clubs, they had not helped to establish any activities for the leisure time of the workmen.

[150] *Labour Voice*, 24 January 1920, p.5.

We do not suggest that it is the business of the churches to inaugurate these undertakings. But the ministers and other religious leaders ought to be to the fore in all movements making for the fuller use of the substantial leisure that now accrues to every mining district. Rev T. M. Roderick may be right when he says that the 'moral conscience' of the district has been thoroughly roused by the movement to establish a club, but does not the 'moral conscience' often turn a blind eye to the real needs of a community?[151]

The whole tone of this comment differs from that of comments made before the war. Whereas previously the church was called on to act in order to achieve results in favour of the working class, to join or even lead the Socialist cause, it seems here that the church was no longer required to press for social reform. The reform will come anyway because of the increasing strength, both political and moral, of the labour movement. The church should therefore fall into line, though its relevance in the whole debate seemed to be minimal.

Considering the opposition of the churches and the labour movement, the incident has an ironic epilogue. Less than two years later, the *Labour Voice* had to record that the Tai'r Gwaith Workingmen's Institute Club had, at the request of the police, been struck off the register as it had become 'a drinking den of the worst kind'.[152]

8. THE 1920S: DISPUTE AND DEPRESSION

It appears that by the late 1920s the chapel and the labour movement had become gradually more estranged, the two great coalfield disputes of 1921 and 1926 resulting in a more overt political consciousness.[153] For Will Paynter the 'big industrial disputes of the 1920s demoralized and made rebels of many men'. He renounced his chapel membership following the General Strike in 1926.[154] Some of the men interviewed by the South Wales Coalfield Project point to the period of the early 1930s as the time when they left the chapels, though it is unclear

---

[151] Ibid., 31 January 1920, p.2.
[152] Ibid., 1 July 1922, p.5.
[153] Ned Gittins, Bedlinog, conversation with Alun Morgan, August 1973, SWML.
[154] Will Paynter, *My Generation*, p.32.

what the significance of this is.[155] Some men would then have
been in their twenties, and no longer under direct parental
control. Henry Lewis, Aber-craf, believed that the chapels lost
their hold on the populace simply by ignoring the plight of the
miners during the 1920s. He accused them of insularity, of
having no interest in external affairs. This, for Lewis, was a
major weakness, as politics was 'the only way to run a country'.
This led him into local politics, believing this to be the sphere
where his Christianity could be made effective. 'Well to me it is
this you see,' he admitted, 'whatever society, if I believe in
Christianity, I'm supposed to try and carry that into society.'[156]

But those years were years of economic hardship and
depression with high unemployment, particularly in single-
industry communities like those of the south Wales valleys. Even
in 1918 the economic future was uncertain. Time and again the
people of Wales would suffer the agonizing cruelties of
unemployment, poverty and degradation. Already by 1925 coal
production was low, as alternative sources, not to mention fuels,
were found.[157] Coal was not the only trade to suffer. Although a
slight upturn of the tinplate industry occurred in 1919, there was
periodic short-time working throughout the 1920s.[158] The
spectre of unemployment hung menacingly over the south Wales
coalfield constantly between the wars. The unemployment
average between 1925 and 1938 was consistently above 20 per
cent and peaked in 1932 at 37.4 per cent. That year single-
industry communities suffered tremendously, with Merthyr
Tydfil recording 62.3 per cent unemployment, Bargoed 68.2 per
cent and Ferndale a massive 79.7 per cent.[159] The report to the
Pilgrim Trust, *Men Without Work*, published in 1938, revealed
that south Wales suffered more than any other area classified as
'depressed'. It had the highest rate of 'long unemployed', or men
who had been employed for no more than three continuous days
in the previous year.[160] There was more time for reading, which

[155] Myrddin Powell, Onllwyn, conversation with Hywel Francis 19 May 1975; Tom
Watkins, conversation; Bob Morris, conversation.
[156] Henry Lewis, conversation.
[157] Cf. D. Howell and C. Barber, 'Wales', in F. M. L. Thompson (ed.), *The Cambridge
Social History of Britain 1750–1950*, I, *Regions and Communities* (Cambridge, 1990), p.307.
[158] P. W. Jackson, 'The interaction of industry and organized religion in a changing
cultural pattern' (MA thesis, University of Wales, 1957), pp.43, 47.
[159] Howell and Barber, 'Wales', p.307.
[160] *Men Without Work: A Report made to the Pilgrim Trust* (Cambridge, 1938), p.16.

meant that they were more open to be influenced by Socialism or Communism. The popularity of reading as a pastime is well documented, although the significance of reading theoretical Socialist books has possibly been overplayed.[161] South Wales miners certainly suffered the whims of a paternal and almost feudal system of deference and patronage, whereby men known as 'trouble-makers' were victimized in the pits. This could have been the result of political awareness in the valleys, where men's vocal support of Socialism either lost them their jobs or made them believe that they forfeited their employment in the class struggle. However, enough incidents abound of local managers and officials revelling in the status of authority and power which they had over the workforce to suggest that claims of victimization are plausible.

The human cost of this was high. In the survey approximately half of the long-term unemployed men who had formerly been miners, and were over the age of forty-five, were 'in some way unfit'.[162] Physical injury was common, the result of accidents in the pit, or the 'occupational hazards' of nystagmus and silicosis. But there was also the psychological and emotional damage which long-term unemployment could bring. A miner aged twenty-seven told Rhys Davies how he had not worked for five years, having been made unemployed at twenty-two to avoid the payment of a man's wage. 'He spoke . . . as though he had already obtained all the employment the world was likely to grant him.' Davies claimed that in order to flourish religion needed prosperity. 'The gaze of the people will not turn upwards at such times, it turns downwards to the stomach and around the denuded dwellings.' He entered a chapel where only twenty people had gathered: fifteen years previously there would have been no empty seats.[163]

Such a situation helped radical and militant political views to spread. South Wales was already regarded as a breeding-ground of Communist and Socialist activity, a charge levelled by the Report of the Royal Commission into Industrial Unrest published in 1917. According to the report, this was due to a

[161] Hywel Francis, 'Survey of miner's institute and welfare hall libraries', *Llafur*, I/2 (1973), 55–64; R. J. Barker, *Valley of Unemployment*, p.39; Lieven, *Senghennydd*, p.230.
[162] *Men Without Work*, pp.68–9, 155.
[163] Rhys Davies, *My Wales* (London, 1937), pp.122–6 *passim*.

small group of committed propagandists who were spreading discontent between capital and labour, and bringing more people in contact with the ILP. The Central Labour College movement, committed to 'independent' working-class education, which in practice meant the propagation of Socialist and Communist economics and class war theories, had also helped to disseminate advanced, radical views.[164] The leadership of the SWMF was now in the hands of young, militant Marxists. A. J. Cook, Arthur Horner and S. O. Davies were three who had replaced their initial religious work with propaganda work for the Socialist and labour cause, and they were in turn led by Frank Hodges, secretary of the MFGB. The 'left-wing outlook' of the south Wales coalfield was well known during the 1920s.[165] Towns, such as Maerdy, became known as centres of left-wing thought. A secret government report of 1919 had branded Clydach, too, a 'hotbed of theoretical Bolshevism',[166] while for Vyrnwy Morgan the Aberavon parliamentary constituency was a 'little Moscow', with Ramsay MacDonald as its MP.[167]

Despite the hardship and the popularity of Socialist thought, the Pilgrim Trust found that the sense of community was greater in the Rhondda than in the other towns they surveyed. The two organizations with the highest rate of social involvement were the trade union and the chapels, with the former only slightly higher than the latter.[168] The Report concluded: 'Comparatively few of those who had played a full part in the life of the Churches or trade unions had dropped out of them as a result of unemployment.'[169]

Following the Great War, the chapel had to compete with other movements for working-class allegiance. Most groups had existed before 1914 but at the cessation of hostilities the SWMF and the labour movement appeared to have grown in confidence and strength, while the Liberal Party and its Nonconformist allies were to a degree in disgrace. This did not result in an automatic and drastic drop in attendance or a decline in social status, but the

---

[164] J. P. M. Millar, *The Labour College Movement* (London, 1979), pp.19–20.
[165] R. Page Arnot, *The South Wales Miners: A History of the South Wales Miners Federation 1914–1926* (Cardiff, 1975), p.220n.
[166] Quoted in Kenneth O. Morgan, *Rebirth of a Nation*, p.194.
[167] J. Vyrnwy Morgan, *Welsh Mind*, p.230.
[168] *Men Without Work*, p.274.
[169] Ibid., p.289.

chapel no longer had a monopoly of influence and provision of social activities for Welsh communities. It now had to share that role with other groups which often held very different ideals to its own.[170]

The confidence of the labour movement and the consequent pressures of allegiance were startlingly revealed during the Taff Merthyr dispute over company unionism in 1934. The village of Bedlinog was split between the families of men loyal to the SWMF and those of men who had defected to the Industrial Union. Bitterness and hostility between the two sides lasted for many years after some men had defied the collective will of the Federation miners.[171] This hostility spilt over into the chapels. Four strike-breakers were regular attenders at Moriah chapel, the organist among them. Hector Bolwell, a personification of the complexities of industrial society at the time, was both a deacon at Moriah and a member of the Council of Action Committee which decided to make a silent protest. A large congregation gathered on the Sunday evening, including many men who had not attended chapel for years. Bolwell, in a show of support and solidarity for his comrades, had gone to sit in the gallery and not in the *Sedd Fawr*. When the opening hymn was announced the strike-breakers alone stood to sing. This continued throughout the service.[172]

Although this incident was apparently unique, it does show how different forces vied for the allegiance of the working class at the time. In Bedlinog, at least, the commitment to social class and to the union outweighed all other considerations. This was an incident when class loyalties were demanded above all and were demonstrated through membership of the SWMF. The men were not ranged directly against the coalowners, but against their colleagues who, in their view, were traitors to their class. This incident shows that in the working-class struggle the true victims were the chapel and religion. The service, at which a large congregation had gathered, was used merely to stigmatize the strike-breakers. The dispute concerned the desire of the majority of miners to have a single union, namely the SWMF. The chapel incident was merely a convenient form of protest.

---

[170] Herbert Morgan, *The Social Task in Wales* (London, 1919), p.82.
[171] Hywel Francis and David Smith, *The Fed*, p.295.
[172] Edgar Evans, conversation with Dai Smith and Hywel Francis, 14 July 1973; cf. Walter Haydn Davies, *Ups and Downs*, p.72; Harry Edwards, conversation.

The minister of Moriah chapel at the time was the Revd Buckley Jones. Although not a member of the Labour Party or any other political body, he had supported the men during the Taff Merthyr strike. This incited some in the church to agitate for his removal.[173] As a result of Buckley Jones's marching with the strikers, Moriah chapel was often full of working men at Sunday evening services: 'he was [regarded as] one of the leaders of the strikers',[174] and was prosecuted for intimidation and unlawful assembly.[175] After the strike those who attended services because of his support left. The minister could still be a leader in his community but no longer on his own terms. His leadership was only sought when it could bring some benefit for the union.

9. CARMARTHEN, GLAMORGAN AND MONMOUTH

As this chapter has concentrated on working-class activities in south Wales, it would at this point be appropriate to introduce some religious statistics to the argument. Nonconformist statistics have proved notoriously difficult to interpret. The existence of two classes of Nonconformist, the full church member or communicant on the one hand, and the adherent, on the other, has made it difficult to assess the number of people with a firm Nonconformist allegiance. Furthermore, membership of a particular chapel did not always or necessarily mean frequent attendance or even residence in the immediate vicinity. It should be remembered that Nonconformist membership was not as significant as its provision of a social culture and its ability to influence those who remained strangers to chapel life. That aside, the statistics for the counties of Carmarthen, Glamorgan and Monmouth are illuminating (table 3.1).

Despite the general difficulties mentioned above, and the absence of figures for the Independent chapels during the most significant years, there is a discernible pattern to be found in these statistics. They reflect the pattern of Wales as a whole (see tables 5.1 and 5.2 in Chapter 5). There was an overall increase in the number of chapel members following the religious revival of 1904–5, but this was short-lived and 1907 marked the beginning

---

[173] Edgar Evans, conversation.
[174] Harry Edwards, conversation.
[175] Hywel Francis and David Smith, *The Fed*, p.241n.

Table 3.1 Nonconformist membership in the counties of Carmarthen, Glamorgan and Monmouth, 1904–1939

Year	CARMARTHEN			GLAMORGAN			MONMOUTH		
	Baptist	Independent	Methodist	Baptist	Independent	Methodist	Baptist	Independent	Methodist
1904	16,295	22,356	10,567	51,266	61,989	39,781	16,839	11,011*	6,096
1905	18,377	22,525	11,103	62,962	64,795	44,162	22,196	13,232*	7,128
1906	18,337	23,436	11,003	65,637	63,581	43,518	21,899	12,435*	6,846
1907	17,996	23,191	11,035	62,206	61,074	43,243	20,965	12,514*	6,576
1908	17,657	22,557	11,319	60,369	61,073	43,500	21,139	12,200*	6,553
1909	17,792	22,535	11,435	59,041	59,917	43,471	19,567	11,980*	6,476
1910	17,824	22,723	11,387	57,046	60,227	43,212	19,095	11,503*	6,538
1911	17,773	22,688	11,468	56,295	59,481	43,236	18,863	11,882*	6,535
1912	17,609	21,980	11,625	55,585	58,681	43,719	18,623	11,487*	6,562
1913	17,528	22,017	11,723	55,467	59,882	44,208	18,454	11,408*	6,704
1914	17,810	20,712	11,838	55,461	58,550	44,678	18,203	11,228*	6,715
1915	17,832	21,537	11,947	56,190	59,141	44,868	18,063	10,974*	6,894
1916	17,921	–	12,048	54,853	–	45,185	17,847	–	6,919
1917	–	–	12,181	–	–	46,098	–	–	6,957
1918	–	–	12,134	–	–	46,498	–	–	7,186
1919	18,216	–	12,144	57,210	–	46,516	18,155	–	7,186
1920	18,231	–	12,283	57,242	–	46,484	18,134	–	7,197
1921	18,008	–	12,284	56,704	–	46,469	18,177	–	7,188
1922	17,948	–	12,293	57,151	–	46,360	18,159	–	7,203
1923	18,152	–	12,019	59,011	–	46,963	18,295	–	7,071
1924	18,205	–	12,192	59,530	–	47,228	19,640	–	7,092
1925	18,299	–	12,332	59,539	–	47,112	20,126	–	7,228
1926	18,627	–	12,176	59,470	–	46,989	20,184	–	7,221
1927	18,890	23,939	12,218	58,596	61,626	46,491	20,367	11,085†	7,065
1928	18,921	25,774	11,950	57,986	60,640	45,797	20,125	10,621†	6,975
1929	18,976	25,765	11,972	56,106	60,593	44,929	19,697	10,174†	6,757
1930	19,016	25,774	11,946	55,829	59,458	45,042	19,258	10,176†	6,694
1931	19,152	25,658	11,895	55,046	55,889	44,762	19,032	9,893†	6,726
1932	19,334	24,465	11,985	54,764	58,572	44,348	18,830	9,777†	6,670
1933	18,970	25,113	11,999	54,575	59,043	43,929	18,600	9,457†	6,572
1934	19,213	25,113	12,062	54,170	57,953	43,672	18,392	9,483†	6,540
1935	19,464	25,189	12,137	53,572	57,933	43,311	18,168	9,320†	6,511
1936	19,192	25,347	12,073	52,895	57,964	42,604	17,865	9,177†	6,290
1937	19,019	25,752	12,077	51,704	55,435	42,210	17,582	8,917†	6,240
1938	18,918	25,752	12,053	51,034	55,392	41,879	16,971	8,684†	6,185
1939	18,914	25,752	12,045	50,830	55,317	41,063	17,195	8,545†	6,189

Source: John Williams, *Digest of Welsh Historical Statistics*, II (Cardiff, 1985), pp.249–345.

Notes:

*These figures include the churches which belonged to the Welsh Union and the English Union.

†These figures include the churches which belonged to the English Union only. Dashes are used where no figures are available.

The figures for the Calvinistic Methodists are those for adherents, namely those who attended, including those who were full communicants. This is probably why the pattern amongst the Methodists is often not quite as clearly discernible as with the Baptists and Independents, with more frequent fluctuations in the figures, particularly for Monmouthshire.

of the decline. Perhaps the most significant aspect is the increase that occurred during and following the Great War. Where figures exist, they point to a steady increase up to the year 1926 and thereafter a steady decline. There was no dramatic growth or decline to be seen at all.

The reasons for this pattern are not entirely clear. In the uncertainty of war people may have turned to religion as the tried and tested stronghold against the onslaught of diabolical powers. But it has to be said that this is unlikely to have been the case, at least initially. It was generally, and genuinely, believed that the war would not last long. Certainly as the weeks and months dragged on and passed inevitably into years, with no end to the fighting in sight, it is possible that people turned to the church in search of divine intervention. If this were the case, however, why did membership continue to increase after the cessation of hostilities? Religion that had been sought simply as a comfort in the hardships of the extraordinary situation of war would hardly be compatible with the general optimism of the immediate post-war years. If this was the status of religion, then there should have been an increase after 1926 in the years of unemployment and economic depression. It should also be noted that the decline in membership, though steady, was not all that great. Even in Glamorgan, which had been most receptive to Socialism and the labour movement and had seen most conflict between them and the religious bodies, the membership figures remained fairly constant (57,000–58,000 for the Baptists, 58,000–59,000 for the Independents, 43,000–44,000 for the Methodists). In fact the Calvinistic Methodists would record their highest figures in Glamorgan in the years 1924–5 and not in the aftermath of the revival. The fact was that the Nonconformists did not lose members in great numbers but rather adherents, the people who made up the massive congregations but held no official church affiliation. Members themselves may have been irregular in attendance or even have moved out of the area in search of work elsewhere, yet they maintained a link with the chapel. Thus, the only tentative conclusion we can offer is this: Nonconformity still exercised a significant influence over many Welshmen during this period. For many reasons the Welsh desired an association with the chapels. It may have encompassed matters of faith; it was certainly a cultural link, one that reminded them of their origins and gave them a sense of home, family and belonging. And this leads to a consideration of perhaps the most significant point in continued chapel allegiance: language and nationality.

10. LANGUAGE AND NATIONALITY

While there were notable exceptions, Dai Dan Evans and Idris Cox being two, language and heredity appear to have been important considerations in the abandonment, or otherwise, of religious affiliation. Cook and Hodges were born outside Wales, while Horner and Paynter were born to families where either one or both immediate forebears were English. Of course, they were as fervent in their religious belief and practice, while it lasted, as any, but the chapel did not have the same cultural and ancestral hold on them that it appears to have had on Welsh-speaking workers. James Griffiths and S. O. Davies may have been infrequent in their chapel attendance, but they never severed their links with it completely, whilst in areas such as the Swansea and Amman valleys where the Welsh language remained strong, chapel attendance remained an important social function until the Second World War and beyond.[176] The Empire Colliery, Glynneath, was known as the chapel colliery because its officials were deacons in the local chapels. Will Arthur recalled that if a collier was looking for work he would merely have to attend chapel on the Sunday and report to the Empire Colliery on Monday morning. While he admitted that this was largely a joke which circulated at the time, he also recorded that when men came seeking work from Aberaman and Aberdare, still predominantly Welsh-language communities at that time, they would invariably go to the Empire, while men from Monmouthshire and the Rhondda would go elsewhere.[177] This does at least hint that the men from Welsh communities had a stronger link with the chapel than did those from Anglicized communities.

That north Wales communities and the social, political and religious loyalties of their inhabitants, were far removed from

---

[176] Cf. Huw Walters, *Canu'r Pwll a'r Pulpud* (Denbigh, 1987), p.242; Brennan, Cooney and Pollins, *Social Change, passim.*
[177] Will Arthur, conversation.

their south Wales counterparts is undeniable. But there was also a diversity within the various communities that makes generalization, though at times helpful, ultimately inaccurate. To claim that there was more than one industrial Wales would seem appropriate in view of the differences in attitude between western and eastern communities, but the language issue, and the culture which it represents, provides an exception even to this geographical generalization. Thus, where the Welsh language remained strong, be it in certain Rhondda communities, the district around Aberdare or in the Amman, Tawe and Gwendraeth valleys, chapel loyalties remained important. It was the break in culture and language which also facilitated a move away from the chapel and its ultimate substitution by Socialist politics and labour activity.

The more conservative attitudes towards religion seem to have been held by those newspapers which were published in Welsh, or at least the Welsh-language columns of those newspapers, even in the *Merthyr Pioneer*. When 'Dewi' wrote his article about 'Democracy' in September 1921, claiming that the *gwerin*'s success would be assured provided they reserve a place for 'the spirit of the Son of Man', it is significant that he was writing through the medium of Welsh.[178] In October 1920 *Y Darian* began to publish regular articles in a 'Social Question Column' written, initially, by the Revd J. Griffiths of Ammanford, hoping to reconcile religion and economics as the two great reforming movements in history.[179] Griffiths claimed that there was no longer any reason why the church should be considered an enemy of labour nor why Socialism should be considered atheistic.[180] However, he still maintained that there was an element in Socialism that 'undermines the Christian religion' (*mynd dan sail y grefydd Gristionogol*) and that therefore Socialists should be differentiated according to their attitude towards religion. This column represented the same attitude that Nonconformist ministers had had towards Socialism before the war: it was materialistic, it could lead to atheism and it needed the spiritual and moral force of Christianity. The two movements needed to work together, the church to recognize the

---

[178] *Merthyr Pioneer*, 3 September 1921, p.6.
[179] *Y Darian*, 14 October 1920, p.2.
[180] Ibid., 6 January 1921, p.8.

needs of the flesh and the labour movement to recognize the needs of the soul. Griffiths told his readers that they needed a 'great ideal' in order to 'inspire men to sanctify their lives again to realize it'. That ideal was the gospel of Jesus Christ and the establishment of the Kingdom of God on earth.[181]

This message, that the labour movement would always require the spiritual salvation which only Christ could bring, was consistently upheld in *Y Dinesydd Cymreig*. H. Monfa Parri sought to remind all involved in Socialist work that true religion could only be achieved through the gospel. A 'peaceful conclusion to the social problems of the world' could only be brought about in the Kingdom announced by Christ on the basis of the Fatherhood of God and the brotherhood of man. This would only happen when men recognized each other to be equal as brothers.[182] Writers in *Y Dinesydd* continued to maintain that individual salvation was not merely important but would be vital before social salvation could be achieved. Only Christ could convert men from selfish individualism to sacrificial social awareness.[183]

Although there were many articles discussing religion and its relationship to the labour movement during the 1920s, their tone can be said to have changed. They no longer called for harmony between church and labour but looked instead to an understanding of religion which virtually rendered the church redundant. But the religious spirit which seemed to belong to the Welsh working class was obviously deemed sufficiently important to attempt to appeal to it. Not unrelated to this connection between the chapel and the language was the advent of the Nationalist movement. At the end of the 1930s D. J. and Noëlle Davies advised that south Wales would never recover from the economic depression until Welshmen took responsibility for the situation through self-determination. Interestingly, they too appealed to religious beliefs to support their economic claims.

> To end, the material facts which are revealed by the Surveys are important and valuable; but they are materialistic and they should be used for the welfare of the spirit. And as we bid farewell to those economists who try to

[181]   Ibid., 3 February 1921, p.1.
[182]   *Y Dinesydd Cymreig*, 29 June 1921, p.3.
[183]   Ibid., 6 July 1921, p.7; 13 July 1921, p.3.

combine hesitating homage to ethics and to the welfare of the whole of humanity and uncritical loyalty to the god of pure economic doctrine as it is understood in England, what word is more apt than that of the prophet Elijah?—'How long halt ye between two opinions? If the Lord be God, follow Him: but if Baal, then follow him.' And to the people of south Wales, and the people of all Wales, in the midst of all their economic misery and their great need, is not the word still true, 'Seek ye first the Kingdom of God and his righteousness'—that is the spiritual welfare of your nation—'and all these things shall be added unto you'? Deliverance will not come from without.[184]

The impact of Nationalism as a political force following the establishment of the Welsh Nationalist Party in 1925 is beyond the scope of this book. However, this quotation does have some significance for the conclusions of this chapter, and for our view of Welsh society at the end of the 1930s. For whatever reason, Nationalism never had the widespread appeal which Socialism had achieved during its early years; neither did it become a serious contender to the Labour Party in the years before the Second World War. But the fact that Nationalists, like the early Socialists, had used religious imagery to express their economic arguments is highly significant. This means that at the very least the Welsh, even in the late 1930s, were still considered to be religious people with spiritual motivations and allegiances. This, together with the report to the Pilgrim Trust, presents a picture of a complex society in which there was no real choice between Christian religion and Socialism but in which the two were held in some kind of tension or even equilibrium by the vast majority of ordinary working people, sufficiently so as to make the use of religious argument an important weapon in political campaigns.

11. Conclusions

Men who were attracted to the labour movement at this time certainly appear to have accepted its presentation as a new religion or, perhaps more accurately, as the fulfilment of the old religion instituted by Jesus. Their expectations having been aroused, they believed the religious spirit to be essential in their efforts to realize their social ideal. They recognized not simply its

[184] D. J. and Noëlle Davies, *Cymoedd Tan Gwmwl* (Denbigh, 1938), p.220.

demands on their loyalty and in varying degrees its doctrines and dogmas, but in some cases its divine origin and commission. The characteristics of this religion were its emphasis on social reform and working-class solidarity, its lack of other-worldly content and its view that man's destiny and salvation should be placed firmly in his own hands on this earth. According to some English labour historians, as the movement after 1896 sought the more practical aim of ensuring its members' election to Parliament, the religious characteristics of the Socialist message ceased.[185] Leonard Smith, for his part, believes it to have continued until 1914, though he offers no specific explanation.[186] In Wales it was certainly the case that the popular 'labour' press continued to see a connection between the labour movement and religion throughout the 1920s and many of the men mentioned in this chapter, whatever their attitude towards organized religion, continued to see their Socialism in the context of religious vocation. That this caused a clash with existing organized religion cannot be doubted, but no firm conclusions can be drawn as to how many men left organized religion or why they did so. Much seems to have depended on an understanding of Socialism and also on the nature and personality of individuals. While those who finally forsook the chapels may have claimed that religion was impractical or based on superstition, there is no single reason for their departure. Morgan Watcyn-Williams, a Calvinistic Methodist minister in Merthyr Tydfil during the 1930s, insisted that fewer than one man in twenty had stayed away from chapel due to an abandonment of religious beliefs.[187] They had merely transferred their sphere of religious activity from the chapel to other areas. However, such protestations partially obscure the fact that a whole group of men did leave the chapel. Some were obviously influenced by Socialist propaganda or rationalist reading, and as uncritical as many were, these were considered satisfactory reasons for abandoning religion. Some men simply became apathetic towards religious observance, the natural result of brutalizing conditions of life and work, or of unemployment, while there is sufficient evidence to show that

[185] S. Yeo, 'A new life: the religion of Socialism, 1883–1886', *History Workshop Journal*, IV–VI (1978–9), 42ff.

[186] Leonard Smith, *Religion and the Rise of Labour* (Keele, 1993), p.84.

[187] Watcyn-Williams, *Khaki to Cloth*, p.171.

many men remained faithful, if not active, members of the chapel.

The religious perceptions which remained in the minds of the working class are more difficult to judge. For some men the adoption of political and economic creeds as moral causes became a substitute religion. But it cannot even be assumed that all religious and spiritual beliefs were cast aside even by those who left the chapels. It was not always the practical which they sought, or at least some came to believe that the practical and material were insufficient. This was the case with W. J. Edwards and Jack Jones, though neither made the move back to organized religion. In later life, having awakened to an awareness of the divine, both seem to have regained a formal and almost traditional belief in the need for devotion. Both men had been reared in the chapel although, interestingly, Edwards attended services more frequently before the death of his mother, while Jones for his part confessed that he had 'turned to God most nights'.[188] This only reveals the complexities of religious belief and practice. Their religion was not orthodox. God was more 'a supreme Power or driving force'[189] than the heavenly Father. All that is certain is that the religion which they retained was personal and individualistic and that the chapel was once again the victim.

South Wales society was at this time a complex amalgam of political loyalties, trade-union allegiance, religious sentiment, sporting interests and with an important place for the public house. What is clear is that while elements in all these movements to some extent opposed the others, none could ever claim the exclusive allegiance of the working class.[190] Overall in this period there was a challenge to orthodox and traditional interpretations of religion. A need for a practical religion was expressed which would influence society and deliver the oppressed working class from their suffering. Many working men believed that this practical religion was to be found in the labour movement. What they did not realize was that a similar challenge, without the class antagonism, was taking place in the religious world.

[188] Jack Jones, *Jack Jones' Unfinished Journey* (London, 1937), p.196.
[189] W. J. Edwards, *From the Valley*, pp.169, 263.
[190] Lieven, *Senghennydd*, p.104; George Ewart Evans, *From Mouths of Men*, p.156.

IV

THE TURNING-POINT 1910–1911:
NONCONFORMITY'S SOCIAL CONSCIENCE

The advent of Socialism presented primarily a theoretical problem for Nonconformists. Chapel people had to consider to what extent Socialist ideology was compatible with the Christian faith. Socialism may not have been specifically defined, but it did stand for economic collectivism of some kind and propagated the concept of justice as being vital to social well-being. Through its apparent concern for the oppressed and its dissemination through the ILP, Socialism became linked to 'labour' organizations, which presented a second, more practical problem for the chapels. How were they to react to the adoption of Socialist ideas by the working class? The Nonconformists, with their tradition of Liberal politics, became increasingly concerned that the estrangement of working-class men from the chapels often accompanied their adoption of Socialism. It was this politicization of 'labour' and the Nonconformist reaction to it which would prove to be most important for the future of the chapels.

The term 'labour' initially referred to a social group, those whose employment required physical exertion. Under the influence of ILP apologists, however, it assumed a political, and most usually Socialist, dimension. Thus, when talking of 'labour', agitators actually referred to the labouring class which, they believed, had a group consciousness arising from its common experience of oppression. 'Labour' then came to represent the social group which would vote in a particular way rather than simply those who worked with their hands. Peter Stead has shown that in Edwardian politics familiarity was of the utmost importance, with the political parties searching for a terminology that would fire the imagination and instil loyalty in its hearers.[1] 'Labour' was a familiar and homely term and working men

[1] Peter Stead, 'The language of Edwardian politics', in D. Smith (ed.), *A People and a Proletariat: Essays in the History of Wales 1780–1980* (London, 1980), *passim*. Also see *The Oxford English Dictionary*, 2nd edn., VIII (Oxford, 1989), p.559.

instinctively understood its meaning. The political party which could make the term its own was assured of success. It was the ILP's definition of 'labour' and Hardie's inspiring oratory which hit the right note in south Wales.

The Liberals were unhappy with this. They recognized that the word 'labour' was being exploited for political ends and, as a result, some sought to distinguish between 'labour' and 'Socialism'. The Revd W. F. Phillips considered that 'labour' was an 'industrial conception' and consequently the 'labour movement' was not to be confused with the Socialist movement, which was a 'political conception'. Such a statement demonstrates the length to which Phillips was prepared to go in his anti-Socialism. The labour movement was precisely a political conception as it sought certain social and industrial improvements which had to be enforced by, and embodied in, law. Phillips's point was that this labour movement was being exploited by 'ambitious and oftentimes unprincipled Socialist agitators for their own profit'. For this reason, the *Monthly Democrat*, which he edited, published balance sheets of the SWMF lodges in order to prove financial irregularities, or to imply that funds were being used for dubious ends. In Phillips's view, Socialism and Christianity were totally incompatible. Socialism had promulgated a common and material cause of human hardship and suffering, rendering men 'the helpless prey of economic forces'.[2] Christianity, on the other hand, sought individual regeneration, recognizing that the human condition was fatally flawed by sin. Phillips believed, however, that such arguments should not affect the relationship between the church and the labour movement because 'the interests of both are identical'. The labour movement which he had in mind was completely non-political. For him, 'labour' and 'Socialism' were not synonymous, a fact which would have to be recognized before the relationship between the working-class movement and the churches could be improved. His advice fell on deaf ears. There was, after all, the suspicion that his protest was inspired by the desire to attract the workers to the Liberal Party. 'Cymro', writing to the *South Wales Daily News* (*SWDN*), proudly boasted in 1907 that the terms Nonconformity and labour were 'almost as

[2] W. F. Phillips, 'Religion and labour week', *The Monthly Democrat* (1912), 106–7.

nearly synonymous as are Nonconformity and Liberalism, or Liberalism and Labour',[3] clearly demonstrating the problem facing Nonconformity at the time. To this correspondent, labour was an industrial phenomenon representing those who laboured, probably in the mines and works of south Wales. It is clear that he expected such men to vote Liberal. Even though aware that 'labour' had by this time a political nuance, this correspondent to the overwhelmingly Liberal *SWDN* was attempting to redress the balance by laying a Liberal claim to it. But in reality those who comprised the 'labour' class, as well as those who represented their interests, were increasingly attracted to Socialism as a political theory. This highlights the complexities and the dangers of the situation. Nonconformity's traditional allegiance to the Liberal Party was losing it support amongst the working class as the latter began to adhere to the politics of the left. Thus, the Nonconformists became aware of the problem of labour: the estrangement of working men from the chapels.

It was a source of pride in Welsh Nonconformity that working men had comprised the vast majority of its members, deacons and ministers.[4] The religious revival of 1904–5 was thought to have strengthened this link. Stories of miners who had stopped swearing, of hauliers who had stopped maltreating their pit ponies, and of religious services being held before the commencement of work abounded in the period.[5] In the space of no more than two years, however, newspapers and journals reported that a profound change in outlook had occurred between Nonconformity and labour. According to a correspondent to *Llais Llafur* in 1906, both movements were 'plant y werin' (the children of the *gwerin*) and therefore identical in aim, outlook and social composition.[6] Within a year the same paper had to admit that a breach was opening between the two groups which would have to be bridged. The newspaper, whose political sympathy was by this time firmly Socialist, noted that hostility had developed between the two movements as a result of

<hr/>

[3] *South Wales Daily News*, 6 July 1907, p.4.

[4] *Llais Llafur*, 10 August 1907, p.3; *Tarian y Gweithiwr*, 28 September 1911, p.1; *Seren Cymru*, 7 February 1919, p.3.

[5] See e.g. Cyril E. Gwyther *The Valley Shall Be Exalted* (London, 1949), p.40; Mabel Bickerstaff, *Something Wonderful Happened* (Liverpool, 1954), pp.75–6.

[6] *Llais Llafur*, 3 February 1906, p.2.

Nonconformist anti-Socialist diatribes.[7] *Y Cronicl* could comment in 1905 that 'in Wales the churches and the world of labour have been hand in hand with each other down the years'.[8] The article claimed that whereas in England the churches were out of step with the lives of working people, this had never been the case in Wales. Less than two years later the same journal had to warn its readers about the dangers of militant Socialism which was 'taking the place of the flame of true worship on the altar of Welsh religion'.[9] As early as 1907 it was recognized that the churches were losing the allegiance of the working class. In that year, *Y Cronicl* stated that the elements which would alienate the working class from the church were already active in the labour movement in south Wales. It is clear that the cause of the problem was the arrival of Socialism and its claim on 'labour'. The growing indifference of a social group which the churches had previously considered loyal can thus be dated to 1906–7, within a year of the end of the revival. It was then that Socialism's claim on labour began to be recognized.

The arrival of the 'Labour Party' as a political alternative for Welshmen was one reason why Nonconformists began to withdraw from overt political activity during the first decade of the twentieth century. The danger that chapel congregations would be divided between followers of the Liberal Party and supporters of labour was recognized as too great a threat to risk any kind of political activity. The problem for Nonconformity was that the working class in this period was, if anything, becoming more politically conscious. As a result, the church's unwillingness to be overtly political was seen as an attempt to retain the status quo. In fact it was not, for the Nonconformist withdrawal from political circles was accompanied by a growing recognition that its spiritual and moral mission required a social expression; but its spokesmen had come to realize that in fact they lacked any real political influence. In such a situation it was considered that to have an effective role in the life of 'labour' the church had to remain outside the political establishment.

Criticism was, as a result, virtually inevitable. Labour groups continually accused the chapels of insularity and impracticality,

[7] Ibid., 9 February 1907, p.1.
[8] 'Hanes y mis', *Y Cronicl* (1905), 190.
[9] 'J.D.J.', 'Nodiadau'r mis', *Y Cronicl* (1907), 262–3.

positing these characteristics as the reason why many were leaving religion behind.[10] It was increasingly claimed that the churches were representing a backward-looking ideal and consequently losing adherents. They were no longer in the 'van of progress' or seen to represent the general feelings of the labour movement.[11] A letter to the *SWDN*, written by William Ellis, claimed that industrialization and the consequent enslavement of men had left no place for religious sentiment. The churches therefore had to 'wake up to and thoroughly realize their position and duty towards the social problem' and take a prominent part in clearing slum housing from the land, improving health and 'thundering out with no uncertain, wavering or equivocal voice against the oppression and economic evils' rampant in society. It was only then that they would regain the confidence of ordinary people.

> The churches will then be real, living bodies, pregnant with life and vitality, abounding in all the attributes of grace and having an irresistible attraction for the legions who are now without their doors, and to whom their appeal is now cold, bloodless and of no avail.[12]

The letter, written in the spirit of Hardie, stated that the church's social inactivity was a result of its apostasy and that Christians were failing to follow 'the teaching of Him whom they profess to serve'. It pointed clearly to the way that labour's estrangement from organized religion was associated with social problems. To regain the respect and allegiance of the working man, the church had to condemn social injustice and seek its removal.

The response of some ministers was simply to join the labour movement. The Revds Daniel Hughes, Pontypool, Rhys J. Huws, Bethesda, J. Jenkins (Gwili),[13] E. K. Jones, Brymbo, J. Edryd Jones, Garnant, Stanley Jones, Caernarfon, W. Rowland Jones, Merthyr, Herbert Morgan, London, James Nicholas, Tonypandy, T. E. Nicholas, Glais, R. Silyn Roberts, Blaenau Ffestiniog, T. M. Roderick, Cwmgors, W. D. Roderick, Rhiwfawr, D. D. Walters

---

[10] *Llais Llafur*, 22 February 1908, p.1; *Labour Leader*, 27 November 1918, p.4; 26 December 1918, p.1.
[11] *Merthyr Pioneer*, 18 January 1913, p.7; *Rhondda Socialist*, 31 (18 January 1913), p.1.
[12] Ibid. The letter was reprinted in both journals.
[13] 'Gwili' was never actually ordained.

(Gwallter Ddu), Newcastle Emlyn, Iona Williams, Llanelli, all came to prominence either as members or active supporters of the ILP. These men were either Independents, Baptists or (Calvinistic) Methodists and thus belonged to mainstream Nonconformity. There were also Unitarian ministers who took an active interest and involvement in the labour movement at this time, men like the Revd D. G. Rees, Bridgend, and the Revd J. Park Davies, who would later become principal at the Presbyterian College, Carmarthen. The reasons for the attachment of these ministers to the labour movement vary considerably. Some claimed to have adopted Socialism, though usually it was seen as essential to achieving social reform rather than as an economic theory. But there was, too, a simple desire to be associated with the struggles and aspirations of the working class. Whatever reason lay behind their support of labour and however they interpreted their Socialism, their presence on labour platforms and their recognition as 'labour' ministers was welcomed unequivocally by the labour press. *Llais Llafur* went as far as to advise labour supporters to join those churches where the ministers had clearly linked themselves to the labour cause.[14] But Nonconformists in general found themselves being increasingly criticized for failing to adopt labour politics and ensuring social reform. The labour movement was presenting its case in emotive, moralistic terms borrowed from religion. It sought the establishment of a more just and righteous social system and thus it expected some compliance or support from the churches. When this was not forthcoming, the Nonconformists had to justify themselves against accusations of impracticality and pious unconcern.[15] The ideological issues posed by the advent of Socialism were soon replaced with the more practical problem of retaining working men within the chapel. By the end of the first decade of the twentieth century, the churches in general and Nonconformists in particular had begun to approach seriously the problem of working-class abandonment of chapel religion and had recognized the need to address the wider social issues which the labour movement had done so much to highlight.

The year 1910 marked a watershed. Increasingly bitter industrial unrest had culminated in the year-long Cambrian

---

[14] *Llais Llafur*, 22 July 1911, p.1.
[15] *Tarian y Gweithiwr*, 14 April 1910, p.4; cf. *Merthyr Pioneer*, 31 January 1914, p.8.

Combine dispute in the Rhondda where Socialist militancy and working-class radicalism boiled over into a demonstration of revolutionary fervour. The authorities were sufficiently concerned to send in battalions of soldiers and Metropolitan Police officers, but they failed to prevent such celebrated incidents as the Tonypandy riots of November 1910. The railway dispute of 1911 would bring troops to south Wales and led to an incident in Llanelli when two men were shot dead by soldiers. While the coalowners were satisfied that this was the result of Socialist agitation,[16] by this time Nonconformists were generally recognizing social injustice and poverty as ultimately responsible for the popularity of Socialist ideas. The problem of labour's estrangement from traditional religious forms would consequently have to include the wider issue of effective social reform.

It was not simply the tide of revolutionary zeal which marked 1910 as a turning-point. From that year the social problem, too, including issues such as living and working conditions, just wage settlements and industrial relationships, reached the top of Nonconformist agendas and began slowly to replace the more overtly political question of Socialism as their main concern. Socialist candour had drawn attention to the specific industrial problems which periodically erupted in the years between 1898 and 1914. Although the underlying reasons for the unrest were more complex than mere political aspiration fuelled by a sense of injustice, it only slowly dawned on Nonconformists that housing, public health and leisure activities had to be improved if a solution to society's problems was to be found. Once the connection was made, they quickly became convinced that conditions in Wales were far worse than those in similar districts in England.[17] The death rate in 1910 was nearly 2 per cent higher for Wales than for England, as were the infant mortality rate and the instances of epidemic diseases.[18] An effective Christian response to the current challenge was required, including practical measures and theological reformulation. It

[16] D. Evans, *Labour Strife in the South Wales Coalfield 1910-1911* (Cardiff, 1911), p.3.
[17] D. L. Thomas and Herbert Morgan, *Housing Conditions in Wales* (London, 1911), p.2. This remained the impression throughout the period, cf. *Labour Voice*, 20 May 1933, p.6.
[18] Thomas and Morgan, *Housing Conditions*, pp.5-6; cf. John Davies, 'Y gydwybod gymdeithasol yng Nghymru rhwng y ddau ryfel byd', in Geraint H. Jenkins (ed.), *Cof Cenedl IV* (Llandysul, 1989), pp.155-78.

was from this point that the three main Welsh Nonconformist denominations made their own attempts to express their basic social principles in a cogent way, and provide chapel members with some practical leadership and advice through the establishment of specific committees to deal with the social problem.

1. DENOMINATIONAL RESPONSES

The first to respond was the Union of Welsh Independents, whose assembly at Lampeter in 1910 marked a watershed in Welsh Nonconformity's treatment of the social problem. Although the chairman's address at Lampeter had dealt with 'The social mission of Christ and his Church', it was Daniel Lleufer Thomas's[19] lecture which highlighted the social problem in Nonconformity. Although he had been chairman of the Swansea branch of the Progressive Theology League, his espousal of the liberal interpretation of Christian doctrine was not the sole inspiration for his social concern. His daily work as stipendiary magistrate for Porth and the Rhondda had brought him into contact with men who were victims of an unjust social system. This made him demand a specifically Christian answer.

In his address, Thomas painted a picture of injustice in which wealth was unevenly distributed and workers condemned to an unhealthy slum-life. Competition, the very principle on which society was based, and the pressure to increase wealth, sometimes even at the expense of morality, were unjustifiable and ought to be changed. The church had restricted its interest to matters of temperance and individual morality. In order to redress the balance he urged the formation of a Welsh Union of Social Service. Rather than study the Bible, he suggested that the older classes in Sunday Schools could study social questions, while every minister should be encouraged to study sociology. The church should organize meetings in individual congregations in order to consider social problems. He wanted the Union to co-operate with other denominations because the social problem, he claimed, was too important an issue to become a matter for denominational rivalry.[20]

---

[19] For Daniel Lleufer Thomas (1863–1940), see *DWB*, pp.939–40.
[20] *Y Tyst*, 17 August 1910, pp.5–6; *Llais Llafur*, 13 August 1910, p.1; *South Wales Daily News*, 28 July 1910.

Although Thomas's priority was to establish some kind of social service committee amongst the Independents, his speech set the tone for the involvement of all the Nonconformist denominations in social matters for the next twenty years or so. The stress was firmly placed on gathering and providing information, which was considered to be a far more important factor than the study of the Bible, and was a notion compatible with the prevailing belief in self-improvement. The secularizing tendencies of the age are apparent, for the understanding of the gospel's social principles was subordinate to an understanding of the actual social issues themselves. Thomas's association with the Progressive Theology League suggests that he was an immanentist with all the pantheistic tendencies which such a position involved. As a result, any distinction between secular and sacred would have blurred in his mind. Thus, the traditional and directly religious exercise of biblical study could be replaced by the study of contemporary social issues. God was immanent in his creation and thus could be served through serving the needs of the created order. Perhaps as important as this specific doctrinal interpretation was the more general Liberal belief that religion's main purpose was to transform the world and build the Kingdom of God. These two ideological factors validated Lleufer Thomas's call on the church to abandon its traditional approach in order to meet the demands of the current social crisis. And there were at least some amongst his audience who agreed with him. Apart from the implications for Christian doctrine and ecclesiology, it was perhaps the ecumenical element in his lecture which was of most abiding significance. Denominational rivalry was common and could on occasion be intense. Thomas's greatest achievement was to encourage ecumenical co-operation and ensure that the social problem achieved a similar level of importance to the traditional Nonconformist topics of education and disestablishment.

Events then moved rapidly. A meeting was held at Gnoll Road English Congregational Church, Neath, on 14 October to discuss 'The relationship of the Independent Churches of Wales and social subjects'.[21] The invitation to attend was extended to all parties interested in the role of the church in the social debate,

[21] *Y Tyst*, 5 October 1910, p.1.

from the Welsh and the English churches. The meeting was
addressed by the Revd Will Reason, secretary of the Social
Service Committee of the Congregational Union of England and
Wales, who described how the committee worked. It was then
decided that such a committee should be formed in the Welsh
Union. It was the churches which belonged to the Welsh Union
that appeared to offer the leadership and enthusiasm required to
take seriously the needs of society. The response of the English-
language churches proved disappointing and the Welsh churches
eventually decided to go ahead alone.[22] Will Reason then
addressed another meeting, this time of the north Wales
Independents at Penygroes, Arfon, on 21 January 1911. Those
present included Principal Thomas Rees of the Bala-Bangor
Theological College and the Revd Stanley Jones, Caernarfon,
who expressed the view that the church should act as society's
conscience, rising 'to create a public opinion on these matters'.[23]
This opinion received endorsement from an unexpected source
by the end of the year and in fact became the policy of Welsh
Nonconformists throughout the period of their social interest and
concern.

Although the work appeared to be proceeding well, the
decision was taken to inaugurate a non-denominational and
independent group whose membership would be open to
individuals, churches and study groups, and so the Welsh School
of Social Service was born. Initially, it was a joint venture
between the Independents and Baptists, with the arrangements
in the hands of Lleufer Thomas, D. Miall Edwards of the
Memorial Theological College, Brecon, and the Revd Gwilym
Davies, Carmarthen. A joint committee was established which
consisted of three representatives of the Independent churches,
namely Lleufer Thomas, the Revd Thomas Richards, Newport,
and Principal Thomas Rees of Bangor, and three Baptists,
namely Professor J. M. Davies of the Baptist College, Cardiff, the
Revd Herbert Morgan and the Revd James Jones, Llandrindod
Wells.[24] They proceeded to organize a conference which met in
Llandrindod Wells, at that time a popular holiday resort, in

[22] Ibid., 25 January 1911, p.9.
[23] Ibid., 1 February 1911, p.3.
[24] Minute Book Welsh School of Social Service 1911–1914, Gwilym Davies Papers,
NLW.

September 1911, and the Welsh School of Social Service was established.[25]

It was the first 'school' of its kind in Britain and Gwilym Davies later claimed that it had helped to popularize the term 'social service'. Its purpose was to engage in the discussion of social problems from a specifically Christian standpoint, with a view to formulating a Christian response. It could then be a 'clearing house' for ideas affecting social agencies in Wales because it would provide a common meeting ground for all men and women who felt a concern for social welfare.[26] The speakers at the first school outlined the principles which should govern the church's involvement in social issues. William George pointed to the polarization of opinions current in Christian thought. The first was that the church's task was exclusively to fit men for the next world, while the second was that the church's sole purpose was in the realm of social service. The school was to represent a middle path, namely the idea that the church was not to involve itself directly in political and social reform, but rather to produce citizens who would apply gospel principles in everyday life. The school should be a 'go-between the Church and the world' which would ensure a Christian input into the debate but would also keep the sanctuary free from social and political divisions and propaganda. The church did, however, have a responsibility to promote a standard of conduct and dissociate itself from those who broke it.[27] Such principles were no different from those propounded elsewhere by Nonconformists interested in social issues.

It was recognized at this very first school that the Liberal Nonconformist hegemony which had prevailed in Welsh chapel life for half a century was at an end. As a result, the church had to act out of its own Christian principles and convictions. For Miall Edwards this meant that the school had to offer a positive contribution to the debate rather than merely show sympathy with the labour movement. For most of the men involved, this contribution was to be expressed in liberal theological terms. Thus, Herbert Morgan could claim that the church's unique contribution was the development of individual character and

---

[25] *Y Tyst*, 20 September 1911, p.6; 27 September 1911, p.12.
[26] Gwilym Davies, *Twenty Five Years of the Welsh School of Social Service 1911–1936* (n.d.), p.1.
[27] *South Wales Daily News*, 7 September 1911, p.6.

human personality. Such a moral conversion was required to make effective any attempts at social reform. It was the Christian gospel alone which provided the dynamic for this individual regeneration along ethical lines. Daniel Lleufer Thomas's contribution was probably the most significant and marked the school's character as separate from that of the churches. If they were to contribute anything worthwhile to the social question, Thomas believed that they should enter the debate with no ulterior motive. It was not to be viewed as a means to gain the support of the working class with a goal of increased membership. Instead, their concern for social conditions was to be the fruit of the 'Christian life', in which brotherly love and the thirst for justice and righteousness reigned.[28] Although its implications were not immediately recognized, the principle of service was certainly embodied in the initial aims of the school.

Arrangements were made at the close of the school to establish an organizing committee consisting of representatives from all the denominations in Wales with the exception of the Roman Catholic Church. There was therefore a genuine desire to keep denominational sectarianism to a minimum, which was a remarkable achievement considering the bitterness of the disestablishment question at the time.[29]

Although the school's advent was generally welcomed by the press,[30] it is difficult to avoid the criticism of 'Toplis' in the *SWDN*, who wanted to know why no working men, or leaders of the working men, were involved. The school had been an 'eclectic body of men' discussing the social question in an 'academic spirit' in a holiday spa town. His comments on the organizing committee for the following year are significant:

> among the members of the committee which sets itself to deal with the economic conditions of the Welsh toilers in the industrial valleys of

[28] Ibid., 8 September 1911, p.5.
[29] Minute Book, meeting at Shrewsbury 17 November 1911. Those added to the committee were Professor D. Phillips, Revd Silyn Roberts, Revd S. N. Jones (Methodists); Revds Gwynfryn Jones, Barmouth, T. Hughes, Llandudno, T. J. Pritchard, Aberdare (Wesleyans); Canon Buckley, Cardiff, Revd D. Williams, Llangyfelach, Revd T. H. Hughes, Blaenau Ffestiniog (Anglican). After the Cardiff conference in December 1911, Revd J. Park Davies (Unitarian), Revd E. Radcliffe and Mr H. D. Phillips, Llandrindod, were added.
[30] *Llais Llafur*, 28 August 1914, p.7; *Merthyr Pioneer*, 7 March 1914, p.4.

Glamorganshire, not one hails from the affected districts and among them
there is not a single pastor of a Welsh church.[31]

The suspicion of paternalism would plague the school for the first
fifteen years of its existence. The stress on expert study and the
prominence of ministers of religion led to the opinion that the
school ignored the view of the working men themselves.
Considering the popularity of proletarian movements at this
time, such a policy was doomed to failure.

The school, however, became an annual event. From 1912 it
was intended that speakers should concentrate on one specific
area of the social problem. That year the meetings were devoted
to matters directly or indirectly related to industrial unrest,
particularly in the coalfield. The proceedings of the 1913 school
were published in book form. It was convened to discuss rural
problems, but two papers entitled 'The Christian philosophy of
life in its relation to the social problem', one by Principal Owen
Prys of the United Theological College, Aberystwyth, the other
by Miall Edwards, gave the church's involvement in social
discussions a philosophical and theological basis.

Owen Prys held that the school might 'generally [do] the duty
that lies nearest to us' but it needed also a vision and ideal that
would only be realized well in the future. The task was the
discovery of such a vision and the attempt to embody it in
society. This vision was provided by the teaching of Christ.
Interestingly, he almost echoed Keir Hardie in his belief that
society could be formed to help the living of Christian life.

> We need to so mould society that men may live their lives as Christ would
> have us live, so that every man shall be treated in society according to the
> great principle of our religion, the infinite worth of the human soul, and
> the dignity of human life.[32]

As a doctrinal theologian, Miall Edwards wanted to see social
concern grounded in theological principles. The central
principles were the Fatherhood of God and its natural

---

[31] *South Wales Daily News*, 9 September 1911, p.9.
[32] Owen Prys, 'The need of a Christian base for social reform', in Gwilym Davies (ed.),
Social Problems in Wales (London, 1913), p.34.

implication, the brotherhood of man, with the establishment of the Kingdom of God as that brotherhood's ethical task.

> The Kingdom of God is the *summum bonum* of Christian ethics, the supreme thing we live for, that which alone can give meaning and value to our life ... Our social, political and commercial life is good to the degree, and only to the degree, in which it realises or promotes the Kingdom of God and His Righteousness.[33]

The foundations having been established, it was the school with its ecumenical and studious approach which became the main focus of Christian social activity in Wales over the next decade. It was only after the pioneering efforts of the Independents were transformed into interdenominational attempts at a social interpretation of Christianity that the Methodists and Baptists, as separate denominations, began to consider the social problem and the responsibility of the church in solving it.

From July 1911 the Welsh Baptists were kept informed of social issues in regular articles in *Seren Cymru* by the Revd E. D. Lewis, Ystalyfera, Glamorgan. Although no economic solution was ever offered, the column did serve to awaken the Baptists to social needs. Lewis's main intention appears to have been to keep matters of religion before the working class rather than to offer solutions to the social problem.

The Baptist Union of Wales formed a Social Service League during its annual assembly held in Mountain Ash in September 1911. Its goal was to study social subjects in the light of the principles enshrined in the gospel and to encourage direct social efforts according to the values of Christ's Kingdom. The League was to form study groups, produce literature and provide lectures and sermons on social issues, and thus to induce members into an 'enlightened mind'. Any person could join the League on payment of one shilling annual subscription, and each minister or church secretary was asked to bring the matter to the attention of his congregation. Men involved on the committee included the Labour MPs William Brace and John Hinds, the

---

[33] D. Miall Edwards, 'The ethical position of Christianity', in Gwilym Davies (ed.), *Social Problems*, pp.49–51.

Revd J. Griffiths, Ammanford, who had contributed articles to *Tarian y Gweithiwr* on the church and labour, the Revds Gwilym Davies, J. Tywi Jones and Herbert Morgan. However, it seems that the League had difficulty in convening regular meetings and so its more important and practical aims were never achieved.[34]

The Calvinistic Methodists convened a committee at Shrewsbury, 28 April 1913, which reported to the General Assembly at Fishguard later that year.[35] Its call was for the church to nurture the conscience of its members and apply 'Kingdom principles' to every practical need in life. It was apparently assumed that everyone knew precisely what those 'Kingdom principles' were. The committee's report recommended that both Connexional assemblies, of the north and of the south, should consider social problems in the light of Christianity. They encouraged further research into each local problem and to see that reform was conducted according to the principles of Christ. The denomination's leaders recommended that the churches form study groups and keep out of party politics. Preachers should be given the opportunity to study economics or sociology, while the Connexion should provide pertinent literature.[36] It also asked the churches not to inaugurate special meetings but rather to discuss social topics in those which already existed.[37] Although the importance of education in social issues was recognized, no literature appears to have been provided by the Methodist Connexion before the Great War.

Although initially the Welsh School of Social Service encouraged the denominations to form social service unions, to research social topics and discover a Christian response to the problems embodied in the social system, it seems that the denominations were mostly content to allow the school to do the work for them. Thus, nothing really came of either the efforts of the Methodist Connexion or the Baptist Social Service League before the war. It seems that those whose interests lay in this direction tended to work through the School of Social Service. A

[34] 'Constitution', Baptist Union of Wales Social Service League, 1911; *Seren Cymru*, 30 June 1922, p.2.
[35] *Blwyddiadur y Methodistiaid Calfinaidd* (1914), 119; cf. *Y Goleuad*, 25 June 1913, p.5.
[36] *Blwyddiadur* (1914), 119–20.
[37] *Y Goleuad*, 25 June 1913, p.5.

full programme had been arranged for Llandrindod in September 1914. The outbreak of war caused a last-minute cancellation as the social problem lost its priority in the face of more pressing needs.

2. THE CARDIFF CONFERENCE

The Welsh School of Social Service was not the only event organized by Nonconformists and churchmen in 1911 which attempted to tackle the social problem head-on. It was ostensibly because of the growing antagonism between labour and the church that a conference was convened at the Park Hall, Cardiff, on 29 December 1911, to discuss the rift and how to heal it. The need for social reform was high on the conference's agenda, particularly as Nonconformists were beginning to recognize that the masses would only be attracted back to the chapel through the propagation of a specifically social Christianity. Unfortunately, the conference was surrounded by controversy even before it assembled. One of the organizing secretaries was, of all people, W. F. Phillips. According to Vernon Hartshorn, he was 'one of the most unscrupulous and vindictive opponents of the Labour Party in South Wales'.[38] When it was discovered that the main speech of the conference would be delivered by Lloyd George, suspicions of political opportunism were rife and probably justified.

Vernon Hartshorn led the attack.[39] The conference was 'foredoomed to failure', he claimed, as it was a 'cunning party device for retaining that political power which Welsh Liberals wield through the Welsh Nonconformist churches'. Considering that the only political figure to be invited was Lloyd George, it would seem that either Hartshorn was correct, or that the organizers were guilty of gross naïveté. Rather than fostering a better understanding between religion and labour, the result would be 'an expression of opinion by a discredited political cauqus [sic]—a ponderous political humbug worked under the

[38] *Labour Leader*, 27 October 1911, p.674.
[39] For Vernon Hartshorn (1872–1931), see *DWB*, p.344; J. M. Bellamy and J. Saville (eds.), *Dictionary of Labour Biography*, I (London, 1972), pp.150–2; Peter Stead, 'Vernon Hartshorn; miners' agent and Cabinet Minister', in S. Williams (ed.), *Glamorgan Historian*, VI (Cowbridge, 1969), pp.83–94.

cloak of religion'.[40] If the main purpose of the conference was to supply the church with a better understanding of the needs of labour, then its failure was already assured; the labour representatives staged a boycott on the grounds of political partisanship. But there were still more difficulties to be faced. Every church and chapel in south Wales was invited to send a delegate to the conference, but the Anglican clergy of Cardiff refused to attend because it appeared to 'have assumed a political complexion'.[41] The day itself did not start auspiciously. The Park Hall proved insufficient to house all who sought entry and some official delegates were turned away.

The conference was divided into two sessions. Those who attended the morning session, which was restricted to ministers and clergy, were informed by the chairman, the Revd H. M. Hughes, Cardiff, that working-class estrangement from religion had been caused by the politicization of labour and the influence of atheistic and immoral Socialism. Any solution to the current state of affairs would have to consider this political and specifically Socialist dimension.[42] The main speaker, the Revd John Morgan Jones, Merthyr, addressed the congregation on 'The relation of the minister to social problems'. He attempted to show that the means to meet the needs of the working class and to create a just society were to be found in the Christian religion. By emphasizing the value of personality and the universal brotherhood of the human race, the gospels had provided the great moral principles to do this. They could not be used to validate contemporary social or political policy, however. Thus, the ministers were made aware of the dangers to religion inherent in the Socialist message, and they were treated to a lesson in Liberal Theology and biblical criticism. None of this addressed the fundamental question of labour's estrangement from the chapels but seemed instead to answer the accusation levelled against the churches that they had no message for industrial society. No attempt was made to offer practical advice on how the ministers could reach the working class. Instead, it became obvious that the church's first task would be to understand its own message. John Morgan Jones gave those

---

[40] *Labour Leader*, 27 October 1911, p.674; cf. *Merthyr Pioneer*, 20 December 1911, p.4.
[41] *Labour Leader*, 22 December 1911, p.812.
[42] *South Wales Daily News*, 30 December 1911, p.9.

present a lesson in what the gospel contained and, equally important, what it did not.

Two important points are revealed by the opening meeting of the Cardiff conference. The first is that the specific problem of labour, namely the working class's estrangement from the chapels, became indelibly associated with the social problem in general. In answering the social question, including such issues as poor housing, dangerous working conditions and unfair wage agreements, the problem of religious indifference would also be solved. This would ultimately take the place of the question of labour in the minds of most Nonconformists because they came to believe that their role was not to fill chapels but to serve the world in the name of Jesus Christ. The second is that political debate was essential. Although Jones stated that the church should not simply adopt the policies of one political party, he offered no alternative policy. This would create obvious problems in a situation which required political solutions but where Nonconformists generally sought to avoid politics.

In the ensuing discussion, various suggestions were made, including the need for the chapels to develop their own specifically social ideal and that the church should lead the social movement. The vicar of Glyntaff, the Revd V. Gower Jones, was one dissenting voice. He disagreed with the content of John Morgan Jones's paper. The Merthyr minister had warned against exploiting the gospel in the name of Socialistic theories. Gower Jones believed that the gospel was equally prone to exploitation in the name of individualism. Few would have disagreed with him had he not remarked that the Sermon on the Mount dealt mainly with temporal matters. This was met with 'loud cries of No'. 'Unfortunately the conference then closed', noted *Llais Llafur* in a damning criticism, 'or we might have been privileged to see more of the poverty of the ministerial mind as far as social questions are concerned.'[43] A Socialist agenda had caused the *Llais* to be selective in its information and to present a negative view of the whole conference. It had wrongly implied that the morning assembly consisted of the more important meeting of the day and had quoted only the negative aspects of Jones's paper. At this time, the *Llais* was at its most radical and it

[13] *Llais Llafur*, 6 January 1912, pp. 1–2.

seems to have been keen to demonstrate the inability of the churches to agree on social policy. It emphasized that the church was totally impractical in its message and practice and had proved itself unable to come to any firm or helpful conclusions over social issues. But the *Llais*'s report was accurate in one respect. Despite having recognized the need to meet the social problem, and the specific issue of labour's estrangement from religion, Nonconformists and the church in general were finding it difficult to offer any realistic solution.

The second session, held in the afternoon, was open to politicians and labour leaders as well as church representatives. It was the more important of the two meetings, with initial addresses by F. B. Meyer and the bishop of Llandaf. The highlight, however, was the address by Lloyd George, which was later published as a sermon supplement to the *Christian Commonwealth*, a journal associated with R. J. Campbell and the 'New Theology'.[44]

It was precisely the type of event at which Lloyd George excelled. He was addressing an assembly of religiously minded Welshmen, many of whom idolized him, on a topic close to their hearts. It was at this time, while he was Chancellor of the Exchequer, that he reached the height of his popularity among his compatriots. In his address, he proceeded to deny that he had attended the conference with any ulterior political motive. He claimed that he was not seeking support for a political party or economic programme but to give his opinion on the relationship between the church and the social problem. The church was to 'create an atmosphere' in which it would be impossible for social justice to be ignored. His attitude to the social problem itself was quasi-socialist: he claimed that it was the community's responsibility to solve the social problem of poverty, bad housing and consequent health problems, for it was only collectively that enough resources could be drawn upon to ensure a satisfactory conclusion. The churches should act the part of the conscience of the community and thus had to awaken the moral outrage against social injustice. As well as publicizing the wrongs, the church should develop a sense of responsibility amongst all its

[44] D. Lloyd George, *The Relation of the Churches to Social Questions*, Christian Commonwealth Sermon Supplements, no. 58 (London, 1912).

individual members who would then work to remove those wrongs. It had to emphasize individual responsibility.[45] But it should not draft acts and issue political propaganda.

> In the old days the churches used to search out heresy among the people, but they never punished it; they used to hand it over to the secular arm. That is exactly what I suggest to the churches today. Let them hunt out evil conditions, let them expose them, drag them to the light of day and when they come to be dealt with, hand them over to the secular arm.[46]

He told the assembly that 'those who are below' could only be redeemed by 'the sacrifice of those who are above'.[47] An article in the *Labour Leader* expressed the hope that he would remember this the next time the question of a minimum wage was raised in Parliament.[48]

The conference concluded with a single resolution, proposed by Daniel Lleufer Thomas, which was passed unanimously.

> In view of the gravity and the urgency of the social problem and the need of studying it in the light of Christian principles and of defining the attitude of the churches towards it, this conference urges the churches to organise means of social study and service.[49]

Such a resolution, proposed by such a man, highlights the paradox of the situation. The Cardiff conference had merely indicated the connection between social conditions and the estrangement of labour from organized religion. No solutions had been offered and the conference had been continually overshadowed by the accusation of political partisanship. Lleufer Thomas, on the other hand, had played a pivotal role in establishing the Welsh School of Social Service, which sought to offer Christian solutions to society's problems. The 'school' had been inaugurated the previous September and had been poorly attended.[50]

[45] Ibid., pp.1–4, *passim.*
[46] Ibid., p.6.
[47] Ibid., cf. *Y Tyst*, 3 January 1912, p.8.
[48] *Labour Leader*, 5 January 1912, p.1.
[49] *South Wales Daily News*, 30 December 1911, p.9.
[50] Davies, *Twenty Five Years of the Welsh School of Social Service*, p.4.

Press reaction generally welcomed the conference as a step towards ultimate reconciliation between the labour movement, or the working class, and the churches. However, even these responses were partisan. 'Dewi Vychan' was pleased that the church and the chapel had come together to discuss such an important matter and that Lloyd George's speech was such an encouragement to the church to lead in seeking social reform. He also believed that 'the best of Wales were there to learn at the feet of the greatest Welshman of his age'.[51] Just as Lloyd George's presence had been a stumbling-block to the conference's critics, so it was a mark of the conference's success for its supporters. According to the *SWDN*, a paper sympathetic to the Liberal Party,

> Henceforth the mission of our Churches in South Wales will be so broadened as to include within its scope, in addition to its strictly spiritual aims, the creation of a civic conscience for better harmony and the improved administration of public health laws.[52]

It is remarkable how, over the next few years, so many religious leaders referred, either directly or indirectly, to Lloyd George's speech as having given the churches a definite policy to enable them to contribute to solving the social problem. This undoubtedly says more about the awe in which 'the Wizard' was held by his Nonconformist compatriots than about the effectiveness of his policy. Although the phrase 'create an atmosphere' did not originate with Lloyd George, his speech gave it a greater authority and validity and the way in which it was repeated in later years is striking.[53] There was even a hint of it in Vernon Hartshorn's writings.

[51] *Y Tyst*, 3 January 1912, p.5.
[52] *South Wales Daily News*, 30 December 1911, p.5.
[53] E.g. *Seren Cymru*, 9 February 1912, p.3; *Y Tyst*, 10 January 1912, p.9; 28 February 1912, p.8; *Llais Llafur*, 13 January 1912, p.7; 30 May 1914, p.4; T. R. Jones, 'Yr Eglwys a phynciau cymdeithas', *Y Drysorfa* (1912), 202; H. C. Williams, 'Cenhadaeth gymdeithasol yr Eglwys', *Seren Gomer* (1920), 16; D. Miall Edwards, *Crefydd a Bywyd* (Dolgellau, 1915), p.347; D. Harford Evans, 'Cyfrifoldeb yr Eglwys', in E. Curig Davies (ed.), *Llef y Gwyliedydd* (Llanelli, 1927), p.140. A similar line is taken, though not necessarily under Lloyd George's influence, by Charles A. Ellwood, *The Reconstruction of Religion* (New York, 1923), p.290; S. E. Keeble, *Christian Responsibility for the Social Order* (London, 1922), p.278; A. E. Garvie, *The Christian Ideal for Human Society* (London, 1930), p.364; T. Rhondda Williams, *The Working Faith of a Liberal Theologian* (London, 1914), p.241.

In the name of God I ask is it not the business of the Christian Church to unite its forces with Labour and bring about a reform in this particular direction, to bring pressure to bear upon governments in such a way that they cannot resist the cries of the disinherited?[54]

Llais Llafur, on the other hand, represented labour, if not Socialist, politics. Its response to the conference was rather more critical, yet even it believed that the conference had raised points which needed to be answered. For one thing there was the question of the conference's political undercurrent.

We are puzzled to know in what capacity the Chancellor of the Exchequer spoke: whether it was as a Liberal Politician, or an ex-president of the Welsh Baptist Union. The Liberal press on the following day made no bones about it. They referred to it as the speech of the Chancellor of the Exchequer. Mr Lloyd George himself emphasised the non-political character of the meeting, but throughout his speech there was just an under-current that suggested that the measures introduced since 1906, Old Age Pensions, the 1909 Budget and the Insurance Act, were on show although there was an effort made not to parade them too openly . . . If another Conference be held, we trust that it will be at least representative of the three political parties, so that the suspicion of the partisanship may be clearly absent. These people on Friday gathered together to discuss the needs and aspirations of the working man, and the working man himself, the chief person concerned, was absent![55]

There was also an objection to the content of the speeches and discussions. The *Llais* reported that those present in the Park Hall were left with the feeling that Lloyd George's speech may have been 'moving towards some social idealism', but ultimately was intended to 'make more efficient Liberal clubs of the Nonconformist churches'.[56] Silas Williams, at least, felt insulted by the Chancellor of the Exchequer's advice to the church. Writing in 1913, he criticized his call for the church to 'go and create an atmosphere'. 'And ever since then', he wrote, 'every fool (*pob aderyn aflan*) says "Go and create an atmosphere." '[57]

[54] *Llais Llafur*, 6 April 1912, p.7; cf. *Y Dinesydd Cymreig*, 5 March 1913, p.7.
[55] *Llais Llafur*, 6 January 1912, p.1.
[56] Ibid., p.4.
[57] *Tarian y Gweithiwr*, 23 January 1913, p.4.

Williams's sardonic response was that this is exactly what the churches had been doing for years.

As a direct result of this conference, a 'Religion and labour week' was held in Cardiff during April 1912. By this time it was considered that the most important task facing the churches and the labour movement was the promotion of a clearer mutual understanding. The object of the week was to demonstrate that the labour movement, the trade unions and Socialism in general were not antagonistic to religion and thus to help them draw closer together in promoting the well-being of the nation.[58] On this occasion, Vernon Hartshorn was present along with Keir Hardie, and W. F. Phillips, never slow to miss a propaganda opportunity, pointed out that Hartshorn and company were now sitting down with the very ministers responsible for the Cardiff conference they had boycotted the previous December.[59] Phillips, though, was misrepresenting Hartshorn's position. He had not objected to the fact that those who organized the conference were ministers but to the apparently political nature of the conference as demonstrated in the invitation to Lloyd George.

In attempting to promote a better understanding between the two groups, the Revd J. Morgan Jones, Cardiff, protested that the churches were not indifferent to the plight of the working class. Such claims were made frequently by labour leaders who sought outright acceptance of their Socialist creeds and active involvement on the part of the churches on behalf of working men. Jones claimed that in Hartshorn the SWMF had a leader who was a 'religious man', and when Hartshorn spoke he made clear that he, too, sought a better understanding between labour and the churches. The need was for an effective force to reform society, and should the desired understanding be achieved, a potent and invincible force for social betterment would have been found. The labour movement and the churches, 'when united and working together, were invincible and irresistible and the reason why they accomplished so little good and slow head-way was because they did not co-operate whole-heartedly'.[60]

[58] *South Wales Daily News*, 30 March 1912, p.3.
[59] W. F. Phillips, 'Religion and labour week', p.106.
[60] *Llais Llafur*, 6 April 1912, p.7.

These speeches represent the general desire prevalent in the pre-war period to see the church and labour movement joining forces. Once this had occurred, social reform was believed to be inevitable as the force supplied by the two movements together would be irresistible. As a result, Hartshorn's remarks were welcomed by many, though they were perhaps not as promising as they at first appeared. He admitted that his argument was not against the religion of Christ, but he was careful not to mention the chapel and the church. When addressing a meeting which mainly comprised ministers of religion, he concentrated on the positive aspects of the work of the chapel but at other times he was vitriolic in his criticism of Nonconformists, as after his defeat in Mid Glamorgan. Hartshorn had suffered the caustic attacks of the amateur Nonconformist politicians more than most and it is understandable that his own reaction to them was so bitter. However, his admission that the two groups should better understand each other and work together was undermined by his demand that the church should follow the labour line rather than bring its own unique contribution into synthesis with the aims of the new movement. This illustrated the more hostile relationship that was beginning to develop, in which, ultimately, the church and labour would go their separate ways. Hardie's rhetoric had encouraged men to believe that the labour movement alone was correctly interpreting the religion of Jesus. Hartshorn appears to have adopted this view, and so sought an adjustment in the position of the church. He was not prepared to recognize a spiritual element in the church's work. For him it was social improvement, for which Christianity needed to join the labour movement, or nothing.

The differences between the labour movement and the churches were by this time deep-set and were in no way resolved by the Cardiff conference or the 'Religion and labour week'. The *SWDN* was, therefore, naïvely optimistic in announcing that religion and labour had finally come to understand each other.[61] It is difficult to see what the Cardiff conference actually achieved. There was possibly consensus, but certainly not unanimity, in the morning session, while the afternoon session was plagued by the underlying political partisanship of the organizers and the

[61] *South Wales Daily News*, 2 April 1912, p.4.

opportunism of Lloyd George. Together with the problems which presented themselves in the weeks leading up to the conference, these factors make it difficult not to conclude that it was virtually a disaster. It is likely that the conference could have done no more than highlight the problem of labour's general estrangement from traditional religious forms, particularly from the chapels. But it also managed to demonstrate the problems of too overt a political involvement, even if it had not set out specifically to do so, and it confirmed that most men who were genuinely concerned about the estrangement of labour linked it clearly to the wider sense of social reform and insisted that further study was the way forward for the church.

The Cardiff conference rightly belongs to the death throes of the old Liberal Nonconformist hegemony rather than to the beginning of a new socially aware religion that held any sympathy with labour politics. It was confirmed that the problem of labour and of the departure of young working men from the church was inherently bound up with social problems, but it made no lasting contribution to the debate. The very fact that men continued to advise the church to 'create an atmosphere' suggests that it was failing to do so. Instead of spurring the churches to a greater understanding of labour, the Cardiff conference seems to have made no difference to the actual situation. In the years that followed, labour, both in an industrial and a political sense, and the churches seemed to follow separate paths.

3. ATTEMPTS AT SOCIAL MISSION

Conferences were vital in recognizing the importance of social issues and encouraging the labour movement and the church to work together in the cause of social reform. They were organized in response to the problem of the working-class drift from the chapels, but concerted local efforts were needed to regain the working man for religion. Examples of such attempts amongst mainstream Nonconformists are not easy to discover, but the efforts of the Revd David Pughe in Merthyr before the war are worthy of mention.

Although the problem was beginning to be recognized before 1914, little had been attempted which broke away from previously accepted patterns of ministry and churchmanship. The problem of Christian witness in a depressed industrial town led to an initiative by the Wesleyans in Merthyr Tydfil to bring a Christian influence to bear upon the working class. They decided to reorganize their English and Welsh churches in the town into a single English Mission, with a ministerial staff of two. The superintendent minister was a Welshman, the Revd David Pughe, who had a reputation for work amongst the working classes as a 'thinker, a student, preacher and a social reformer'. During a pastorate in the north-east of England, he became known throughout Durham and Northumberland as the 'Pitmen's Parson', having fought and won several battles on the miners' behalf. The junior minister, the Revd Percy Hallding, who was known 'to have social sympathies', was stationed at Dowlais. Even the *Merthyr Pioneer* found it possible to comment that 'The Wesleyan Conference, in sending these two men to Merthyr, has . . . done signal service in the interests of unconventional religion and social evangelism'.[62]

Pughe inaugurated Brotherhood Movement meetings in Merthyr to try to reach the unchurched men of the district. Speakers tended to adopt either Socialistic subjects or at least spoke on the social problem, particularly in its relation to the churches. Pughe himself admitted to believing in spiritual individualism and a kind of economic collectivism in response to the need to stem the flow of young men from the chapels. The need, in his view, was to differentiate between Socialism and religion and to demonstrate that, as they had separate tasks, both could be held together. Religion was 'a conception of the unseen which makes for righteousness', while Socialism was a 'belief in active propaganda for securing complete public ownership of the principal means of production, distribution and exchange'. Socialism, therefore, had nothing to do with religion. Socialism might well be 'a practical application' of Christian ideals, and he was prepared to admit that many Socialists whom he knew believed in the advent of a 'golden age' far more keenly than many Christians believed in the ultimate coming of the Kingdom. It was a mistake, however, to believe that material improvement would bring about eternal happiness. He believed

---

[62] *Merthyr Pioneer*, 7 September 1912, p.4.

that it was only the existence of an eternal and spiritual authority 'to whom man must go and report' that gave substance to any claim that altruism was a duty. Although Christ's teachings could be applied to the complex problems of modern life, the gospel could also offer much more. It alone could 'satisfy the eternal longings of the human heart'. He believed that even when material needs were met, spiritual needs would remain.[63]

It may appear that Pughe was not initiating any radically different form of Christian witness, but this would be to misunderstand the fashions of the time. Christian ministers, particularly Nonconformist ones, were expected to offer a particular kind of religious service, including hymn-singing, preaching and prayer. To an extent this had been superseded in the Brotherhood meetings in favour of rational argument and debate concerning the burning issues of the day. Although this made politics inevitable, Pughe had correctly perceived that this was the main concern of many ordinary people. He had also realized that one of the labour movement's strengths was that it gave working men the opportunity to air their grievances. In addressing the issues closest to their hearts, he demonstrated once again the way in which the social question was linked to the estrangement of labour from the church; he also attempted to show that the church had a contribution to make.

Three years before commencing his Merthyr ministry, Pughe lectured in the town on 'Riches and poverty'. It was a daring address in which he welcomed current interest in social issues and declared that he had considered himself a Socialist for twenty years. The system that placed wealth in the hands of the few, he claimed, was wrong.[64] It is not surprising therefore that the *Merthyr Pioneer* welcomed his appointment. Following the establishment of the Merthyr mission, however, he seems to have considered his task to have been to convince the working class not of his social sympathies but of their need to consider spiritual issues. This in some ways reflects the changing nature of the problem of labour. Although initially the need was for the church to express its sympathy with the working class and to offer practical help, the problem was now perceived as one of

---

[63] Ibid., 21 September 1912, p.3.
[64] *Merthyr Express*, 24 April 1909, p.7.

preventing leakage from the chapels. Thus, Pughe emphasized the need for individual regeneration as a prerequisite for social renewal. The impression gained from the local press is that he was relatively successful in attracting men to his Brotherhood meetings, which were separate from the Sunday acts of worship. His activity was not daring by modern standards but his efforts were in some respects unique as an attempt to bring religion to the working man almost on the working man's terms.

4. PRINCIPLES AND THEOLOGY

Various factors influenced the development of a Nonconformist social conscience before the war. The labour movement's swingeing criticism of Christian inaction and the growing popularity of Socialist politics certainly contributed to the growth of Nonconformist social thought, as did the gradual estrangement of young men from the chapels. It was generally assumed that a sympathy with the plight of the working class, which would include practical advice for social reform, would enable labour's return to the religious fold.[65] Thus, in expressing social concern the Nonconformists were responding partly to the situation which they perceived to exist beyond the chapel walls.

The development of a social conscience was also, in part, the result of Nonconformity's withdrawal from direct political involvement. By 1914 Nonconformists were, in general, unwilling to link their new-found social beliefs with the pro- gramme of individual political parties. This resulted in a productive period when the social implications of Christianity were explored by men of vision and enthusiasm, without the distractions of political argument and partisanship. This was in part the ethos of the Welsh School of Social Service and, ostensibly at least, the Cardiff conference. Ministers warned each other not to be concerned with political matters, though the complexities of the situation were highlighted by the fact that some who adopted this position still dedicated their books to Lloyd George.[66] Eschewing politics proved ultimately to be the greatest failing of Nonconformist social activity in the period.

---

[65] T. R. Jones, 'Yr Eglwys a phynciau cymdeithas', *Y Drysorfa* (1912), 200.
[66] E.g. J. H. Howard, *Cristionogaeth a Chymdeithas* (Liverpool, 1914), p.114.

The fact was that the social problem required political measures to ensure the amelioration of living and working conditions. They therefore needed the courage to come down on one side or the other, a policy which would be urged particularly by Herbert Morgan in 1918.[67] In not doing so, Nonconformists ultimately failed to convince working men that they had any worthwhile contribution to make to the social and political debate.

It should be noted that Nonconformists were already playing an important and active role in one area of social reform, namely temperance. In the view of many, intemperance, and consequently personal moral responsibility, remained the major reason for poverty and slum-life. The Revd D. J. Lewis, Tumble, in an address to the Union of Welsh Independents, insisted that sobriety was required before social reform was possible, otherwise the church's complaint would soon be 'better houses but worse men'.[68] While it cannot be denied that Nonconformity became obsessive about alcohol, it is also true that their concern with temperance issues formed the basis for a social plan that was compatible with traditional Nonconformist theology. Temperance concern opened the way for a wider treatment of social issues,[69] but its implementation was considered by some to be the only necessary reform.

Nonconformity's alliance with temperance movements largely belonged to a period when men were considered responsible for their environment. When legislation to curb the drink trade was called for, Nonconformists unwittingly conceded the vital principle that government could be used to promote, and even enforce, good living. This was vital for any formulation of social theology and policies. So, too, was the realization which had dawned upon some younger Nonconformists that not only did people create their environment but the environment was a factor in creating human character. Nonconformists were gradually realizing that the hardships endured by the vast majority of ordinary people were the result of external forces beyond their

[67] Herbert Morgan, 'The church and labour: a symposium', *The Welsh Outlook* (1918), 127–8; cf. John Adams, 'Safle yr Eglwys Gristionogol yngwyneb cynhyrfiadau'r oes mewn diwydiannau a chymdeithasiaeth', *Y Dysgedydd* (1912), 164.

[68] *Y Tyst*, 9 July 1913, p.6; cf. *Seren Cymru*, 2 June 1911, p.3.

[69] *Y Tyst*, 2 October 1912, p.4; cf. R. Dervel Roberts, 'Perthynas dirwest a chwestiynau cymdeithasol', Union of Welsh Independents, Reports, 1912, Liverpool, pp.286, 294.

control, caused by 'the oppression, greed and rapaciousness of the bosses'.[70] Ordinary people had to fight a constant battle with oppressive economic and social forces which left them with no time or inclination to consider spiritual truths. As a result, it was perceived that social problems were hindering the church's spiritual work and that any future religious revival would have to be preceded by radical social reform. Thus, to an extent, Nonconformists adopted social reform because they had a duty to destroy social conditions which they perceived to be harmful to personal and spiritual development,[71] and, at least in part, in order to safeguard their own spirituality and role in society.

The recognition that environment could have a formative effect on the individual prompted an ideological change as Nonconformists came to believe that an environment could be created which would enhance character development.[72] Spiritual success was now perceived as being attainable only if the main principles of religion were embodied in social habits and institutions. Similarly, only when the population was materially secure could appropriate attention be given to spiritual matters. The principle was simple. The hardship of industrial life itself made consideration of the spiritual dimension impossible.

This demonstrates the difficulty for Nonconformists. Individual evangelical conversion, perceived as central to the gospel message, became impossible as people's lives were taken over by the industrial machine. Yet many Nonconformists, including those who actively sought social reform, were convinced that individual conversion was the paramount necessity. While some sought a compromise in which personal faith and social reform were held to be of equal importance, they were compelled to point to the spiritual work of the church since they believed that society was increasingly ignoring the higher moral values.[73]

The point was well expressed by religious conservatives such as W. T. Glyn Evans, London, who claimed that the church's only mission was to equip men for the next world. This, he

[70] T. R. Jones, 'Yr Eglwys', p.201; cf. T. E. Nicholas, 'Yr Eglwys a phynciau cymdeithas', *Y Geninen* (1914), 21.

[71] T. R. Jones, 'Yr Eglwys', p.200; *Merthyr Pioneer*, 22 February 1913, p.4.

[72] *Y Tyst*, 2 October 1912, p.4; see also G. A. Edwards, 'Galwad gymdeithasol Crist', *Y Drysorfa* (1924), 162; Thomas Lewis, 'Cyfrifoldeb yr Eglwys', *Y Dysgedydd* (1918), 313; Charles Jones, 'Crefydd Crist a'n problemau cymdeithasol', *Yr Eurgrawn* (1919), 61.

[73] *Y Darian*, 29 January 1914, p.7; cf. *South Wales Daily News*, 7 September 1911, p.6.

posited, had been the traditional aim of the Christian church and should not be exchanged for social reform. It was also true, however, that making men fit for the next world would automatically make them better inhabitants of this world.[74] The church's task was to develop individual character through the principles and teaching of the gospel and to encourage its adherents to put them into practice in their daily lives. But they should not enter directly into social questions for this would lead to divisions within the sanctuary. In Evans's view the church should only be involved in movements which were totally spiritual and whose sole concern was the communion between man and God.[75]

This demonstrates the problem which Nonconformists initially faced in their social activity. They brought to the specific problems of the twentieth century a deeply held belief in the responsibility of the individual before God. They sought to retain this emphasis despite Socialist propaganda which suggested that men were victims of their environment and thus not individually responsible for their destiny. Socialism had argued that man could be improved morally if he was given better living and working conditions, more leisure time and higher wages. If treated as a person, man would be raised to new moral heights by his environment. Nonconformists had been aware of the implicit threat to Christianity contained in the Socialist message and, as a result, they argued that Christianity offered not merely a different but a more effective way of achieving the desired result of social reform. Christianity sought the regeneration of the individual, a moral conversion that would result in a renewed attitude, and a recognition of personal responsibility towards society.[76] It was, thus, through the conversion of the individual that social improvement would be guaranteed. Such a redemptive process secured the primacy of the moral and spiritual aspects of life over the material and physical. It insisted that moral principles be embodied initially in individual life and then in society. This was, in some ways, merely a new

[74] W.T.Glyn Evans, 'A ddylai yr Eglwysi yn uniongyrchol bleidio a hyrwyddo diwygiadau cymdeithasol?', *Y Dysgedydd* (1912), 82.
[75] Ibid., p.83; cf. J. H. Howard, *Cristionogaeth*, p.79.
[76] J. H. Howard, *Cristionogaeth*, p.96; *Blwyddiadur y Methodistiaid Calfinaidd* (1912), 120; *Seren Cymru*, 21 July 1911, p.3; 22 March 1912, p.6; D. Powell, 'Perthynas yr Eglwys a chwestiynau cymdeithasol', *Y Greal* (1913), 187.

application of the traditional doctrine of redemption. The church would continue to preach the need for individual regeneration though it would henceforth be interpreted as the development of human personality. Such individuals would automatically affect society for the better, but would also exchange personal interests for social ones.[77] Thus, individual regeneration was specifically orientated toward the service of the wider community. Man was still the object of the church's mission, but he was now envisaged as *man in society* rather than as man in isolation. In turn, it was argued, the individual character could only be perfected through service and self-sacrifice.[78] The underlying tension between recognizing social need and an unwillingness to disregard the traditional importance of individual salvation characterized Nonconformist thought throughout these years. Viewing individual regeneration as the only effective way to social reform was a logical response to the current challenge.

This redemptive scheme was inspired by the tenets of philosophical Idealism adopted by liberal Nonconformists and given its first exposition in Welsh by the Independent minister, the Revd David Adams.[79] Idealism held that the natural and unstoppable progression of history was towards the ultimate harmony of the whole universe. God was no longer to be found far and above the material creation but was in fact immanent within it, the spiritual reality at the heart of all living beings. The presence of the immanent God was the dynamic which made progress not merely a possibility but an inevitability. Adams had attempted to synthesize the claims of Idealism, particularly that found in the work of G. W. F. Hegel, with the claims of Darwin and modern science and then to use this knowledge in theological formulation. His was a didactic and doctrinal contribution rather than a specifically social theology but he laid

[77] T. R. Jones, 'Yr Eglwys', p.201; *Seren Cymru*, 2 June 1911, p.3; *Y Goleuad*, 12 November 1913, p.12; Richard Morgan, *Cristionogaeth yn Iachawdwriaeth Dynoliaeth* (Bangor, 1912), p.17.

[78] *Merthyr Pioneer*, 14 October 1911, p.9; cf. J. H. Howard, *Cristionogaeth*, pp.97, 116, 122; John Evans, 'Y deffroad cymdeithasol presenol ei genhadaeth', Union of Welsh Independents Reports, 1911, Aberaman, p.202.

[79] For David Adams (1845–1923), see *DWB*, p.3; E. Keri Evans and W. Parri Huws, *Cofiant y Parch. David Adams* (Liverpool, 1924); Glyn Richards, *Datblygiad Rhyddfrydiaeth Ddiwinyddol ymhlith yr Annibynwyr* (Swansea, 1957), pp.11–17; W. Eifion Powell, 'Cyfraniad diwinyddol David Adams (1845–1923)', *Y Traethodydd* (1979), 162–70.

the foundations on which other liberal modernists, most notably
Herbert Morgan, Thomas Rees and D. Miall Edwards, would
build. Nonconformists like these applied their Idealism through
their preaching of a social interpretation of the gospel. They
implied that reform and eventual perfection were unavoidable
provided that men and women were morally regenerated.
Alongside Neo-Hegelian Idealism, Nonconformists also used the
insights of Kantian philosophy and its emphasis on the moral
imperative in the message of Christianity. Thus it was the
individual's duty to apply the spiritual principles encapsulated in
Jesus's teaching to his or her social life. The church needed to
express the life of the Kingdom, interpreted as the perfect social
state in which man's relationship to God and his relationships
with others were fulfilled. Thus social improvement hinged on
the establishment of moral ideals as the governing principles in
personal conduct and social institutions. This, rather than
housing reform and improved wages, would ensure success.[80]
The ideals which Nonconformist social thought emphasized
were those of Liberal Theology: the inherent value of man
stemming from the universal brotherhood of the race under the
general Fatherhood of God, the need for men to serve each other
as brothers and the establishment of the Kingdom of God as the
moral task of regenerated individuals.[81] The prevailing theology,
in fact, considered that when the brotherhood of man as a
natural corollary of the Fatherhood of God was established on
earth, then the Kingdom of God would be ushered in.[82]

5. THE KINGDOM, GOD'S FATHERHOOD AND MAN'S BROTHERHOOD

Liberal Theology, in its most recent form, appeared to be
particularly predisposed to a social interpretation of religion. It
had specifically called for an application of the Christian message

[80] Gwilym Owen, 'Trefn Cristionogol cymdeithas', *Seren Gomer* (1924), 221.

[81] E.g. H. Jones Davies, 'Yr Iachawdwriaeth yn bersonol ac yn gymdeithasol', *Y Drysorfa* (1924), 139; Charles Jones, 'Crefydd', p.60; D. Miall Edwards, 'Teyrnas Dduw', NLW MSS 17671B; D. Wyre Lewis, 'Crist a'r werin', *Seren Gomer* (1920), 264; T. T. Jones, 'Y gweinidog a'r bywyd cyhoeddus', *Seren Gomer* (1924), 113; *Y Darian*, 20 March 1924, p.9; *Y Goleuad*, 3 May 1918, p.6.

[82] E.g. J. Jenkins (Gwili), 'Iawnderau dyn', *Y Geninen* (1914), 63; Richard Morgan, *Cristionogaeth*, p.3; cf. J. H. Howard, *Cristionogaeth*, p.6.

to the life of this world. Albrecht Ritschl's emphasis on the concept of 'value', and the primacy of the Kingdom in the teaching of Jesus as the ethical task of his followers, naturally led to a consideration of social needs. 'Value' pointed men out of themselves into an appreciation of the eternal values of truth, goodness and beauty, the apprehension of which was eclipsed by an unaesthetic environment, the result of abject poverty. In order to support liberal theological claims, a specifically social ideal had to be offered and it was found in the concept of God's Kingdom, which transferred the emphasis in redemption from the individual to society as the object of God's love.[83] Adolf Harnack, a pupil of Ritschl, drew attention to the infinite value of humankind as the children of God, and thus the object of divine love. In his famous lectures in Berlin, 1899–1900, *Das Wesen des Christentums* (English edition, *What is Christianity?* London, 1901), he drew specific attention to Jesus's comments on the fundamental human need for shelter, sustenance and, rather more obscurely (yet vital in the conditions of the time), cleanliness. Harnack declared that it was for the community to ensure that all individuals received these. All individual needs, as well as the needs of society as a whole, would be met, according to Harnack, in the concept of the Kingdom of God.[84] Harnack delineated the Kingdom in its relation to the individual who, through the Fatherhood of God, had been raised to the level of supreme value. In that state, according to him, the individual had a duty to exercise the commandment to love in all situations. The 'essence' (*Wesen*) of Christianity was thus a message of moral value and responsibility primarily concerned with the individual.[85] This was the basic doctrinal inspiration for the Welsh Nonconformists, though they gave it their own evangelical thrust.

The accomplishment of social reform would ultimately rest on the provision of a successful and effective moral dynamic. Nonconformists emphasized that reform depended entirely on the

---

[83] A. E. Garvie, *The Ritschlian Theology* (Edinburgh, 1899), pp.251–2.

[84] Adolf Harnack, *What is Christianity?* (London, 1901), pp.63, 100–1.

[85] Stephen Neill and Tom Wright, *The Interpretation of the New Testament 1861–1986* (Oxford, 1988), pp.144–5.

conversion of individuals through the gospel.[86] There was no suggestion of a political programme, introduction of better wages, fairer industrial practices, or a clearing of poor housing, but simply the need for individual regeneration. Regeneration was considered to engender moral responsibility towards others rather than to redefine the relationship between God and man. Although it concerned the spiritual government of men by God, his Fatherhood tended to be subordinated to the brotherhood which was its natural consequence. The relationship that should exist between men was one of mutual service, and the church, it was claimed, existed to make such relationships possible.[87] In this, Nonconformists sought to preserve Christianity's unique message of individual redemption and also to institute social concern.[88] Through moral regeneration, man would make the effort to produce a better world, but it all depended on recognizing God's Fatherhood.[89]

The motif of the brotherhood of man was popular amongst labour and Socialist agitators, though they tended to restrict its relevance to the working class. Nonconformists seeking to retain the superiority of the Christian message had long questioned the basis of such a brotherhood. They claimed that man's brotherhood depended entirely on recognizing God's Fatherhood, which could only be found in the church's teaching. It was, they claimed, a recognition of the relationship between Fatherhood and brotherhood which promoted the infinite value of the human soul.[90] God's Fatherhood had always featured in

[86] E.g. *Seren Cymru*, 21 July 1911, p.3; 30 August 1912, pp.3–4; 21 February 1913, p.3; *Y Tyst*, 14 September 1910, p.3; 13 January 1911, p.8; 9 May 1923, p.8; J. H. Howard, *Cristionogaeth*, p.97; Richard Jones, 'The Church and social questions', *The Welsh Outlook* (1914), 251; T. R. Jones, 'Yr Eglwys', p.200; see also Owen Evans, 'Yr Eglwys ei lle a'i swyddogaeth', *Yr Eurgrawn* (1915), 294; H. P. Roberts, 'Perthynas crefydd a bywyd', *Y Drysorfa* (1918), 189; H. T. Owen, 'Crefydd yr oes', *Y Drysorfa* (1921), 128; H. C. Williams, 'Cenhadaeth gymdeithasol yr Eglwys', *Seren Gomer* (1920), 16; G. M. Ll. Davies, 'The Kingdom', *The Treasury* (1921), 1–2; Gwilym Owen, 'Trefn Cristionogol cymdeithas', *Seren Cymru* (1924), 226.

[87] T. R. Jones, 'Yr Eglwys', p.199.

[88] Ibid., p.201; cf. *Y Goleuad*, 8 September 1913, p.12.

[89] Richard Morgan, *Cristionogaeth*, pp.8, 17, 64.

[90] *Y Tyst*, 14 September 1910 p.3; 26 July 1911, p.6; 5 January 1912, p.4; *Seren Cymru*, 9 February 1912, p.3; *Y Goleuad*, 12 November 1913, p.12; *Y Darian*, 27 March 1924, p.6; T. R. Jones, 'Yr Eglwys', p.201; J. H. Howard, *Cristionogaeth*, pp.77, 80; 'The secret of social welfare and progress', Box 4, E. K. Jones Papers, NLW; J. J. Jones, 'Efengyl a gwasanaeth', Union of Welsh Independents, Reports, 1912, Liverpool, p.403; G. A. Edwards, 'Galwad', pp.161, 163; Charles Jones, 'Crefydd', pp.60, 101; John Morgan Jones, 'The relation of the minister to social questions', *The Treasury* (1914), 52; see also Herbert Morgan, *Diwydiant yng Nghymru*, Traethodau'r Deyrnas, no. 2 (Wrexham, 1924), p.14; J. H. Howard, *Which Jesus? Young Britain's Choice* (Dolgellau, 1926).

orthodox theology, but by this period its meaning had changed. Man's value was no longer to be interpreted in the context of God's redemptive plan. His infinite worth was instead a direct result of God being his Father. This was the primary inspiration for the church's involvement in the social debate. The church was to oppose anything which impinged on human dignity and value, and to urge church members to go out into the world in a spirit of self-sacrifice and service.

There was, however, a latent concern that this social emphasis would lead to God being displaced and that man would become the central object of religion. Religion was not merely humanitarian service but was meant to lead towards God in worship, piety and prayer. Those who recognized the danger sought to promote a synthesis where worship of God became synonymous with service of mankind. Both were held to be equally important, inspired by Jesus's identification of both the commandment to love God and the commandment to love neighbour as central to the Law (Matthew 27: 34–40; Mark 12: 29–31):

> there is a place for prayer, and to assist the poor; there is a place for preaching, and to attend to the sick; there is a place to sing praises in the sanctuary, and to teach the young how to earn an honest and honourable living; it all belongs to pure and undefiled religion. God is worshipped by serving men.[91]

The emphasis in religion was undoubtedly changing not merely from the theological to the practical and from eternal to temporal concerns, but also away from God and towards man.

It is striking that the image of God's Fatherhood was used almost solely to promote fraternity. It was considered to be the moral dynamic that would naturally establish better relationships between men of different social strata as they recognized their brotherhood to be a direct consequence of God's common Fatherhood. Social differences would not disappear; men would simply view their fellows in a different light.[92] It is strange that Nonconformists were not more anxious to emphasize the

---

[91] T. R. Jones, 'Yr Eglwys', p.202; cf. Owen Jones, 'Perthynas dyn a chymdeithas', *Y Drysorfa* (1921), 409; Charles Jones, 'Crefydd', p.60.
[92] John Adams, 'Safle yr Eglwys', p.164.

difference between the Socialists' idea of brotherhood, based on a common humanity, and the Christian idea of a spiritual brotherhood rooted in God's common Fatherhood. The crux of the matter was sonship, though this was rarely given prominence at this time.[93]

This was the unavoidable result of contemporary Nonconformist thought. Under the influence of philosophical Idealism, younger Nonconformists had emphasized God's immanence, which was generally accepted as being theologically valid. The danger would only emerge through its over-emphasis. A God who is exclusively immanent becomes something less than objectively personal, being instead a divine element in creation. The notion of Fatherhood then either becomes superfluous or requires radical reinterpretation. The resulting tension between God's immanence and the need for a more personal Father-God was never resolved. In ignoring the motif of sonship, the focus of man's brotherhood, namely God as the common Father, was also lost. The injustices of industrial society were obviously pointing to the fact that men did not naturally recognize each other as members of one family. They lacked the point of reference from which they would recognize their fellows as worthy of respect, love and life. Welsh Nonconformists were either too busy trying to reinterpret theology according to the intellectual concepts of the age, or merely emphasizing man's innate dignity, to construct a satisfactory theological argument. While an emphasis on man's brotherhood may have endeared them to certain sections of the labour movement, the lack of theological reasoning would ultimately prevent them from achieving any specifically Christian response to the social question.

6. THE KINGDOM OF GOD

The advent of a vociferous and critical labour movement had coincided with a rediscovery of the Kingdom of God as the central aspect of Jesus's teaching. This was a crucial step in the

[93] Exceptions were Ben Evans, 'Y nefoedd newydd a'r ddaear newydd', Union of Welsh Independents Reports, 1913, Swansea, p.648; 'Yr Eglwys a'r byd', H. M. Hughes Papers, no. 35, NLW; *Seren Cymru*, 9 February 1912, p.3; P. T. Forsyth, *Socialism, the Church and the Poor* (London, 1908), pp.6, 71.

development of a Christian social conscience. The church's neglect of the Kingdom of God was rightly identified as rendering it unable to sympathize with working men. The creeds concentrated almost exclusively on Christ's metaphysical claims, with no mention of the specifics of Jesus's teaching, while the church's mission had concentrated on individual conversion specifically orientated towards an after-life. Consequently, many within the labour movement considered the church to be on the side of the rich, or at least to support the status quo. For well over a century, theology and biblical studies had been trying to discover the historical Jesus behind the gospel accounts. Through this, Jesus lost the ontological divinity accorded him by the church's traditional creeds in favour of the claims of an enlightened humanity. He became far more of a moral teacher and leader of the people than the divine saviour of mankind. Despite the fact that Nonconformists insisted that Jesus was not merely a teacher but the saviour,[94] they too had come to emphasize the contemporary relevance of his teaching.[95] Central to Jesus's teaching was not the formation of a church but the announcement that 'the Kingdom of God is at hand'. Some Nonconformists began to propagate an understanding of the Kingdom which was virtually indistinguishable from that of the Socialists. It became an ethical, far more than an eschatological or apocalyptic, concept in which man became the appointed means of its establishment on earth. Undoubtedly, this was in part a response to the intellectual need of the time, when the social problem was uppermost in the minds of thinking men, though Nonconformity itself still clung to the concept of man's individual responsibility. The Kingdom was the state wherein the Fatherhood of God and the brotherhood of man would reach their fulfilment.[96] Inspiration for this interpretation came from the Ritschlian theology. For Ritschl, man was not justified in order to perform his moral task, but was justified as he

[94] *Seren Cymru*, 5 January 1912, p.5; 19 January 1912, pp.3–4; *Y Tyst*, 23 August 1911, p.6; Edward Jones, 'Y deffroad cymdeithasol presenol ei beryglon', Union of Welsh Independents Reports, 1911, Aberaman, p.211; cf. P. T. Forsyth, *Socialism*, p.55; 'Yr Eglwys a'r byd', H. M. Hughes Papers, no. 35, NLW; Isaac Parry Griffith, 'Iesu Grist fel esiampl', *Y Drysorfa* (1937), 56.

[95] *Y Tyst*, 26 July 1911, p.7.

[96] W. Davies, 'Cenhadaeth gymdeithasol Crist a'i Eglwys', Union of Welsh Independents Reports, 1910, Lampeter, p.18.

performed his moral task.[97] Thus, while the Kingdom became the inspiration for social reform, the task of establishing it became man's moral responsibility. Man's role in constructing the Kingdom raised him to the level of partnership with the divine; it was this which ensured his eternal value.[98]

The motif of the Kingdom of God, like that of the brotherhood of man, had been commandeered by the labour movement. Keir Hardie often used it in his speeches. For Hardie it referred exclusively to this world.[99] It represented the perfect social system in which all were given a fair chance to live 'life in its fullness'. For Welsh Nonconformists, the Kingdom provided the right image to meet both individual and social need. It helped to retain the belief that society could only be reformed through the individual, but it also insisted on the need for social purity. It was 'sufficiently great and high to secure every privilege and freedom to the personal, consistent with the basic truths of life and existence'.[100] But labour's interpretation of the Kingdom had made it a material concept while Nonconformists sought to retain it as a spiritual one; for them it referred to the state where God ruled, rather than the state of material equality. In some ways the image of the Kingdom suffered the same fate as the word 'labour'. It was sufficient to inspire men and had the advantage of granting divine approval for the organization that could claim it as its own. Although the church had reclaimed the concept of the Kingdom for itself and attempted to purge it of the materialistic claims of the Socialists, it was never defined in any rigorous or scholarly detail. Those Nonconformists who were concerned with social reform tended to use the term to inspire rather than to explain.

It was the combination of philosophical Idealism and Liberal Theology, especially as espoused by Ritschl and Harnack, that became popular amongst Welsh Nonconformist theologians during the next twenty years or so. This was the intellectual background for the Liberal Modernists who exercised so much

---

[97] See A. E. Garvie, *Ritschlian Theology*, pp.251–2; cf. James Orr, *The Ritschlian Theology and the Evangelical Faith* (London, 1898), pp.78–9, 158–60.

[98] H. Jones Davies, 'Yr Iachawdwriaeth', p.138; Owen Jones, 'Perthynas Dyn', pp.406, 410.; see also E. Griffith-Jones, *Providence Divine and Human*, II, *The Dominion of Man* (London, 1926), p.237.

[99] E.g. *Merthyr Pioneer*, 6 May 1911, p.5; 9 March 1912, p.6.

[100] *Seren Cymru*, 30 August 1912, pp.3–4.

influence in Welsh chapel and social life at this time, men who would come to greater prominence after 1918. The main doctrinal and historical posts in the two Congregational theological seminaries were held by Modernists. Thomas Rees, Principal at the Bala-Bangor College from 1909, John Morgan Jones, Professor of Church History and later Principal at the same college, and D. Miall Edwards, Professor of Christian Doctrine and Philosophy of Religion at the Memorial College, Brecon, were the three main protagonists of a social exposition of theological truth. They supported the call for social Christianity in periodicals, books, from the platform and pulpit. Their influence on generations of ministerial candidates was immense. Together with the Baptist Herbert Morgan, they formed a kind of unofficial caucus which maintained the pressure for a religiously inspired social movement in the next decade. They had all come to prominence before the war, but their major contributions, mainly in the didactic field of theological literature, would come after 1918.

7. CONCLUSIONS

By the outbreak of the Great War, social issues were firmly placed, if not at the top of the agenda, then very near it for Welsh Nonconformists. The ideological foundations for the development of a social theology had been laid in the fields of doctrine and philosophy and in this Nonconformist theologians merely reflected the common conception of religion as a dynamic for social renewal. *Llais Llafur* commented in 1914 that 'it is widely agreed that it is the duty of every true Christian to work for such material conditions as well as to ensure to every man, woman and child the opportunity of developing their God-given powers to the uttermost'.[101] Herbert Morgan, also writing in 1914, had made it clear that it was not the concept of salvation which working men found incredible but its interpretation in individualist and moralist terms. They had come to believe that salvation could only truly be achieved if society as a whole was

---

[101] *Llais Llafur*, 30 May 1914, p.4.

redeemed.[102] Morgan published these ideas in the first issue of *The Welsh Outlook*, a journal whose specific aim was to link Christianity with new ideas of social reform as a 'credible alternative' to militant labour and Socialist politics.[103] By then the call for the church to respond to social problems was gaining increasing support. When war finally came, it did not change this trend but directed the attention of most people to the more pressing problem of defeating the enemy.

There can be no doubt that Nonconformity was, in this period, breaking with its past. Having achieved virtually all their political aims by the turn of the century, Nonconformists had to find new causes to fight. Although they had been awakened to the plight of the working class, Nonconformists were also searching for a way of approach other than through politics, partly as a result of their recognition that they held very little influence in the Liberal Party. This would ultimately be deepened by the disillusionment which many Nonconformists would feel at their betrayal by the Liberal Party during the Great War. The emphasis on political activism which had been uppermost in chapel policy for the previous half-century was abandoned in favour of a practical definition of their specifically spiritual gospel under the influence of the most recent philosophical and theological trends. Overt political involvement or active social agitation might imperil what they increasingly considered to be their most important contribution.

> The present social and political commotions call on the churches not to lose their position and Christian self-possession, and in caring for her first and chief message, she will prove herself a blessing on social paths and in politics. If Christians wish to be better citizens they must first of all be better Churchmen.[104]

Despite their awareness that 'labour' had been politicized, their reaction, in withdrawing from political activity, was certain to do Nonconformists more harm than good. At the very time

---

[102] Herbert Morgan, 'The religious outlook in Wales', *The Welsh Outlook* (1914), 13; cf. John Adams, 'Safle yr Eglwys', p.164.
[103] Gwyn Jenkins, 'The Welsh Outlook 1914–1933', *The National Library of Wales Journal*, XXIV/4 (1986), 465.
[104] *Tarian y Gweithiwr*, 14 April 1910, p.4.

when 'labour' was becoming more politically orientated, Nonconformity was becoming less obviously political and sought to articulate a distinctly Christian answer to social problems. Such a policy was unlikely to win working men back to chapel religion.

The problem of the estrangement of labour and its connection with the social question raised the issue of the nature of the church's role in society. There can be little doubt that labour agitators generally expected political agitation at the very least and quite often they expected more practical contributions from the churches. But Nonconformists did not move in that direction. By and large they sought to inform themselves, believing that once they had been educated about social issues they could educate the people.

More than anything else, Welsh Nonconformity had to discover a way of effectively presenting the message of the gospel which preserved its uniqueness and eternal significance as well as making a contribution to the social problem and stemming the flow of labour men from the chapels. Both issues were intimately connected and Nonconformists were in some small way attempting to meet the ideological and social needs of the day. But Nonconformity would never really recover its previous status in society because it had eschewed the only path that might have ensured success: namely, a spiritually informed commitment to politics.

V

BUILDING JERUSALEM: NONCONFORMITY AND POST-WAR RECONSTRUCTION

The silence on social issues which prevailed among Welsh Nonconformists during the war years is striking. Most Welshmen, both those who had been attracted to the labour movement and those who remained committed to the chapel, recognized that the need to win the conflict should be the priority of all righteous citizens. One notable exception to this pattern of compliance could be found on the pages of the pacifist journal, *Y Deyrnas* (The Kingdom). Inaugurated by Thomas Rees, noted Socialists like Herbert Morgan and T. E. Nicholas, along with other ministers who supported social reform, contributed articles to the journal. John Morgan Jones, Bangor, published a series of articles dealing with the social principles embodied in the teaching of Jesus and found in the New Testament under the title 'Gwersi'r Deyrnas' (The Lessons of the Kingdom). The journal finally ceased production in 1919, having faithfully supported the claims of the individual conscience, the primary need for real peace in a war-torn Europe and a recognition that higher principles of justice and fairness needed to be built into the social fabric nationally and internationally in order to end the possibility of future conflict. In promulgating these principles, the Nonconformist contributors to *Y Deyrnas* believed that they were promoting the principles of the Kingdom of God and actively seeking its establishment. That it did not fully materialize at the time was the inevitable result of mankind's folly in preferring war to peace and injustice to righteousness. The outbreak of war understandably brought tensions to the work of Welsh Nonconformist theologians. D. Miall Edwards possibly demonstrates this better than most. Unlike those mentioned above, Edwards was not attracted to uncompromising pacifism. He made no criticism of the war itself, rather he emphasized the materialism *on all sides* which had led directly to war. In such a time of crisis the church, he maintained, should remain silent on controversial issues and become a haven for broken souls.[1]

By 1918, however, the time was considered right for the churches once again to turn their attention to the alienation of the working class from religion. Herbert Morgan co-ordinated a symposium in *The Welsh Outlook* to which readers were invited to give their opinions on the complexities of the issue. The problem of the estrangement of 'labour' from the chapel had been 'on hold' since the beginning of the war. Why it was decided to return to it in 1918 is unclear. It is possible that minds were beginning to turn to the need for rebuilding that would follow the cessation of hostilities. Certainly, the church needed to concentrate on making provisions for the working men who had, by and large, been fighting the war for the past four years. However the war's end was not in sight when the symposium was announced. It seems, therefore, that Herbert Morgan believed that, war or no, the issue could not be ignored any longer because it held important ramifications for labour, the church and society as a whole. Although he claimed that the situation in Wales was not as serious as it was in England, it nevertheless required the urgent consideration of the churches. Unless something was done quickly, the rift between labour and the churches which had continued unabated during the war would adversely affect not only religion but also social progress and national well-being.[2] Morgan's intention was to draw attention to the issues at stake and thus inspire a renewed effort to answer the problems and bring a greater degree of mutual trust and co-operation. The symposium attempted to discover why working men were leaving the churches. The answers which were received were summed up by Morgan under two headings, 'Indifference' and 'Insincerity'.

The indifference shown by labour centred on its unwillingness to recognize spiritual needs and values. The labour movement's teachings were generally suspect, its aims being materialistic and its methods revolutionary, connected to the preaching of hatred and class warfare. The church's indifference centred on its

---

[1] See T. Robin Chapman, 'Argyfwng ffydd D. Miall Edwards, 1916–1923', *Y Traethodydd* (1982), 188–92.

[2] Herbert Morgan, 'The church and labour: a symposium', *The Welsh Outlook* (1918), 42.

unwillingness to recognize how iniquitous the social order
actually was. Morgan claimed that this charge was expressed by
many who had remained within the church as well as those who
had left it for the labour movement. It is significant that the
charge of insincerity was only levelled against a church whose
'teaching [was] felt to be faulty and unconvincing to the modern
mind'.[3] The church was charged with taking too much notice of
the moneyed people within its ranks and whenever it attempted
to remain neutral in social matters it was perceived as supporting
the status quo. There was also evidence of hostility towards those
ministers who advocated a Holy War during the 1914–18
conflict, a war from which they had been exempt.

Once again, the symposium emphasized the need for better
mutual understanding between the labour movement and the
churches. But Morgan's advice to the church did not stop there.
The church required a far wider ethic than a narrow
confinement to abstention from evil practices which had hitherto
characterized its moral code. Instead, it needed to develop a
courageous policy which would eventually mean supporting one
side or the other in both the social debate and labour disputes.[4]
He stated that this should be the result of applying the principles
of the Christian faith and not a mere reaction to the growing
popularity of the labour cause. However, the tendency of the
replies, as well as Morgan's own political sympathies, lay entirely
with the labour movement.[5]

The symposium ended with a rallying cry to all men to work
for a better world. This was probably as much as Morgan could
do and was undoubtedly the correct emphasis considering that
hostilities, though not over, were slowly abating. But there is a
sense of anticlimax in the final words of the symposium. His
search for a leader who would bring the two movements closer
together, and thus achieve the human utopia he perceived as
central to the vision of both, would prove ultimately futile.

> This is a time which calls pre-eminently for common action from all men
> of goodwill. The world's need is too bitter and our problems are too
> obstinate to be dealt with by any group of men, however well-intentioned,

[3] Ibid., p.95.
[4] Ibid., pp.127–8.
[5] Cf. ibid., p.165.

if they have to act in isolation. It is a time for closing the ranks, not by way
of surrender but by way of good faith and clearer vision. It would be a
calamity if, after such a promising beginning as the *Welsh Outlook* has made,
matters were to lapse back into their old unhappy state. Better things are
possible, especially in Wales. Who will be our Moses?[6]

The symposium highlighted several problems, not least the
fact that nobody seemed prepared to do anything. The same
attitudes and grievances were expressed in 1918 as during the
Cardiff conference of 1911 and before. The general consensus
was once more affirmed to be in favour of greater co-operation.
The issue of labour as a political as well as an industrial concept,
though not directly referred to, is present in the discussion. And
there is just a hint that here, too, there was an ulterior political
motive.

When Herbert Morgan collated the evidence for the
symposium, he may have already been sure of his selection by
the ILP as its candidate for the Neath constituency in the
impending general election. Even if he did not know this, he was
at that time enjoying a fair degree of popularity within the ILP in
south Wales. His was undoubtedly a welcome support for the
nascent labour movement. Outspoken and with an unwavering
faith in the ILP programme, and above all a leading
Nonconformist minister, Herbert Morgan represented the kind
of Welshman the ILP had always sought to secure to convey
their message to other Welshmen. His rejection by the electors of
Neath in 1918 was almost certainly due to his uncompromising
pacifism, although certain sections of the labour press believed
that the electorate, made up as it was of mainly working men,
would reject political pastors.[7] This marked a turning-point for
Nonconformity, the labour movement, relations between the
two, and for Herbert Morgan himself. Nonconformity was
increasingly attempting its own specifically religious answers to
the social problem which would take it away from the specific
problem of labour. After 1918 the labour movement had grown
sufficiently in confidence as not to need such a close relationship
with the churches, partly because its agitators believed in the self-

---

[6] Ibid., p.199.
[7] *Llais Llafur*, 4 January 1919, p.2; *Merthyr Pioneer*, 7 December 1918, p.2.

sufficiency of their case, but also because of the opinion that the churches had disgraced themselves during the war. It was not so much that relations mutually cooled but that the chapel's involvement with the labour movement was no longer a live issue. Herbert Morgan left the ministry in 1920 to become the Director of Extra-Mural Studies at the University College of Wales, Aberystwyth. Gradually he came to emphasize the importance of the church for its own sake, even reminding the Welsh Baptists in his presidential address to the Union meetings of 1945 of the need for devotion and public worship.[8]

1. NONCONFORMITY AND POLITICS: THE 1920S

The *Welsh Outlook*'s symposium, like the Cardiff conference before it, attempted to analyse the specific problem of 'labour'. Some working men had left the chapel following the development of a political consciousness. The labour movement had sought a political solution to the innumerable problems of industrial society, problems which were all too familiar to the 'labour' class. With Socialists giving voice to the issues which concerned them most, working men were beginning to turn away from the chapel and its apparent support of the status quo. Nonconformists rightly recognized that the working class had been wooed away from the chapels by the labour movement, which was prepared to agitate for social reform. However, they did not consider their involvement in the social problem to be a political issue. Idealism, the current philosophical trend, had forced them to emphasize ideas and principles rather than to seek to offer any practical advice. This, together with the advent of a Labour Party and the growing disillusionment with Liberal policy, resulted in a desire amongst Nonconformists to distance themselves from political activity. Certainly, following the 1918 election, the appearance of Nonconformist ministers on Labour, or even Liberal, platforms became rare indeed. This was in part due to the disillusionment felt with the Liberal Party and partly due to Nonconformity's growing unease since 1910 that it had become over-political to the detriment of its spiritual mission.

---

[8] *Seren Cymru*, 27 July 1945, pp.1, 2, 8.

While there were some exceptions,[9] on the whole Nonconformist ministers kept away from political platforms. They sought to be less political at a time when the working class was claiming its political rights. This would ultimately hinder the chapels in their search for a solution to the social problem. It also ensured that Nonconformity's task of reaching the working class would be all the more difficult.

With hindsight, the election of 1918 was the turning-point. Both the Revd Herbert Morgan and the Revd T. E. Nicholas had stood for Parliament, Morgan at Neath and Nicholas at Aberdare, and had been heavily defeated apparently because of their pacifism during the war. From that time onwards, Nonconformists seem to have sensed that the days of their political influence were over, while the labour movement's confidence in its own ability to achieve its ideals and desires became much more marked. In the 1920s the chapels and the labour movement would go their separate ways, no longer calling for co-operation in the struggle for social reform. The situation was vastly different from that in pre-1918 south Wales, as demonstrated by the Revd Ben Wilson's low-key tour of the area in 1923.[10] He noted that 'the returns at the last general election furnish abundant evidence that public opinion has changed and that Labour principles . . . are now being generously adopted'. His visit hardly received a mention in the press and it is ironic that while Wilson was visiting Cwmllynfell and Brynaman, the report in the *Labour Voice* noted that the local ILP branch which had welcomed him fourteen years previously was now 'defunct'.[11] Neither the dissemination of Socialism by a Christian minister nor the call for a partnership between the labour movement and the churches was deemed particularly newsworthy after the war.

The abstention from direct political activity by the Nonconformists ensured that at least some within the labour movement would continue to criticize the chapels and their social inaction. Rhys J. Davies, MP for Westhoughton,

---

[9] Ibid., 3 January 1919, p.3; *Labour Voice*, 11 November 1922, p.6; J. Graham Jones, 'Welsh politics between the wars: the personnel of labour', *Transactions of the Honourable Society of Cymmrodorion* (1983), 179.

[10] *Labour Voice*, 27 January 1923, p.3.

[11] Ibid., 10 February 1923, p.4; 17 February 1923, p.4.

complained in *Y Tyst* in 1924 that there was still much 'coldness' between the church and Labour Party which arose from ignorance and prejudice. The Labour Party sought better treatment for the widows and children, pensions for coalminers as well as for soldiers, and a house for each family. This agenda, he considered, was not inconsistent with the gospel.[12] The Labour Party desired a better social order in which the government ensured work for all or, failing that, support that would keep men from poverty. Significantly, the editor of *Y Tyst*, Beriah Gwynfe Evans,[13] felt compelled to answer Davies's remarks. He suggested that any preacher who preached party politics was wandering from his commission. Despite an attempt to be fair, the editorial did have the flavour of Liberal support.[14] The controversy continued with a contribution from the Socialist firebrand, the Revd D. D. Walters, 'Gwallter Ddu', who wrote to explain that Liberalism and Conservatism were not Christian for they sought only their own profits and not justice. Furthermore, they drew up no policies specifically for the *gwerin*. R. Price Morgan believed that *Y Tyst* should awaken young minds to decide which means were best to give fair play to 'the bottom dog'.[15] The editor responded by claiming that he was neither rich nor a landowner yet he had always voted Liberal. Furthermore, any strength which the Labour Party possessed it drew from the Liberal elements in its policy.

Despite the fact that these political issues were even in 1924 beginning to sound old-fashioned, as Nonconformists were generally no longer interested in political movements, the significant thing is that the controversy no longer focused on Socialism *per se*. For whatever reason, the debate about the efficacy of Socialism had come to an end. The issue now was the need for the churches to recognize 'labour' as a political force, rather than Socialism as the only valid political theory. This was revealed in both positive and negative ways. Some Nonconformists did recognize the politicization of labour, while it was still important for the labour movement to publicize that the Revd Thomas Shankland and Principal Thomas Rees had

[12] *Y Tyst*, 10 January 1924, p.5.
[13] For Beriah Gwynfe Evans (1848–1927), see *DWB*, pp.220–1.
[14] *Y Tyst*, 17 January 1924, p.5.
[15] Ibid., 14 February 1924, p.2.

switched their allegiance from a bankrupt Liberalism to labour politics, even though they were not necessarily active supporters of the Labour Party.[16] The pleasure felt in labour circles at such defections was still considerable in 1923, because both men had a history of enthusiastic and active support for the Liberal Party. It is also true that chapels were still wary of the 'red menace' and ministers were, consequently, still not totally free to follow their individual conscience over matters of politics. Some chapels maintained a narrow-minded political sectarianism, as demonstrated by the sporadic reports of problems faced by ministers who adopted Socialism, as late even as 1929.[17]

On the whole, however, the fate of many of the pre-war political pastors was either to withdraw to post-war obscurity, to an honourable silence, or else to change direction, a move which usually meant leaving the ministry. R. Silyn Roberts, Herbert Morgan, T. E. Nicholas and 'Gwili' have already been mentioned. James Nicholas became pastor of Castle Street Baptist chapel, London, in 1916, following a year's service in France with the YMCA. Iona Williams left Llanelli in 1913 and never ministered in Wales again. Daniel Hughes appears to have continued to preach politics from his pulpit, much to the chagrin of his congregation.[18] As for the others, such as the Rodericks, some continued to sit on local councils, while Rhys J. Huws died in 1917. On the whole, the shift within Nonconformity away from politics meant that most of these men took a far less prominent role in public and political life after the war. The fact that they did not enter more fully into the labour movement suggests that it no longer embodied their social and spiritual ideals. For Silyn Roberts, Herbert Morgan and T. E. Nicholas, the converse was probably true, namely, that Nonconformity had failed to encapsulate a true and effective gospel.

After the war Nonconformists tended to concentrate on the wider issue of the social problem rather than on more exclusively political concerns. This was in part a recognition of the unique opportunity for social reconstruction which offered itself to the post-war world and partly the result of theological developments.

---

[16] *Labour Voice*, 28 April 1923, p.2.

[17] *Y Dinesydd Cymreig*, 26 June 1929, p.5.

[18] See A. H. Jones, *His Lordship's Obedient Servant: Recollections of a South Wales Borderer* (Llandysul, 1987), p.35.

While Nonconformists considered that their concentration on social reform would naturally enable them to reach 'labour' with their gospel, it also meant that the specific problem of working-class abandonment of religious affiliation was virtually ignored.

As well as the diminishing importance of Nonconformity's political allegiance, the 1920s offered Nonconformist ministers a particular opportunity to demonstrate their sympathy with the working class. The succession of labour disputes and the Depression which took hold from the end of the General Strike in 1926 required exactly the kind of sympathetic and practical response which Nonconformists believed would reach the class known as 'labour'. The Revd J. Derlwyn Evans of Bethesda church, Ynysmeudwy, called on those involved in the lock-out following the General Strike not to absent themselves from church but 'to join together in earnest prayer for peace and justice in the present crisis'. Courageously, he announced that he was prepared to suffer with them and take a cut in wages while the dispute continued, an act much appreciated by his congregation.[19] The Association of Glamorganshire Independents, meeting at Pant-teg chapel, Ystalyfera, on 8 July 1926, passed a sympathetic resolution calling on the government to 'place in legal power the measures that are recommended by the last Commission'. They congratulated the workforce on their 'peaceful, quiet spirit in their adversity', and called on all churches and members 'to display the deepest sympathy and the utmost generosity' in attempting to ease and reduce the suffering of the miners during the lock-out.[20] They also announced that only the principles and spirit of the gospel of Christ could bring about a just and lasting settlement.

Not all workmen were satisfied that the churches were doing everything they could to help their cause during the long dispute. A miner of forty years' experience signing himself 'the Lover of Justice' (*Carwr Cyfiawnder*) and writing to *Y Tyst*, insisted that Bolshevism and Marxism could never help the workers. He was critical of ministers for not offering leadership to the working class in their struggle.

[19] *Labour Voice*, 31 July 1926, p.6.
[20] *Y Tyst*, 15 July 1926, p.11.

The field is the world: and the minister's job is to teach justice to the people, and pronounce judgement against injustice. The country's Parliament should be informed that no worker could raise his family on two pound a week, and ask whether the master's profits or the worker's maintenance is most important.

For this correspondent, the 1926 strike was an opportunity for the church to raise its voice against the 'oppression and godlessness' of the age.[21] Notably, Beriah Gwynfe Evans placed a note with the letter protesting that it was not the duty of ministers of the gospel to take sides but to preach the principles of the gospel and address them to the needs of the age. The fault, he claimed, was on both sides and not just on the side of the owners.

It becomes increasingly clear during the 1920s that the ministers and the chapels generally were more prepared than ever before to offer their sympathy and support to those suffering the hardships of life in economically depressed industrial areas. The Maerdy churches, for example, sent a delegation to the Board of Guardians in Pontypridd in 1927 calling for increased relief, while the SWMF lodge invited ministers of religion to sit on its strike and distress committees.[22] Churches passed resolutions during periods of industrial dispute and also on behalf of those who were imprisoned following industrial disturbances.[23] The response to 'labour' as a social phenomenon was apparent here more than anywhere else, as working men trying to support their families were forced to exist under conditions that made life difficult. Ministers demonstrated not a political preference but compassion for those who suffered, and solidarity with those whose cause was righteous. This dictated that their response be *apolitical*, and led to the criticisms of men like 'Carwr Cyfiawnder'.

There were exceptions. H. Cefni Jones, for example, had recognized that the concept of a 'general strike' had political overtones. He insisted that the workers had lacked true leadership, having chosen instead to follow the instructions of

[21] Ibid., 11 November 1926, p.10.
[22] Stuart Macintyre, *Little Moscows: Communism and Working Class Militancy in Inter-War Britain* (London, 1980), pp.159–60.
[23] Ibid.; *Llais Llafur*, 2 January 1926, p.4.

men of dubious motive and intention. Writing to *Y Goleuad*, he claimed that the workman who strikes despite his agreement to work has committed as much of an injustice as if the owners had withheld his pay. He blamed the misunderstanding of the concept of justice on the churches' inability to proffer adequate advice during the strike. Because of this, the workers had been turning to men whose religion was suspect, to say the least. The strike had attempted to hold the nation to ransom, and had attacked the most vulnerable in society by withholding necessary goods. It was also immoral, as even workers' rights could only be safeguarded by moral and reasonable persuasion. The church must be awakened to the dangers of the situation and proclaim them aloud. 'It is as though the day the Communists long for has arrived', he wrote in dramatic vein.

> Millions are on strike for weeks, and there is no hope of a settlement. Starvation stalks the land. The children cry for food. Seeing them enrages the fathers. Starvation turns quiet workmen into rapacious beasts. They swarm to the market places. The policemen fail to keep order. Merchants are struck dead for seeking help to stop them. The owner of the works happens to be nearby at the time. He lies in a pool of his blood on the road. A regiment of soldiers arrive. Listen to the firing. Look at the crowd fleeing and trampling the defenceless in their hurry . . . Caring institutions, established by the Churches of Christ, have been hopelessly scattered; and God has been conquered. The old minister weeps copiously saying to himself between sighs. Oh! if only we had seen in time where strikes would lead them.[24]

Such a message was hardly helpful. It merely suggested that the church supported the political and social status quo, there being no mention of the justice of the men's demands during the strike, or of the intransigence of the mine owners. There is no mention of the conditions of hardship brought upon the industrial workers through insanitary housing, dangerous working practices and conditions, and the economic depression of the period. It is hardly surprising that working men believed that the church had no message of comfort and no way of helping them in their very real predicament.

---

[24] *Y Goleuad*, 19 January 1927, p.9.

2. THE 1920S: DECADE OF THE KINGDOM

By the 1920s the main themes of theological liberalism were advanced as embodying the central message of Christianity. The same familiar images were emphasized: the Fatherhood of God, brotherhood of man and the ethical task of the Kingdom. These ideas, kept 'on hold' during the war years, re-emerged to greater prominence after 1918 through journals such as *Yr Efrydydd*. The mood after the war was one of relief accompanied by optimism for a better future. Political and religious groups very quickly grasped this unique opportunity to create a better environment and to place the great principles of justice, brotherhood, equality and co-operation at the centre of all human activity and relations. Although little was achieved in practical terms, the 1920s more than any other decade were the years of the Kingdom, as Nonconformists exploited its inspirational potential.

It was the ideal of the Kingdom of God, interpreted as 'the sum of God's purpose for the world',[25] which lay behind the formation of *Urdd y Deyrnas* (the Order of the Kingdom) at the beginning of the decade. Inspired by the work of the inter-denominational and students' movement, the SCM, the *Urdd* became the chief focus of non-sectarian religious activity amongst the youth of Wales. The *Urdd* sought to instigate a 'great campaign' which would seek to establish the Kingdom of God on earth[26] by bringing Christ's lordship to bear on all aspects of life.[27] It aimed to provide a focus for specific Christian social thought amongst young people outside the colleges and, to an extent, outside the churches. Those who wished to 'understand the Christian faith, discover the Christian way and live the Christian life' would be welcomed into the *Urdd*.[28] The goal was not to encourage church membership but to foster 'individual consecration, study and service' as a means of building the Kingdom of God on earth.[29] Study of the social implications of the gospel was encouraged along with study of local issues and a recognition of individual responsibility.

[25] Owen Griffith, 'Urdd y Deyrnas', *Yr Efrydydd*, III/2 (15 January 1923), 44.
[26] D.Miall Edwards, 'Nodiadau golygyddol', *Yr Efrydydd*, II/2 (15 March 1922), 49.
[27] Owen Griffith, 'Urdd y Deyrnas', p.45.
[28] 'Mudiad yr "Auxiliary" yng Nghymru: cyfansoddiad dros dro', *Yr Efrydydd*, II/4 (15 June 1922), 96.
[29] D. Miall Edwards, 'Nodiadau golygyddol', *Yr Efrydydd*, III/4 (15 June 1922), 74.

In conferences and local study groups throughout the decade, the *Urdd* propagated the idea that religious faith was geared towards, and essential for, true social reform. It drew on the prevailing Liberal Theology to emphasize the need for a concerted effort by its members to promote, in their own area, the ideals of the Kingdom, with the added assurance that reform would be inevitable if energized by the idealism and enthusiasm of youth. Thus, for example, the 1923 conference discussed 'Personality', while that of 1926 discussed 'Christian citizenship'. The value and responsibility of the individual were once again axiomatic. Those who were involved in the *Urdd* included educationalists such as Gwenan Jones, literary figures such as T. H. Parry-Williams, ministers and theologians such as Professor David Phillips and Professor David Williams, both of whom were involved in ministerial training for the Calvinistic Methodist denomination at Bala, and John Morgan Jones (Merthyr). Most prominent, however, were those whose names would become associated with the wider attempts at social Christianity in this period: Herbert Morgan, D. Miall Edwards and John Morgan Jones (Bangor).

The *Urdd* attempted to infuse culture and a religious spirit into Welsh youth. Thus, essential to its mission was the publication of *Traethodau'r Deyrnas* (Essays of the Kingdom) written by prominent Welsh scholars and educators. Of the twelve Welsh and six English pamphlets published, some dealt directly with social issues,[30] individual morality,[31] religion and culture,[32] and the remainder with general literary and cultural topics.[33] Of the second series only three numbers actually appeared.[34] Most of *Traethodau'r Deyrnas* shared the conviction that contemporary society was seriously flawed,[35] that it was essential that a new

---

[30] Herbert Morgan, *Diwydiant yng Nghymru*, no. 3 (Wrexham, 1924); David Thomas, *Y Deyrnas a Phroblemau Cymdeithasol*, no. 6 (Wrexham, 1924).

[31] Dorothy E. Roberts, *Oriau Hamdden ac Adloniant*, no. 9 (Wrexham, 1924).

[32] E. Morgan Humphreys, *Cymru a'r Wasg*, no. 10 (Wrexham, 1924); D. Miall Edwards and M. E. Davies, *Cyflwr Crefydd yng Nghymru*, no. 1 (Wrexham, 1924); D. Miall Edwards, *Religion in Wales*, English ser., no. 3 (Wrexham, 1926).

[33] Ifor Williams, *Llenyddiaeth Gymraeg Fore*, no. 8 (Wrexham, 1924); T. Gwynn Jones, *The Culture and Tradition of Wales*, English ser., no.5 (Wrexham, 1926); Saunders Lewis, *An Introduction to Welsh Literature*, English ser., no.1 (Wrexham, 1926).

[34] Thomas Lewis, *Yr Hen Destament a Beirniadaeth Ddiweddar*, 2nd ser., no. 1 (Wrexham, 1930); Ifor Williams, *Llenyddiaeth Gymraeg a Chrefydd*, 2nd ser., no. 2 (Wrexham, 1930); D. Llewelyn Williams, *Cyflwr Iechyd yng Nghymru*, 2nd ser., no. 3 (Wrexham, 1930).

[35] David Thomas, *Y Deyrnas*, pp.3–4.

society be created[36] and that the church was the only movement able to achieve that by promoting individual morality. Jesus had come to found a perfect society, the Kingdom of God,[37] the establishment of which should be the church's priority.

In 1927 D. Miall Edwards edited a collection of essays entitled *Efengyl y Deyrnas* (The Gospel of the Kingdom) on behalf of the Council of the Union of Welsh Independents.[38] Its subtitle, 'Essays on moral and social matters' (*Traethodau ar faterion moesol a chymdeithasol*), demonstrated the essential association between social reform and individual regeneration. Among the issues it raised were the social message of the gospel, gambling, relations between the sexes, the adolescent, the drink trade, the international problem. All this serves to show that by the 1920s the social problem had become comprehensive. Instead of being restricted to solving industrial problems, it was now concerned with a wider vision of a perfect society, the Kingdom of God, where issues of personal and social morality were embodied within the social fabric. This was no longer to be accomplished merely on a local scale but was to be international. More crucially, Nonconformists were emphasizing that social reform required the inspiration and moral dynamic of religion in order to be effective.

The image of the Kingdom was invoked as an all-encompassing concept which would not merely include the establishment of a just and pleasing environment but would also require a higher standard of morality and culturalization on the part of each individual. Thus, the overriding issue in the establishment of the Kingdom in liberal Nonconformist theology was a recognition of the sanctity of human personality. All aspects of society including industry had to be restructured to make this their primary consideration. Industry had 'no *raison d'être* except as a means of supplying the whole community with certain commodities which are necessary to all'.[39] It was no longer to be used merely to gain profits for the few but to serve the needs of the many.[40] This would mean replacing competition

---

[36] Ibid., p.6.
[37] Ibid., p.7.
[38] D. Miall Edwards (ed.), *Efengyl y Deyrnas* (Bala, 1927).
[39] Herbert Morgan, *The Social Task in Wales* (London, 1919), p.49.
[40] J. H. Howard, *Cristionogaeth a Chymdeithas* (Liverpool, 1914), p.65; Herbert Morgan, *Diwydiant yng Nghymru*, p.10.

with the ideal of co-operation,[41] and having the development of character as the desired goal.[42] All this confirmed that the Kingdom was considered to be a human and not a divine activity, an ethical rather than an apocalyptic concept. Herbert Morgan's words made room for both. 'From the religious point of view [the Kingdom of God] is a gift to be enjoyed: from the ethical point of view it is a task to be accomplished—not in another life but here and now.'[43] In practice, however, the latter tended to take precedence over the former. It was for the denominations to attempt to put this theology into practice to rebuild the world after the devastation of the Great War. In varying ways, and with varying success, the church bodies attempted to do just that.

3. POST-1918 DENOMINATIONAL EFFORTS

There can be little doubt that many within the labour movement regarded the church as an irrelevance. They perceived traditional Nonconformist religion as silent in the face of misery and hardship as well as powerless to transform the status quo. Ironically, Welsh Nonconformists spent more energy discussing social issues during the 1920s than in any other period.

The Calvinistic Methodists led the way after the war with the establishment of their Reconstruction Commission, whose brief was to discuss all areas of the Connexion's life and, where necessary, to recommend change. Five committees were convened, the fifth being concerned with social issues. This reflected the importance which they attached to the social problem and the role of the church in offering solutions. The fifth committee published two reports in 1921, one by the North Wales Assembly, published in Welsh,[44] the other by the South Wales Assembly, published in English.[45] Governed as they were by

---

[41] *The Social Task*, p.50; *Diwydiant yng Nghymru*, p.13; cf. Thomas Rowlands, 'Crefydd a bywyd yr oes', *Yr Eurgrawn* (1926), 345–6; Charles Jones, 'Crefydd Crist a'n problemau cymdeithasol', *Yr Eurgrawn* (1919), 220; 'G.J.', 'Bywyd personol a threfn cymdeithas', *Yr Efrydydd*, XI/2 (November 1934), 30, 33.

[42] *The Social Task in Wales*, p.50.

[43] Ibid., p.87.

[44] *Comisiwn Ad-drefnu y Methodistiaid Calfinaidd; Adroddiad Pwyllgor V Ar Yr Eglwys a Chwestiynau Cymdeithasol* (Caernarfon, 1921) [hereafter *NW*].

[45] *South Wales Calvinistic Methodist Association Reconstruction Commission: The Report of the Fifth Committee on the Church and Social Questions* (Cardiff, 1921) [hereafter *SW*].

Liberal Theology, the reports could find no direct help in the gospel to solve social problems but only principles gleaned from the teaching of Jesus. Both reports were united in enunciating the same principles which should govern social reform, but they differed over the practical role which the church should play.

According to the reports, social questions were, in fact, issues of morality,[46] stemming from an ignorance of the spiritual dimension in life. Overconcentration on the material had corrupted society and thus it was only in the great ethical principles underlying Jesus's teaching that a solution could be found. These were expressed in the by-then-familiar liberal terminology of the Fatherhood of God and the consequent brotherhood of all men.[47] This meant that each individual was of supreme value,[48] and that through the process of individual salvation social questions became the concern of the church.[49] As a result, the reports advised that industry needed to put its priorities in order. Profit should only be considered after the paying of running costs and a decent wage for the workers.[50] Industry, after all, existed for man.[51] The need for individual salvation, leading to consecration in the service of mankind with the goal of establishing the Kingdom of God, was emphasized in both reports.[52]

The Kingdom of God was hailed as the most helpful of Christian images in the debate.[53] The Kingdom was God's family, but men and women were only fitted for the Kingdom individually.[54] The reports thus adopted the policy of concentrating on individual rebirth to nobler aims and principles, emphasizing the moral dynamic of religion which was the legacy of Kant. Once this had occurred, the individual was to aim at Christian citizenship worthy of Christ's gospel. This was to begin in terms of personal morality but must be expressed in the family, and then in civic, national and international terms.[55] Any

---

[46] *NW*, pp.7–8.
[47] *NW*, pp.8, 61.
[48] *NW*, pp.10, 63; *SW*, p.27.
[49] *NW*, p.4; *SW*, p.12.
[50] *NW*, p.39; *SW*, p.32.
[51] *NW*, p.36.
[52] *NW*, pp.11–12; *SW*, pp.14, 19, 34.
[53] *NW*, p.15.
[54] *NW*, p.31.
[55] *NW*, p.58.

attempt to reform society had to be centred on the concept of the family, which was a sphere of activity which everyone could influence and in which everyone held certain responsibilities. Inspiration for social renewal could be found in the doctrine of the Trinity which, it was posited, implied a social rather than an individual salvation.[56] As God was Father, men should live as brothers. God the Son demonstrated the need to destroy evil in all parts of life and God the Spirit demonstrated the immanence of God.

As the central element in Jesus's teaching was, according to this interpretation, the value of personality, it is somewhat surprising that the North Wales Report advocated the practice of eugenics, the pseudo-science which claimed to ensure the propagation of only the higher elements in society. In practice, it could only mean the sterilization of the so-called 'unfit'.

> Connecting the chaste and the unchaste, spoiling the life of the innocent through hereditary corruption, multiplying tendencies dangerous to the prosperity of the human race, and bringing children who will be nothing but disabled and deficient into the world is not only cruelty, but unfaithfulness to Christ. In the healthy and happy child He finds the most perfect plan of the Kingdom of God.[57]

This sinister policy found no place in the South Wales Report, but was alarmingly common amongst Nonconformists dealing with social issues at this time. Such an attitude became untenable in the light of Nazi attempts to establish a super-race and the revelations of the concentration camps.

The Revd J. Puleston Jones believed that the English Report was a document of superior quality to the Welsh, mainly because of its linguistic style.[58] Its superiority was reflected in more ways than that of expression. The advice given to the church by the South Wales Report was clearer. It offered the idea of stewardship as a concrete policy to help solve social problems,[59] and identified a threefold mission for the church to put into practice. It had the 'prophetic function of social criticism' and

[56] *NW*, p.16.
[57] *NW*, p.29.
[58] *Y Goleuad*, 14 September 1921, p.9.
[59] *SW*, pp.9, 33.

therefore had to act as the conscience of society. Secondly, it had the 'evangelical function of social inspiration', with the responsibility to hold the ideal of the Kingdom of God before society. Finally, it had the 'pastoral function of social sympathy' which included care for the weak, poor, erring and fallen.[60] The primary function of the church was still seen in terms of individual salvation, but it had to recognize its responsibility to society. Like the report to the General Assembly in 1913, this report recommended that ministerial candidates study social science, that the denomination prepare suitable handbooks on social issues, that candidates be prepared to work ecumenically and that each local monthly meeting and presbytery should study the social question as it affected the locality.[61]

The Reconstruction Committee report was to be the handbook for the 'Campaign for Morals and Religion' (*Ymgyrch Moes a Chrefydd*) launched by the Calvinistic Methodists at a conference held in Llandrindod Wells on 14 August 1921. According to Nonconformist theory at the time, the need was not merely for a perfect social system but also for a state in which individuals could achieve full character development. The campaign should be viewed in the context of a comprehensive vision of social purity rather than as the death throes of a theological and ethical conservatism. It sought to educate people about the dangers of the drink trade, moral impurity and religious indifference. Its traditionalist concern with the issues of individual morality and temperance was seen in the context of the establishment of God's Kingdom, and the campaign's organizers hoped to achieve most of its aims within five years. Primarily it sought to provide information for the churches through the production of literature and the holding of lectures, and to do so in union with other denominations if possible. This was reflected in the presence at this meeting of Principal William Edwards of the South Wales Baptist College and of the Revd H. Elfed Lewis of the Independents.[62]

Despite arguing for practising personal morality within a better social environment, these aims reveal that there were many amongst the Methodists whose ethical goals, ideals and

---

[60] *SW*, pp.30–1.
[61] *SW*, p.40.
[62] *Y Goleuad*, 24 July 1921, p.4; 24 August 1921, p.9.

outlook had not been affected by the pressing social needs that had risen from rapid industrialization and the destruction of war. The campaign was not primarily concerned with specific economic and social problems but with the 'terrible . . . moral condition' of individual citizens in the country.[63] It was ethical and religious considerations rather than concern for the plight of the working class which gave rise to the campaign.

Like so much Nonconformist social thought, the main argument was that once the churches were convinced of the importance of ethical issues, society could be similarly persuaded.[64] This reflected theological liberalism's faith in enlightening the mind and its consequent belief in education almost as a part of the process of salvation. The aim, then, was a general culturalization of the individual through the promotion of personal morality and education. In order to achieve this, the campaign advocated a concentration on temperance education in the Sunday Schools and the promotion of purity and honesty in the spheres of labour and commerce. As part of a general promotion of social purity, it sought to explain the advantages and dangers of leisure time, the evil of gambling and the necessity of Sabbath observance. Although the problems of capital and labour were mentioned, they were not given priority and the campaign tended to rely on advocating a better personal relationship between the representatives of both sides, primarily in order to maintain the importance of individual responsibility.

The campaign certainly received much publicity from *Y Goleuad*, the weekly newspaper of the Calvinistic Methodists.[65] It is, however, difficult to assess whether or not it succeeded. The overall impression gained from contemporary evidence is that calls for greater moral effort tended to be lost as far more pressing concerns, such as unemployment and the drift away from the chapel, came to the fore. More important than its success was its historical significance. Apart from the prominence of Liberal Theology, emphasizing human responsibility, it also demonstrates that Nonconformists were keen not to return to any kind of political activism but to offer something that was

[63] Gwilym Davies, 'A Welsh social diary', *The Welsh Outlook* (1920), 125.
[64] *Y Goleuad*, 7 September 1921, p.10.
[65] E.g. *Y Goleuad*, 9 November 1921, p.15; 30 November 1921, p.4; 21 December 1921, p.12; 28 December 1921, p.9; 22 February 1922, p.4; 20 September 1922, p.12.

more uniquely part of their message. As a result, it did not adopt the politics of any particular party or advocate social reform through parliamentary activity. Nor did the Nonconformists wholly accept the labour movement's claim that the individual could be renewed through social reform. Instead, they maintained their evangelical stress on the importance of individual morality in society. That the Calvinistic Methodists were still emphasizing a traditional approach demonstrates the inherent conservatism of some elements within Welsh Nonconformity, but it also shows that they considered the traditional Christian standpoint to be a vitally important part of their message and a crucial step towards establishing the Kingdom. The historical significance of the campaign also lies in the fact that in its stress on educating the public, individual morality and responsibility, and the recognition and identification of all aspects of the social question, Nonconformists had grasped that the social problem was a wider issue than the supply of better housing and higher wages. It involved the moral character of each citizen.

The Reconstruction Committee reports and the Campaign for Morals and Religion demonstrate how important the wider issues of the social problem had become for Methodists at the beginning of the 1920s. They had grasped that as society moved towards perfection, there were social implications to the teaching of Jesus which needed to be expressed. They also recognized the complexities of the social question which included the need for improvements to the environment alongside the moral regeneration of individuals. And they succeeded in doing this without linking these beliefs to the policies of any specific political party. As the churches at this time considered themselves to be the guardians of eternal moral values and principles, it was in the field of practical advice that nothing was achieved. Although the Methodists now had a statement of denominational policy, this proved difficult to put into practice.

The Council of the Union of Welsh Independents appointed a committee of three in September 1921 to give expression to the church's social mission. The presence on the committee of Thomas Rees and D. Miall Edwards as exponents of theological liberalism and the need for a religious social dynamic is hardly surprising. The third member of the group was the Revd R. E. Peregrine, who would feature prominently in movements for practical relief in deprived areas of the industrial south. They reported in September 1922, when four other names, the Revds H. M. Hughes, O. L. Roberts, H. Elfed Lewis and W. Parri Huws, were added to consider the questions further. The report, *Cenadwri Cymdeithasol yr Efengyl* (The Social Mission of the Gospel), published in 1923, was intended as an aid to the churches' reflection rather than a blueprint for social reform.[66] Unlike that of the Methodists, this report was never intended to represent an official denominational view of social matters. It could only be forwarded to the churches for their further consideration. Although the earlier Methodist report was used by the committee, this report is clearly marked by the particular views of two of its authors, Thomas Rees and D. Miall Edwards.

The report called on the church to recognize that the life of the individual was inherently bound up with the life of society as a whole (p.9). The influence of Hegelian philosophy was seen in the report's emphasis on society as a unified whole whose problems were inter-related. If Christian principles could be established at the root of society, reform would be instituted and the Kingdom of God established (p.41). However, the authors were quick to point out that no direct advice could be found in the words and teaching of Jesus. Instead, attitudes would have to be gleaned from his words, the governing principles of his life, modern knowledge and the consistency in Christ's teaching. The basics were the Fatherhood of God and the establishment of the Kingdom as central to Jesus's teaching (pp.8–9).

The report stressed the moral responsibility of every individual. As all men possessed infinite value as the object of God's love, they were to act in service and love towards each other. The social mission, therefore, must begin with the individual, for only through regenerated people could the perfect society be formed. The need for knowledge and education was repeated (p.11), as was the importance of the family (p.19), and the evil of drunkenness (p.20). The church needed to develop into a society of people (p.21) and free itself from political parties (p.23). Within industry, these principles needed to be expressed as providing an antidote to the depersonalization of relations through industrial expansion. Industry had lost the human

---

[66] *Cenadwri Cymdeithasol yr Efengyl* (Swansea, 1923).

element (p.24). Again, the individual responsibility of the worker to his employer and the employer to his employee was stressed (p.25). Although legislation could have been seen as the way to enforce this, the liberal stress on morality and moral persuasion led the church to seek a different path. Naïve it may have been, but it at least made sense. The principle of service needed to be embodied as the governing element in all aspects of life, including industry (p.26). Money and capital should be used to ensure that men have 'life and have it more abundantly' (p.27). Thus, man's stewardship of capital, but also of his labour, needed to be recognized and then used to demonstrate the responsibility of each individual towards society (p.33). The report identified the question of international peace as the most important social question of the age (p.38).

Social issues were, then, important enough in the 1920s for reports to be commissioned by the denominations. They reflected the general optimism that a new society was about to be built and the need for such a society to be firmly grounded in moral principles. Perhaps most significant is the fact that rather than beginning with a critique of society, both the Methodists and Independents interpreted the gospel in terms of social reform. To criticize social practice directly would have been an inherently political activity.

After the war, the Baptists tended to lag behind the Calvinistic Methodists and Independents in social matters. A social issues column, begun in 1919 by 'J.G.' (probably the Revd J. Griffiths, Ammanford) in *Seren Cymru*, soon disappeared.[67] When the Revd D. Wyre Lewis, Rhosllannerchrugog, introduced the 'Social Questions' column in *Seren Cymru* in 1922, this demonstrated a renewed interest in solving social problems, even though it was based on the policy of saving the individual as the most effective means to social renewal.[68] Wyre Lewis, too, emphasized the need for service. 'Doubtless one of the most revolutionary ideas that Christ introduced to the world was that service is the meaning of life, "be a servant to all". Service is the law of the life of the Kingdom.'

Admittedly, before knowing what service the church could offer it had to understand the needs of the world and therefore

---

[67] *Seren Cymru*, 31 March 1919, p.2.
[68] Ibid., 30 June 1922, p.2.

further study was required. Lewis did stress, however, that the church serves the world primarily through presenting God as worthy of worship and devotion.[69] Following that, the worshippers must leave the sanctuary in order to defeat the evil elements in the world. He identified two kinds of evil: that which was essentially evil but could appear good, such as war, gambling and the drink trade. These must simply be condemned and eradicated. The other was the essentially good which sometimes appears as evil, such as sport, commerce and politics. The church needed to redeem these activities by giving them a higher moral orientation. There were two things necessary in the mission of the churches: they had to ensure that individuals were moral enough to withstand evil practices, but also seek the removal of the causes of evil, not simply its consequences. This latter intention required the formation of specific policies, an activity which the Baptists, like the other Nonconformists, had patently neglected. Lewis probably envisaged the formation of a public conscience as Lloyd George had advised in Cardiff. Apart from insisting that it was necessary, little was done to accomplish even this.

4. THE EPISTLE OF ST JAMES

It was primarily the perceived relevance of the Epistle of St James to the social question,[70] and the belief that social renewal would follow individual human enlightenment, that encouraged the four Nonconformist denominations to study that letter in their adult Sunday Schools during 1922. Here, at least, the need for education was partially met, even though the ultimate inspiration was a desire for scriptural rather than social understanding. The timing was significant, coming as preparations were being made for the Copec conference in 1924 and following a six-month lock-out in the coalfield in 1921.

Of the four official handbooks, three were reprints of previous editions. Puleston Jones had first published *Epistol Iago* for the Calvinistic Methodists in 1898, the year of the fateful strike in the coalfield. William Morris's Baptist handbook had appeared

---

[69] Ibid., 8 December 1922, p.6.
[70] E.g. *Llais Llafur*, 3 May 1913, p.2.

within a year of the revival in 1906. The Congregationalist Miall
Edwards's offering had been published in 1911, the year of the
Cardiff conference and the establishment of the Welsh School of
Social Service, and only months after the Tonypandy riots. Only
the Wesleyan Thomas Rowlands's handbook was written
especially for the occasion.

As was to be expected, it was the epistle's emphasis on the
practical embodiment of religious faith that was most strongly
present in these books, and the fact that James did not
differentiate between faith and works but between 'dead faith'
and 'live faith'.[71] In other words, the acceptance of Christ should
lead to a difference in the life of the believer. Faith and works
were not to be divorced.[72] Puleston Jones recognized that James
promoted the kind of Christianity directed towards solving social
problems. The first stage was man's salvation. Once saved, men
could redeem society.[73]

Although most authors were aware that a call for practical
Christianity was vital in an age of social problems,[74] they tended
to restrict themselves to explaining the text without applying it to
current needs. This was typical of the biblical criticism of the
day, with its belief that each generation had a duty to apply
spiritual truth in the best way. Miall Edwards's volume was by
far the best book, not merely in erudition and scholarly rigour,
but also in its presentation of a mission to address current
problems in James's words. More than the others, he recognized
the ability of James to speak to the age and he set out to express
its social message, though always along the lines of his own
theological liberalism and philosophical Idealism. Thus, he
emphasized the need for men to act towards each other in a
spirit of grace, which should not be compromised by the
environment and social situation in which individuals found
themselves. Social differences, he claimed, would lose their
significance if men acted in such a way.[75] The social problem
would thus be removed if individuals recognized their

[71] Thomas Rowlands, *Gwerslyfr ar Epistol Iago* (Bangor, 1922), pp.43, 51; W. Morris,
Esponiad ar Epistol Iago (2nd edn. Tonypandy, 1922), pp.57–8; D. Miall Edwards, *Epistol
Cyffredinol Iago* (2nd edn. Swansea, 1922), pp.xi, xx, xxi.
[72] Thomas Rowlands, *Gwerslyfr*, p.56.
[73] J. Puleston Jones, *Epistol Iago* (2nd edn., Caernarfon, 1922), p.lxv.
[74] W. Morris, *Esponiad*, pp.26–7; D. Miall Edwards, *Epistol*, p.xxii.
[75] D. Miall Edwards, *Epistol*, pp.xxi, xxii.

responsibility to each other as personalities and also as men in different social strata.[76] Moral considerations, the actions of individual men, rather than social reform *per se* were therefore the top priority. It was a question of practising the principles of the Sermon on the Mount and the Epistle of St James.[77]

5. ECUMENICAL ACTIVITIES

Arrangements were made to reconvene the Welsh School of Social Service in 1919. In contrast to the Campaign for Morals and Religion, the school tended to emphasize the need not for individual moral regeneration but for social measures to improve the surroundings of men and women.[78] Thus, the Welsh churches were taking measures, however small and conservative, to meet the two aspects of the social problem which they had identified, namely the regeneration of the individual and the application of moral and spiritual principles to society's needs. Both the school and the campaign tended to believe that the key to solving the social problem was education, and thus the primary objective from 1919 was to inform the public. The school attempted to do this through different sections, each providing enlightened information and advice on specific areas of social need. Initially, sections were planned to concentrate on issues of education, public health and housing, women's work, social life in Wales, the religious life of the people, citizenship and local authority, rural life and industry, public morals and international issues. This reflected both the concerns of the pre-war schools and the needs of the post-war world, particularly as the school looked to international concerns and to the issue of the employment of women. By 1921 the sections had been modified slightly. Education, rural problems, public health and international matters remained and were accompanied by the issue of women's suffrage and the need for penal reform. If anything, this reflected the commitment of the school to the proposed national conference on Christian politics and

---

[76] Ibid., p.39.
[77] Ibid., p.xx.
[78] Cf. e.g. Herbert Morgan, 'The church and citizenship', *The Welsh Outlook* (1922), 22; G. A. Edwards, 'Cristionogaeth a diwydiant', *Yr Efrydydd*, III/1 (October 1922), 14, 16.

citizenship, definite plans for which were put in place in the same year.[79]

Lleufer Thomas, believing that the school had a sufficiently mature grasp of social Christianity, suggested in 1920 that that the delegates formulate a confession of faith. Such a confession would express the school's social belief, based on the principle of human brotherhood and the inherent value of personality as the centre of Jesus's teaching.[80] As nothing actually came of this, Miall Edwards's warning to the school in the same year is highly significant, namely that they should not forget the permanent elements in the church's message, such as the supremacy of the spiritual over the physical, the truth of the Christian revelation of God and man, the sovereignty and moral authority of Christ and the establishment of God's Kingdom on earth. All this demonstrated his theological liberalism and also that in his attitudes towards society, politics and religion he was basically conservative. But he had correctly assessed the danger inherent in the school's policy. Gradually, the school's emphasis changed from looking for a Christian response to the social problem to providing a place for expert discussion. This became more marked after 1925 when the school evolved into a private study-week held at Caerleon College. In so doing, the school removed itself from public attention. According to Ben Bowen Thomas, with this move 'the urgency of offering Christian guidance to Wales tended to be subordinated to the tentative submission of expert, cautious and enlightened advice to the general public'.[81]

Miall Edwards seems to have become less involved in the school after 1924. Why this was so is unclear. It could be because he disapproved of the direction it was taking, or because he became more involved in national and international conferences, or merely because he was not considered to be an expert in practical social matters and consequently his contributions were not invited. Whatever the reason, in losing Edwards the school lost its most able theologian, and this was reflected in the path it decided to take. Theology and even theological principles

[79] See *The United School of Social Service for Wales* (n.d.), p.4; Minute Book of Welsh School of Social Service, 1919–22, Gwilym Davies Papers, NLW.

[80] Newspaper cuttings in Gwilym Davies Papers, NLW.

[81] Ben Bowen Thomas, 'Gwilym Davies and the Welsh School of Social Service', in I. G. Jones (ed.), *Gwilym Davies: A Tribute* (Llandysul, 1972), p.29.

expressed in anything but the most superficial manner were no longer considered important.

The question facing the school was how it could promote its conclusions and continue to proffer advice to the populace, both those connected with the churches and those who were not. Propaganda had never been a priority and a conscious decision was taken not to begin such work after the Great War. Instead it was felt that the school should remain simply a common meeting ground.[82] In order to disseminate the school's principles more fully, it was suggested that it offer help to working men to establish their own local associations of social welfare. One local group was formed at Aberdare.[83] The very fact that the school chose to concentrate on providing information rather than holding public meetings suggests that it no longer considered the presentation of a specifically Christian answer to social problems to be a priority. Studying the problems within their social context became all-important.

The school would have achieved more success had it listened to its more radical members. Herbert Morgan advocated a far more direct and detailed approach on the part of the churches, producing a blueprint for their members to follow. The church had been handicapped by

> . . . a kind of timidity which shelters itself behind the contention that the real task of the corporate Christian society is to enunciate general principles and to leave their particular application to individual Christians. The motive behind this cautious policy is a fear that the unity of the group may be jeopardized by disagreement with regard to practical action.[84]

In one sweep, Morgan dismissed the activity on which the Nonconformist churches and the Welsh School of Social Service had chosen to concentrate. He believed that individuals could not be left to work out how Christian principles should be applied; they needed a 'corporate, coherent and practical witness to the Christian life'. Morgan's address was an attempt to encourage the church to accept a wider vision and responsibility

---

[82] *The United School of Social Service for Wales* (n.d.), p.10.

[83] Minute Book; also Gwilym Davies, 'A Welsh social diary', *The Welsh Outlook* (1920), 297.

[84] Herbert Morgan, *The Social Task*, p.21.

as well as to express clearly how its great principles could be applied. This meant that it had to stop emphasizing narrow individualistic interpretations of values such as temperance, chastity, industry and honesty. The church needed to adopt social rather than individual motivation: 'The minor morality which ministers to respectability and self-advancement must make way for the larger and more creative ethic of the Kingdom, with love and service as its watchwords.'[85]

Herbert Morgan had consistently espoused a more direct approach to social problems since the days when he contemplated a career in Parliament. It had, however, been rejected by the majority of Welsh Nonconformist theologians in favour of the safer route of enunciating principles which should underlie social activity and communal life. Morgan had rightly perceived that it could never be enough to demonstrate principles without showing how they could be applied. The irony is that he tended to look elsewhere for leadership.[86] His greatest fault, and the fault of most Nonconformists, was to expect others to apply the general principles to the concrete situations of life. The greatest weakness of the school was that Nonconformists rightly expected it to fulfil this task, and it never really did so.

Far more typical of the general attitude to social issues was the address by the Revd G. A. Edwards on 'Christianity and Industry' to the 1922 school. Edwards, who would later become a professor at the theological college at Bala and then Principal at Aberystwyth, was at this time a minister in Bangor. In him the Calvinistic Methodists had for the first time a representative in the social debate whose motives were untainted by a suspicion of political partisanship.

According to Edwards, the industrial system devalued the individual and thus presented a challenge to Christianity.[87] During the early 1920s the idea that industry had no position in society unless it served mankind as a whole was expressed more strongly than ever.[88] The fact that the industrial system tended to ignore the personality of the worker meant for Edwards that the

---

[85] Ibid., p.23.
[86] Herbert Morgan, 'The church and labour: a symposium', *The Welsh Outlook* (1918), 199.
[87] G. A. Edwards, 'Cristionogaeth', p.14.
[88] E.g. Gwilym Owen, 'Trefn Cristionogol cymdeithas', *Seren Gomer* (1924), 224; Herbert Morgan, *The Social Task*, p.49.

reform of the individual was insufficient. The system itself was at fault for preventing industrialists from effecting improvements as these would result in a loss of competitiveness. Edwards believed that the Christian's task in the world was to perfect his relationship with God, with his fellow men and with the world around, and although the church had in the past emphasized the first two, the last aspect had been neglected. Despite all this, Edwards maintained that the church's task was to recognize the responsibilities of its members in society, to research the notable problems of the age, to pronounce Christ's general standpoint on life in this world and then to encourage the recognition of responsibility by his followers in the face of these facts. In other words, it needed to gather and disseminate information. The strictly economic and political questions should be left to the experts. The church, however, should constantly announce that no system could survive unless it was based on the principles of Christianity.[89] Unfortunately, Edwards had not taken Herbert Morgan's advice of making the principles more concrete. Somewhat frustratingly, in school after school, different men tended to say the same thing, that Christianity provided the only principles on which a fair and just society could be established. They had reached the stage of identifying those principles through the influence of theological liberalism but seemed unable to go any further. Nonconformists appear to have consistently failed to capitalize on their opportunities. The early 1920s were years of increasing membership within the Non-conformist churches. Although detailed statistics for the Welsh Independents are not available, the figures for the Baptists and Calvinistic Methodists increased consistently, reaching a peak in 1926–7 (see table 5.1). Despite this, and the ascendancy of Liberal Theology, it seems that the churches were unable to do any more than protest that they had a contribution to make. It went largely ignored by the wider social movement and was thus generally not acted upon by the churches themselves.

The period between 1921 and 1924 was probably the most important in the history of the school. The atmosphere was still filled with religious optimism and anticipation. The denominations had produced reports on the social problem because they

[89] G. A. Edwards, 'Cristionogaeth', pp.16–17.

Table 5.1 Membership figures for the three main Nonconformist denominations in Wales, 1920–1930

Year	Baptists	Independents	Calvinistic Methodists
1920	125,068	–	187,220
1921	123,798	–	187,260
1922	124,511	–	187,746
1923	126,933	–	188,412
1924	129,009	–	189,323
1925	129,734	–	189,323
1926	130,098	–	189,727
1927	129,758	134,971	189,132
1928	128,747	129,732	187,892
1929	126,203	129,382	186,194
1930	125,704	125,806	185,827

Source: John Williams, *Digest of Welsh Historical Statistics*, II (Cardiff, 1985), pp.249–345.

considered that mankind was presented with an unprecedented opportunity to rebuild society along lines of justice and peace. An international brotherhood under the universal Fatherhood of God would finally be established according to the purpose of Jesus's mission. Such a theological understanding, vague as it was, underpinned most of the social activity amongst Nonconformists in Wales and the rest of Britain during the decade, and such concepts were consistently held at the school's annual conferences in this period.[90] It was also the period of preparation for the great national and international ecumenical conferences on Christianity and social issues.

The year 1925 marked a watershed for the school. It was decided that one major piece of research should be undertaken each year, that it should continue to concentrate on the particular problems of adolescence, encourage members to co-operate with the denominational Social Service Unions and to use the school as a link between Wales and the Copec Continuation Committee. In that year, however, the school moved to Caerleon and thereafter never really had a permanent home. It lost its public

[90] Cf. Herbert Morgan, 'The church and citizenship', p.21; Gwilym Owen, 'Trefn Cristnogol', p.217.

and, to an extent, its original objectives. Expert and detailed study could not be relied on to bring a specifically Christian response to the problem of post-war society in Wales. Certainly, from this point, the school appears to have been little more than an irrelevance. Its concentration on understanding the social problem to the detriment of reform itself was a major weakness. Throughout its history no resolutions of any weight and no petitions to Parliament or anywhere else were advanced. In 1930 the topic of discussion was a comparative study of social life in Wales and Denmark.[91] The social problem had by then become little more than an academic topic for too many of its members. The discussions lost their urgency and, in so doing, their relevance. Possibly the greatest achievement of the school was to foster ecumenical relations, particularly considering the bitterness which had marked the campaign for disestablishment of the Anglican Church in Wales. But the initial optimism and promise were soon dispelled as the school became little more than a talking-shop.

6. COPEC

The school was committed to the Conference on Christian Politics, Economics and Citizenship held in Birmingham in 1924.[92] Preparations for the conference had begun in February 1920, when a council of 300 was convened under the chairmanship of William Temple and vice-chairmanship of Alfred Garvie. The council prepared twelve different questionnaires of which almost 200,000 copies were circulated during spring 1922. From these and group discussions twelve reports were prepared and they formed the basis of discussion at the actual conference. There were 1,500 delegates representing all the Christian denominations in Britain except the Roman Catholics, although there were Catholics present and some had served on the commissions. *Y Tyst* hailed the conference as 'the most important Christian movement since the days of the Apostolic Church',[93] while G. A. Edwards asked, 'Is it too much to believe that this is

[91] Gwilym Davies, *Twenty-Five Years of the Welsh School of Social Service, 1911–1936* (n.d.), p.2.
[92] For Copec, see Will Reason (ed.), *The Proceedings of C.O.P.E.C.* (London, 1924).
[93] *Y Tyst*, 27 March 1924, p.1.

the most important Conference for a long time (*ers tro byd*)?'[94] The conference received so much publicity that the acronym COPEC virtually became accepted as a new word and it often appeared with lower-case lettering (Copec).

The underlying conviction of the conference reflected the primacy of theological liberalism. It was expressed in the belief that God's Fatherhood over the human family provided the dynamic for individual conversion that would lead to a wider service of mankind and the establishment of a just society. All the reports were underpinned by the same basic axiom: that it was possible for men to build the Kingdom of God as a response to the fundamental demand of Christ's teaching:[95] 'Doubtless the Kingdom of God stands for the depths of truth and experience which is greater than any social system as such. But although the Kingdom of God stands for more than social reform, it cannot mean any less than that.'[96]

In the correspondence to members of the original organizing committee, one essential condition was required: all members should be 'really concerned with the coming of the Kingdom of God and what can be done to bring it about'.[97] The conference held that the traditional emphasis on the individual's salvation was of utmost importance, but that each individual was not separate from society: 'Man must be saved in his entirety and in the unity of his person socially as well as individually, physically as well as spiritually, otherwise it is not "man" who is saved but rather some worthless apparition which is called a "soul".'[98] Copec set itself the task of expressing the social implications of the gospel. Then, its delegates were committed to preach those implications and put them into practice.[99] In this the chief role of the conference was to enlighten the minds of men and women through the provision of expert reports surveying all aspects of social life.[100] This would create a public opinion sympathetic to social change.

---

[94] *Y Goleuad*, 19 March 1924, p.8.

[95] Copec Reports, I, *The Nature of God and His Purpose for the World*, *passim*; also D. Miall Edwards, 'Natur Duw a'i bwrpas ynglŷn â'r byd', *Yr Efrydydd*, I/1 (October 1924), 5.

[96] Ysgol Gwasanaeth Cymdeithasol dros Gymru, *Yr Efengyl Gymdeithasol: Cynhadledd i ymdrin â Gwleidyddiaeth, Economeg a Dinasyddiaeth o Safbwynt Cristnogaeth* (n.d.), p.4.

[97] Letter to David Thomas, 3 March 1921, David Thomas Papers, NLW.

[98] *Yr Efengyl Gymdeithasol*, pp.4–5.

[99] Ibid., p.7; Ben Bowen Thomas, *Cenadwri Copec* (Wrexham, 1924), p.10.

[100] Charles E. Raven, *The Meaning of Copec* (n.d.).

Four major problems were identified by Copec: the need for decent housing, employment, an education system which was orientated towards the full development of the human personality, and international peace. According to Copec, Jesus Christ offered an answer to all these issues, but his answer had been entrusted to the church and could only be made real through its members' obedience to him. The conference called on all Christians to seek assiduously for answers to these problems and then to apply them to everyday life.[101] According to Thomas Rees, Copec marked a conversion to social thought on the part of the church.[102]

Copec attempted to give a systematic and wide-ranging Christian treatment of the recognized social problems of the day. These found expression in reports which, although lacking in positive direction, are redolent of a hope for a better future. All Copec could achieve was to encourage church members to stir up a Christian social conscience and to establish study groups that would treat the social problem. It achieved a remarkable level of co-operation between denominations which became a stimulus for future ecumenical projects, but due to its diversity it could not, and probably dared not, give any firm guidance on specific issues. More than anything, religious leaders throughout Britain were seeking to demonstrate through Copec that Christianity had an invaluable contribution to make to the social debate.[103] It seems, however, that they omitted to express any clear guidance on what that contribution should be. It was the protest of a church claiming desperately to have the vital message for social reform in a context where its witness was increasingly being ignored.

The details of the discussions and the reports published are not directly important. Many Welshmen had been involved in the planning stage of Copec. Gwilym Davies had been invited to join the executive committee, while D. Miall Edwards, John Morgan Jones (Bangor), Thomas Rees, Herbert Morgan, Daniel Lleufer Thomas, David Thomas (Talysarn, Gwynedd), Owen Prys and David Phillips (Bala Theological College) belonged to the general committee. As well as this, the Welsh School of Social

---

[101] William Temple, 'Copec', *Yr Efrydydd*, IV/4 (June 1924), 105.
[102] *Y Darian*, 21 August 1924, p.4.
[103] Cf. Raven, *Meaning of Copec*.

Service was recognized by the organizers as a pioneer in the field of Christian social concern.[104] However, very few Welshmen actually had prominent roles in the conference itself. There was a general recognition that Copec could only be a beginning and that much more work was needed.[105] However, nobody really knew how it could be continued. Its primary task was the identification of the eternal moral principles on which a just society could be built. Copec's major failing was an inability to translate those principles into practical policies. Many believed that it heralded a new period when the social mission of the gospel should be understood and the Kingdom of God made real in commerce, politics and citizenship. Following the reports, the conference considered that the next step would be to create a deep conviction in the conscience of each church member in order to 'Christianize civilization'.[106] In the words of Thomas Rees, 'there is a need to think, to persuade, to convince and to create the spirit of love and co-operation, and we must go to it to do that ourselves in Wales.'[107]

Certainly Copec engendered much publicity. A Copec Continuation Committee was established and numerous regional conferences organized.[108] During the main conference it was decided that the meetings of the 1924 School of Social Service should become a regional Copec conference, while one of the most successful Copec groups was based in Bangor.[109] A Copec conference was held in the city on 29 November 1924 and a Copec group established, whose members included Principal Thomas Rees and the Revd G. A. Edwards. In co-operation with the council, the group undertook a housing survey in Bangor. The council appointed a temporary sanitary inspector and contributed £30 towards costs, while the Copec group gave £50 and recruited eighty women to conduct the survey. Between

[104] Letter to David Thomas, 20 December 1920, David Thomas Papers, NLW.
[105] G. A. Edwards, 'Gwaith cymdeithasol yr Eglwys', *Yr Efrydydd*, I/11 (August 1925), 299; Ben Bowen Thomas, *Cenadwri Copec*, p.16; *Y Darian*, 16 October 1924, p.6; 11 December 1924, p.6; *Seren Cymru*, 4 April 1924, p.4; *Y Tyst*, 23 April 1925, p.9; *Y Goleuad*, 19 March 1924, p.8; 23 April 1924, p.8; Hugh Martin, 'The meaning of Copec', *The Welsh Outlook* (1924), 260; *The Treasury* (1925), 158.
[106] 'Copec a Chymru', *Yr Efrydydd*, II/6 (March 1926), 165.
[107] *Y Tyst*, 17 April 1924, pp.2–3; *Copec* (a pamphlet published by the Welsh School of Social Service, n.d.).
[108] Hugh Martin, 'Meaning of Copec', p.26.
[109] *Y Goleuad*, 23 April 1924, p.9; 10 December 1924, p.9.

April and August 1926, 2,261 houses were surveyed and 35 per cent of them were found to be overcrowded and of poor condition. The Copec group would later buy a plot of land and build twenty houses, let at rents of 5s. to a total of 122 people. Each house cost £400 to build, which was met by donations and subsidies. Rather than stimulating a more comprehensive building programme, however, the venture seemed to relieve the council of all concern for housing conditions.[110] Despite this, the success of the Bangor Copec group should not be dismissed entirely. It may not have achieved very much, but it demonstrated the ability of a group of ordinary people inspired by their Christian faith to recognize the need for social reform and in some small way to achieve improvements for the least fortunate in society. Unfortunately, the Bangor group appears to have been unique. Although Miall Edwards made strenuous efforts to promote Copec through lectures and addresses,[111] no other Copec groups or district conferences were formed in Wales. Despite all the publicity that Copec received in the denominational press at the time, within two years the Welsh School of Social Service was warning people that the publication of the Copec reports was a beginning and not an end. They needed continued study.[112] Copec ultimately failed to catch the imagination of the public, but more crucially it failed to catch the imagination of the ordinary church-goer.

7. STOCKHOLM

Part of the follow-up to Copec was the 'International Conference on Life and Work' held in Stockholm in 1925.[113] Despite official representation from the Union of Welsh Independents and the Presbyterian Church of Wales, this conference was even more remote from the people of Wales than Copec had been. Both *Y*

---

[110] P. Ellis Jones, *Bangor 1883–1983: A Study in Municipal Government* (Cardiff, 1986), pp.152–4; G. A. Edwards, 'A north Wales housing experiment', *The Welsh Outlook* (1928), 37.

[111] *Labour Voice*, 19 October 1924, p.1; *Y Tyst*, 8 May 1924, p.9.

[112] *Seren Cymru*, 29 January 1926, p.2; *Y Goleuad*, 27 January 1926, p.9.

[113] For details, see G. K. A. Bell (ed.), *The Stockholm Conference on Life and Work 1925: Official Report* (London, 1926); Edward Shillito, *Life and Work: The Universal Christian Conference on Life and Work in Stockholm, 1925* (London, 1926).

Tyst and *Y Goleuad* published detailed conference reports.[114] Far
from adding to the social understanding of Christianity, the chief
significance of the Stockholm conference was that it expressed a
theological reaction which would soon challenge the premisses of
theological liberalism.

The advent of an international conference was hailed by Miall
Edwards as the opportunity for Wales to take its place on the
world stage. The principles embodied in the conference reports
reflected the value and moral responsibility of the individual.
The church was to preach individual salvation and also to
assume its role as society's conscience.[115] The ideas mentioned
included the supreme value of the human soul, man's
stewardship over property, the need for co-operation between
capital and labour, and that industry ought to be based on
service and not on profits.[116] A committee was established to
ensure that the work would continue.[117]

The Stockholm conference was convened to underline the fact
that in the post-war world the social question had to be viewed in
an international context. As at Copec, the delegates at
Stockholm were generally optimistic in their belief that the
Kingdom of God could be established among mankind. The
Right Revd F. T. Woods, bishop of Winchester, in his opening
sermon at Stockholm Cathedral, echoed this faith. 'We believe in
the Kingdom of Heaven', he said. 'We are conspirators for its
establishment. That is why we are here. That is the meaning of
the conference.'[118] But it was during the Stockholm meetings
that the Liberal Theology of Britain and America came to grief.
Continental theologians were dismissive of Anglo-Saxon
optimism that the Kingdom of God could be built, while the
Britons were dismayed by the German contingent's pessimism.
'The bitter experiences of the last few years coloured the ideas of
these Germans,' claimed D. Miall Edwards. 'One could hear a

---

[114] The official representatives were D. Miall Edwards for the Union of Welsh
Independents, Revds E. O. Davies and E. R. Jones for the Presbyterian Church of Wales.
See reports in *Y Tyst*, 3 September 1925, p.1; 10 September 1925, p.7; 24 September
1925, p.6; *Y Goleuad*, 2 September 1925, p.8; 9 September 1925, p.8; 23 September 1925,
p.8; 7 October 1925, p.8.
[115] *Y Tyst*, 3 September 1925, p.1.
[116] *The Welsh Outlook* (1925), 189.
[117] *Y Tyst*, 24 September 1925, p.6.
[118] G. K. A. Bell, *Stockholm Conference*, p.38.

deep undertone of disappointment and hopelessness in their words.'[119]

The difference, however, was not merely dictated by a sense of hopelessness in defeat but by a completely different theological premiss. The division was between those who saw the Kingdom as an ethical concept, dependent on the actions of man, and those who believed it to be an apocalyptic concept, one which depended entirely on the actions of God.[120] Miall Edwards seems to have missed this completely. Because they rejected man's ethical role in building the Kingdom and left it as an individual experience in the heart of the believer, he could see no theological relevance in what the German theologians had to say. Edwards had himself advocated the improvement of society through the individual, but, in his view, the individual needed a social ideal to work towards and that ideal was the Kingdom.

It was not their disagreement with the Germans which was most disconcerting. Rather it was that the liberal theologians by and large refused to take their continental colleagues' theological stance at all seriously. They failed to realize that the reality of war had completely shattered the liberal belief in the automatic progress of mankind towards a new heaven and a new earth. For the German delegation it was not the ignominy of defeat but the fact of war which had swept aside the very foundations of Liberal Theology and had engendered in them a fresh understanding of man's sinfulness, his estrangement from God and his consequent need of redemption. It is a sad fact that ecumenical and international attempts to provide a genuinely Christian response to social problems should falter partly through an inability to understand different theological positions.

Stockholm represents the high point of Christian social activity, but instead of foreshadowing a more realistic embodiment of Christianity in social terms, it heralded a period of decline. It also marked the beginning of a theological reaction which would increase in strength and popularity to become a virtual norm after the Second World War. The Stockholm conference marked the end of Welsh Nonconformity's real interest in conferences. The continuation committee which later

---

[119] *Y Tyst*, 24 September 1925, p.6.
[120] A. E. Garvie, *The Christian Ideal for Human Society* (London, 1930), p.42.

established the Universal Council for Life and Work organized conferences in 1932 on unemployment, in 1933 on 'The church and the social order' at Rengsdorf, in 1934 on 'The church and the modern problem of the state' at Paris. In 1937 a conference was held in Oxford for the churches to 'survey their task'.[121] Although some Welshmen attended this last meeting, nothing but a passing reference was made to any of them in the press.[122]

8. INDIVIDUAL ATTEMPTS AT SOCIAL MISSION

Following the Great War, and particularly after the economic depression of the late 1920s, some ministers grasped the opportunity of presenting a slightly different practice of religion as they attempted to make the Christian message relevant to the working class. The recurring industrial unrest during the 1920s pointed accusingly to the inherent injustice of the social system. There was almost constant industrial strife, especially in the south Wales coalfield, with 1921 and 1926 standing out as particularly serious years. From 1926 the country was plunged into economic depression and the church was faced with the problem of mass unemployment and consequent utter degradation of the population, particularly with the introduction of the means test in 1931. During these two decades between the world wars, there were localized attempts, led by individual ministers, to help the impoverished communities of industrial south Wales.

R. J. Barker arrived in Tonypandy in September 1924 as minister of the Wesleyan Methodist Central Hall. The popularity of his message and methods was recalled by George Thomas, later speaker of the House of Commons: 'His sermons were never less than forty-five minutes long, yet people would queue for an hour before the service to get in and there were seldom less than a thousand to listen to him.'[123] In theology, Barker was a classic liberal, recognizing the divine in Jesus because of the inherent values of his life and death. God was 'the sum of human perfections' and 'the truly human is the truly divine'.

---

[121] J. H. Oldham (ed.), *Oxford Conference on Church, Community and State 1937: The Churches Survey Their Task* (London, 1937), p.15.
[122] Ibid., pp.291–306; listed are Revd Dr Richard Jones, Llandinam, Professor Joseph Jones, Brecon, Revd R. T. Evans, Swansea, Revd Professor W. R. Williams, Tanybryn.
[123] George Thomas, *George Thomas Mr Speaker* (London, 1985), p.29.

Consequently, 'when we look into the face of the perfect Man we see the Glory of God'.[124] As a result of this, Barker came to believe that men had to be helped to achieve moral perfection and not hindered by their environment and social status. For the men in south Wales who were plunged into an economic depression and unemployment following the General Strike of 1926, this was made virtually impossible. The distress in the Rhondda was at its worst during the years 1928–9, when the Cambrian Combine went into liquidation. It was during this time, with the Central Hall busy distributing clothing and arranging the adoption of families by others living in areas where the economic distress was not so great, that Barker began to perceive of Christianity as offering a social order in which all men were one and whose mutual care would alleviate the problems caused by social differences.[125] From this grew the idea for the Community House in Trealaw on which work commenced in spring 1928.[126]

The House was a place for employed and unemployed people of the district to meet for fellowship in the milk bar. It offered them a place to air their grievances through debate, to learn and practise crafts such as book-binding, toy-making and carpentry, as well as giving them opportunities for physical activity in the gymnasium. The ideal was fellowship in industry and human relationships, and the centre of the venture was the chapel to whose services all were invited, though none compelled, to attend. More than anything the Community House offered men, displaced by the social system and brutalized by irregularity of employment, a sense of belonging and sympathy.[127] Its whole ethos was rooted in the ideal that individuals should know Christ in order properly to serve their fellows. Service required that men assist in cases of poverty and also that they rid society of that poverty.[128] It seems that the Community House was relatively successful in attracting the men of the district to a form of religion which broke away from the Sabbath respectability and other-world piety of traditional Nonconformity.

[124] R. J. Barker, *Christ in the Valley of Unemployment* (London, 1936), p.50.
[125] Ibid., p.78.
[126] Ibid., p.86.
[127] Cyril E. Gwyther, 'Sidelights on religion and politics in the Rhondda Valley 1906–1926', *Llafur*, III/1 (1980), p.38.
[128] R. J. Barker, *Valley of Unemployment*, p.27; George Thomas, *George Thomas*, p.29.

The efforts of Leon Atkin were quite different from this.[129] His ministry has the appearance of continual confrontation with authority while, at the same time, he drew attention to, and provided for, the distress caused by depression and unemployment, particularly following the introduction of the means test. Atkin was sent to Risca in 1930 as a probationary minister with the Wesleyan Methodists. On arrival he discovered that the church was empty and the labour exchange full. A visit to the labour exchange followed, and this resulted in a year-long debate with local Communists on the subject of 'Christianity or Communism' at the Workingman's Institute, and to a packed church on Sundays. After a year Atkin went to the new Methodist Central Hall in Bargoed, paid for in part by a massive donation from Joseph Rank.

> With cinema seats for a thousand—which had to be filled; a cinematograph projection box; the last word in kitchens—waiting to be used, and enough extra-rooms to provide a hostel for the homeless, the Central Hall realised the practical Christian's dream of a seven-day religion.

The Central Hall was indeed open seven days a week. The unemployed were able to have free shaves and hair-cuts, while a workshop to repair shoes was established in the Hall. The unemployed could have their boots repaired for the cost of the leather. At other times meals were available. As a response to the means test, whereby some were denied help if a member of their family earned above the minimum allowed by the Act, twenty-eight men were lodged in the Central Hall to stop the flood of young men out of the area in search of work. As a result of this change of address, they were entitled to benefit. Threatened with 'obstructing the administration of His Majesty's Government', Atkin was told that he was liable to prosecution unless he sent the men back to their homes. He refused and lost the sympathy of his denomination. Following typically caustic remarks and a threatened libel suit, the Wesleyan authorities sought to send him to Cornwall which, it was thought, would have fewer distractions than south Wales. He refused to go and resigned from the ministry.

---

[129] Unless otherwise stated, the following information comes from a collection of newspapers loaned by the family of the Revd Leon Atkin. Most have no references.

Churches in Cardiff, Mountain Ash and Swansea asked him
to preach with a view to becoming their minister. He spent most
of the rest of his life as minister of St Paul's Congregational
Church, Swansea. During the 1930s he preached the
unemployed man's cause in sermons on 'Pews, pulpits and
pantries', 'Can a man be a Christian on the dole?', 'Moses and
the means test', all of which filled the church and brought
detectives to take notes each Sunday. The crypt of St Paul's
became a haven for the elderly, for down-and-outs and drug
addicts as Atkin attempted to give expression to his idea of
'practical' Christianity. From 1936 he sat as a Labour member of
Swansea Council. He had joined the Labour Party at the age of
sixteen 'as the intelligent sequel to my conversion to Christianity
at the age of fourteen'.[130] His nomination to the council was not
renewed in 1947 and he resigned his membership of the Labour
Party, successfully standing instead as the 'People's Candidate'.
All this he saw as 'a practical extension of my work as a minister'.

Atkin was unique. Not only was he a political minister in a
decade when most ministers were concentrating on more directly
religious matters but he was a rebel who was never at home in
any movement which he had not established himself. This
brought him in conflict with the Labour Party, but it also
ensured that most of his efforts were individualist and never
likely to do more than offer help to alleviate some suffering.
Everything he ever did was done alone, and almost always to
provoke authority, both ecclesiastical and civil, to take seriously
the needs of the least fortunate in society. He certainly was not
perfect. He had a weakness for alcohol, a particularly ironic vice
considering Welsh Nonconformity's obsession with temperance.
In his view this was the cause of his initial rejection by his fellow
ministers in Swansea. Atkin was often to be seen in local taverns
and achieved notoriety after being spotted in an advanced state
of intoxication in the company of Dylan Thomas. Despite this
weakness, or perhaps because of it, his efforts for the moral
outcasts and society's victims at great personal expense led
people to the almost inevitable conclusion that 'the Kingdom of
Heaven is of such as these'.

---

[130] Letter to Swansea Labour Association, 16 September 1947: copy in private family
collection.

The efforts of the Revd T. Alban Davies, Congregationalist minister of Bethesda, Ton Pentre, ensured that the suffering caused by the economic depression in single-industry communities remained a national concern. Daily sustenance had become an impossibility for many and Davies confessed that the suffering which resulted radicalized him thoroughly. Yet the churches appeared to be silent.[131] In theology he belonged to the predominant liberal school and thus the Kingdom for him was the goal of man's social and moral effort.[132] As a result, Davies was at the forefront of relief work in the Rhondda during the years of depression after the General Strike.[133] He kept the problems of the Rhondda alive in denominational and national circles. He drew attention to horrifying overcrowding[134] and to the chronic unemployment suffered in the Valleys since the disastrous lock-out of 1921. He warned that the situation was promoting Communism 'with [its] parochial spirit and [its] half and half, prejudiced and divisionary vision', as well as a violently anti-religious tendency in the area.[135] Rhondda ministers, all too aware of the threat of extreme political views, sent out an appeal in 1928 to help families suffering hardship as a result of unemployment. They requested money, clothes and shoes.[136] The appeal continued into 1930.[137] During that year the Con- gregational Union of England and Wales distributed clothing in areas most affected by unemployment. Of the three distribution centres established, two were located in south Wales, one in Cardiff and the other in Merthyr.[138]

Anxious to achieve positive reform, the Rhondda ministers sent a deputation to the Prime Minister, Ramsay MacDonald, in 1935 to argue for help for depressed areas. MacDonald showed a distinct lack of interest and concern for the plight of the

[131] T. Alban Davies, 'Impressions of life in the Rhondda Valley', in K. S. Harris (ed.), *Rhondda Past and Future* (Ferndale, 1974), p.15.

[132] Union of Welsh Independents Report, 1932, Denbigh, p.117; also R. Tudur Jones, *Yr Undeb* (Swansea, 1975), p.229.

[133] R. Tudur Jones, *Hanes Annibynwyr Cymru* (Swansea, 1966), p.284; *Y Tyst*, 26 January 1928, p.1; 2 February 1928, pp.8–9; 16 February 1928, p.9; 17 January 1929, p.3.

[134] *Y Tyst*, 26 January 1928, p.9.

[135] Ibid., 2 February 1928, p.9.

[136] Ibid., 22 November 1928, p.9; 17 January 1929, p.3; cf. T. Alban Davies, 'Distress in the Rhondda Valleys', *The Welsh Outlook* (1929), 10.

[137] *Y Tyst*, 20 December 1930, p.10.

[138] R. Tudur Jones, *Congregationalism in England, 1662–1962* (London, 1962), p.421; also *Congregational Year Book* (1930), 80. The third centre was in Durham.

unemployed in the Rhondda. For Alban Davies the meeting only served to demonstrate the inability of even a Prime Minister raised in the Labour Party to understand the problems of depression 200 miles from Westminster. 'You could see that the only thing he had on his mind', Davies later claimed, 'was his trip to an international conference in Stresa on the following day.'[139] This was a political watershed for Davies. He came to believe that for any improvement Wales had to control her own affairs and he moved into the nationalist camp.[140]

MacDonald had suggested that the Rhondda ministers investigate the situation and make their own proposals. Following his advice, they established the 'Rhondda Churches' Social Council' (*Cyngor Cymdeithasol Eglwysi'r Rhondda*) to gather information on the social and economic situation. However, they did not return to Downing Street for more than two years by which time Neville Chamberlain was Prime Minister. Davies found him to be 'as cold as an iceberg'.[141] This deputation resulted in similar disillusionment.[142] No solutions were formulated, and Chamberlain matched MacDonald in his unwillingness to act or even be moved by what he heard.

Alban Davies's ministry highlights the two major weaknesses of Nonconformist social activity in Wales and its allegiance to Liberal Theology. First, Nonconformists had no political voice in what was essentially a political matter. Events had forced Nonconformists in the Rhondda to return to some kind of political activity. Although their inspiration was compassion for the unemployed rather than support of party policy, it was a direct political action to approach the Prime Minister. The social movements of the period never contemplated even such a moderate gesture as this.

The second major weakness was that, despite the profile which social issues had achieved in Christian publications and conferences, Welsh Nonconformists had signally failed to translate them into practical measures. This almost certainly lies behind Davies's accusation of the church's 'silence'. Silent it had

[139] T. Alban Davies, 'Impressions of life', pp.16–17; also G. Alban Davies 'A son of the manse', in Meic Stephens (ed.), *A Rhondda Anthology* (Bridgend, 1993), p.136.
[140] T. Alban Davies, 'Impressions of life', pp.15–17; G. Alban Davies, 'Son of the manse', p.137.
[141] T. Alban Davies, 'Impressions of life', p.17.
[142] *Y Tyst*, 10 June 1937, p.4.

not been. There were twelve Copec reports, a report from Stockholm, not to mention the plethora of publications which dealt with the church and the social issue. What had struck Davies was that when the people needed clothing and sustenance, the church could neither provide them nor ensure that they were provided by the appropriate authority. Such criticism came as a natural result of the theology which Davies and others had adopted. Human personality was of ultimate value and thus possessed certain innate and basic rights, while its moral task was to build the Kingdom where everyone's need would be supplied. The most damning indictment of the whole period is that despite the general acceptance of such theology, very little of a practical nature ever came of it. In the end, the task of immediate relief for the suffering masses depended on the energy and compassion of individual local ministers like Alban Davies. In the dark days of the economic depression, his witness and ministry in the Rhondda stand out as a radiant beacon offering hope to a population ravaged by the cruelties of unemployment and poverty. There can be no more fitting epitaph to a man who merely tried to live out his Lord's commission to be salt and light in the world.

A further example of Liberal Theology taken to its logical conclusion is to be found in the history of Tom Nefyn Williams's brief association with Tumble, which demonstrates how theological controversy prevented a social expression of the Christian faith. Interestingly, it was not the clash between the prevailing theological liberalism and the newer Dialectic Theology of the continent that caused this controversy, but the clash between the ultra-liberal, almost humanistic theology of a young minister and the conservatism of a denomination committed to a Calvinistic Confession of Faith. It highlighted the importance of Christian doctrine and the consequent need for the one thing more than any other that was lacking during this period, a truly doctrinal formulation of the social implications of the gospel.

Tom Nefyn Williams[143] arrived in Tumble in the Gwendraeth valley of east Carmarthenshire in 1925. One of his first actions was to bring the people who had left the church following the

---

[143] For Tom Nefyn Williams (1895–1958), see his autobiography *Yr Ymchwil* (Denbigh, 1949); also William Morris (ed.), *Tom Nefyn* (Caernarfon, 1962).

adoption of left-wing politics back into contact with church members and activity.[144] A tension soon developed within the congregation between those members who desired a total separation of spiritual and political matters and those who believed that the church should lead in the '*gwerin*'s battle'.[145] Nonconformity suffered due to the political differences between the Liberal and the Socialist in the pews. This tension within the chapel congregations occurred in the context of the general withdrawal of ministers from overt political activity, and who then maintained a tactful silence on contentious issues. Williams made no such withdrawal and saw a need for his religious faith and practice to be linked to social action that would inevitably lead him into political debate. Interestingly, however, when the opportunity presented itself for him to stand as a Labour MP at the invitation of the Ceredigion Labour Party, he declined.[146] This decision suggests that he believed the Christian ministry to be the appropriate sphere of his activity.

The issue which excited Williams more than any during his ministry was that of housing. He considered that the building of an impressive chapel to worship God while the worshippers lived in slum conditions was nothing but 'empty worship' (*coeg addoli*). As a result, he surveyed the houses belonging to the coal company on the High Street, making notes of their condition. After the survey, he sent a circular to all company managers and shareholders detailing the condition of the houses, believing that this in itself would create a 'conscience in favour of improvement'.[147]

Williams's theology was orientated towards liberal modernism and a practical application of his beliefs:

> . . . devotion without responsibility is not enough; prayer without work is not enough; the Father's satisfaction on the Mount of Transfiguration is not enough without satisfying the father of the epileptic boy on the plain. That is the experiment (*yr arbraw*), its ecclesiological aspect and its social work.[148]

---

[144] *Yr Ymchwil*, p.99.
[145] Ibid., pp.155–6.
[146] *Y Darian*, 14 March 1929, p.1.
[147] *Yr Ymchwil*, pp.117–18.
[148] Ibid., p.121.

But the argument became one of theological beliefs rather than of the embodiment of Christian principles in personal and social life:

> . . . the whole matter came to revolve around the difficulties of metaphysics. There was no word of the simple experiment (*arbraw syml*), nor of the zealous support of over 230 chapel members. There was no word about the protest against imprisoning the miners, nor the struggle to repair the High Street. There was no word about establishing the movement to win back for religion those who had placed their whole trust in the politics of the left, nor of the slovenly and insignificant, personal effort at following Jesus Christ.[149]

In order to make a clear statement of his theological views Williams produced a pamphlet, *Y Ffordd yr Edrychaf ar Bethau* (The Way I Look at Things). Although he protested that it was intended as a 'confidential document',[150] it was clear that he wanted the Methodist Connexion to pronounce judgement on his theological views.[151] His work at this time was surrounded by the air of a martyr whose fate was to suffer persecution, for he must have known that his theological views were unacceptable to the Methodists. Theologically, Williams was an immanentist. He referred to God as the 'great Spirit that seeks to realize itself in the expression and life of the world' (p.11). He spoke of this experience as that of the 'good, the true and the beautiful' (p.15), and these were the three eternal elements which he saw as the basis of the Trinity (p.18). God was revealed in the presence of true humanity, orientated towards self-sacrificial service and love within the world. Jesus was the supreme example of this humanity, and salvation was achieved through the moral influence of Christ, which led men and women to commune with the eternal (p.17). Despite calls for clemency,[152] Williams was expelled on grounds of heterodoxy from the Calvinistic Methodist Connexion at the Nantgaredig Association in August 1928.[153]

[149] Ibid., p.129.
[150] Ibid., p.132.
[151] Tom Nefyn Williams, *Y Ffordd yr Edrychaf ar Bethau* (Dolgellau, 1928), p.3.
[152] *Y Darian*, 3 May 1928, p.2; R. J. Jones, *Troi'r Dail* (Swansea, 1962), p.79.
[153] For the announcement see William Morris (ed.), *Tom Nefyn*, p.28; also *Y Goleuad*, 5 September 1928, p.2.

To an extent, Williams's ideas were a natural progression within theological liberalism and revealed the distinct influence of Idealist thought. The creation and the divine creator had, in his mind, formed one great Whole, with moral principles forming the basis of the universe. As a result, every human action became an act of worship and every experience a means of receiving grace. As everyday life was exalted by the presence of the immanent God, the chapel, with its religious services and prayer meetings, would lose its status. On the other hand, however, Williams's ideas did not reflect those of Wales's foremost liberal theologians. The chief characteristics found in their work were the eternal value of humankind based on the Fatherhood of God and the brotherhood of man. The goal of creation was the establishment of the Kingdom of God on earth through human sanctification and effort. There was, however, no mention of the Kingdom, God the Father or the brotherhood of man in Williams's work. Instead, he presented an impersonal God known only as a force in the universe, a force which could be experienced in life but not one that could be known personally. While Liberal Theology was generally assumed to lend itself naturally to social concern, Williams's theological statement made no direct reference to social and political work. His theology was not specifically geared towards practical and social applications of the faith.

In many ways Williams was a theological anachronism. The ideas he expressed were not new: the current theological ideas were those of the Dialectic School on the continent led by Karl Barth, Emil Brunner and others, and were far removed from Williams's own views at this period. His significance is therefore difficult to assess. He was a minister who, under the conviction that he was fulfilling Christ's commission, tried to apply his Christianity in a practical way and bring improvement to the social conditions of his village. In returning to the Calvinistic Methodist Church in 1932, Williams, at least by implication, recanted the views contained in *Y Ffordd yr Edrychaf ar Bethau*. He was therefore left without a social or theological understanding other than that of his denomination. He was not an important national or denominational figure and he never achieved prominence again. After a short period of notoriety, which ensures his mention in the history books, he fades almost into obscurity.

The importance of the incident lies not in the inadequacy of the Methodist response. Methodists had every right to reject a minister who refused to conform to their theological beliefs.[154] What it does show is that very often social concern went hand in hand with a theological liberalism which occasionally went far beyond what was acceptable even in a predominantly liberal environment. By 1928 it seems that it was the theological controversy which this aroused, far more than the scandalous social conditions prevalent in the western valleys, that was considered important. What was theologically right and acceptable was gradually becoming the primary concern of Welsh Nonconformists. Judging from the absence of any direct social references in *Y Ffordd yr Edrychaf ar Bethau*, the conclusion must be that Williams concurred with this view, even though he had also been convinced at the time of his expulsion that the 'church must secure better houses for the people, and do away with slums before the lower classes could be saved'.[155]

Nonconformist efforts can be contrasted with those of the Anglican Church. Disestablished from 1920, the Church in Wales looked to consolidate its position and establish its own identity. As a result, it tended to be rather cautious in issues of non-ecclesiastical policy. Having said that, there were exceptions, such as the charismatic Timothy Rees, enthroned as bishop of Llandaf in 1931. From the beginning of his episcopate, Rees had declared an interest in the lives of those who suffered in the depressed areas of his diocese. He gathered about him groups of working men and industrialists who eventually formed the Llandaf Industrial Committee, which formulated plans to tackle economic hardship and unemployment, and formed a deputation to the minister of labour in 1935. Again, such an initiative brought some relief to those living in the depressed districts, mostly, perhaps, as a demonstration of solidarity. But these initiatives depended on the strength and commitment of certain individuals. The Church in Wales, on the whole, had other concerns during this period.[156]

---

[154] See Kenneth O. Morgan, *Rebirth of a Nation: Wales 1880–1980* (Oxford, 1981), pp.199–200.

[155] *The Tom Nefyn Controversy: An Account of the Crisis in Welsh Calvinistic Methodism* (Port Talbot, 1929), pp.33–4.

[156] See D. T. W. Price, *A History of the Church in Wales in the Twentieth Century* (Penarth, 1990), p.18; J. L. Rees, *Timothy Rees of Mirfield and Llandaff: A Biography* (London, 1945);

9. THE CHAPEL AND UNEMPLOYMENT

It is important to recognize that by the time these men, Barker, Atkin, Davies, Williams and Rees, were faced with the problem of labour, the situation had changed dramatically from the period before the Great War and the activities of David Pughe and the Cardiff conference. Instead of the estrangement of the industrial workers from the churches, they were having to deal with the problem of unemployment. It was, therefore, not the inherent value of man in his field of employment that was the underlying principle of their work but the inherent value of man who deserved employment and required work in order to live his life to the full. The five men were dealing with the specific problem of labour in the conviction that the church had a unique mission to the oppressed in society. They did not seek a solution to the more general problems of society, nor did they offer distinctively political solutions. Although Atkin was a local councillor even he tended to see his work as primarily spiritual. He supported a political party which he believed to be compatible with his own vision and principles. These ministers simply sought to serve the working class in some way, thus ensuring that the church became a relevant part in their lives. As this occurred they hoped that the working class would come into closer union with the church. In achieving this, however, they would also help, in some small way, to alleviate the suffering caused by the social problem.

Despite the efforts of these men, there is a sense in which the churches were failing to keep up with events during the 1920s and to reinterpret their message to meet the vastly different social conditions which had to be faced at the end of the decade. Nonconformist social concern had been provoked by issues of industrial hardship and injustice, particularly the dangerous and unhealthy living and working conditions endured by so many. Following the General Strike, unemployment became the main social problem. Although unemployment, which cheapened human personality and rendered men worthless, could be challenged by the principles of Liberal Theology,

Nonconformists did not really know how they should or could react to it. The Revd E. Wyn Roberts recognized the good work done by churches which opened their buildings as meeting places and workshops for the unemployed. Though he was convinced something should be done, he did not know how to proceed.[157] The Glamorgan Congregationalists passed a resolution in 1935 which sought to reflect Christian principles in the face of unemployment. The resolution was that:

> loyalty to Christ compels us to believe that man is more important than a system, industry and wealth and on account of that, [we] are of the opinion that a society that turns aside thousands of its best workers and leaves them to an idle life, is either self-condemned or guilty of neglecting its duties and liability.

In addition to their protest, they also offered a practical scheme to help to nullify the effects of economic depression. They suggested that the school-leaving age be raised; that pensions should be paid at the age of sixty; that the hours of labour should be reduced without any corresponding reduction in wages; and that the unemployed should receive reasonable maintenance and be provided with useful leisure activities.[158] Some of these the churches could have instituted themselves but others required the determined effort of the government of the day, which reflected how political the issues actually were. The question was: how were the Congregationalists to get their voices heard by those in power? In fact, they made no real attempt to be heard. According to the principles Nonconformists had established since 1910, concrete social change depended on MPs who had been so influenced by the preaching of an ethical gospel that they would fight for justice through Parliament. This was a far more difficult task than it initially appeared, and though their protest was a genuine expression of sympathy, it was ultimately futile.

The issue of the church's relationship to politics was, then, of seminal importance. Ministers like the Revd Morgan Watcyn-Williams had hoped for a 'new synthesis' of politics and religion following the war in order to build a better future. He had

---

[157] *Y Goleuad*, 17 May 1933, p.8.
[158] *Labour Voice*, 1 June 1935, p.1.

believed that the building of a new society was fundamentally a political task, and as religion had a contribution to make, it too was political. As far as he was concerned religion and politics needed each other to be most effective. Thus, 'a religion that had no political implications, and a politics which is without religious inspiration are alike dead'.[159] But he came to believe that the 'politics of the Lord's Prayer' were required where the Kingdom is established on earth, and daily bread and forgiveness are available to all.[160] He was convinced that the call to excise politics from religion was the result of people believing that 'mercy and the love of the Kingdom of God were out of place in industrial employment'. He believed that mercy would find political and social expression through the establishing and building of Jerusalem, the Holy City.[161] This was to be accomplished, of course, through man's moral effort.

The Revd Llewelyn Boyer believed that the apparent popularity of Communism amongst some elements of society had arisen as a protest against the failure of the church to give any definite leadership in political and social matters. His advice was that the church itself should devise a specifically Christian political policy. The possibilities of such a proposal were wide-ranging but what precisely Boyer intended is unclear as he, too, ultimately believed that the church should concentrate on individual regeneration.[162]

The argument was advanced that politics should be kept out of the church but that the church should not be kept out of politics. The glibness with which this was argued is startling, as was the amazing ability to ignore the need and possibility for even Christian principles to be embodied in practical policies.[163] The overriding concern was that the church should not actively support one political party over another. The church could influence politics by supplying men of high moral character who would devote their personal lives to the establishment of better political systems for the service of mankind. It was the direct and specific political comments by ministers from pulpits which were

[159] Morgan Watcyn-Williams, *From Khaki to Cloth* (Caernarfon, 1949), p.115.
[160] *Idem, When the Shoe Pinches* (London, 1936), p.78.
[161] *Idem, The Beatitudes in the Modern World* (London, 1935), pp.80–1.
[162] *Y Tyst*, 28 March 1935, p.10; 4 April 1935, p.10.
[163] D. R. Jones, 'Yr Eglwys a gwleidyddiaeth', *Y Dysgedydd* (1927), 179.

rejected. If social and political issues were to be treated at all
from the pulpit, then ministers were generally expected to restrict
their comments to the preaching of principles. There was
nothing new in this. For twenty years or so Nonconformists had
argued that the church should remain separate from political
movements and to a great extent this had been accomplished.
The fact that the argument was still being promulgated in the
1930s suggests, however, that some Nonconformists at least had
maintained a political link or argued for its necessity. Herbert
Morgan had continually argued a similar thesis and, significantly, a view prevailed amongst the industrial population that the
church should take sides and preach politics. The response of the
Young People's Guild at Bethesda chapel, Ynysmeudwy, to the
question 'Should ministers preach politics?' late in 1927 was a
resounding 'Yes'.[164] It is not clear whether the young people
intended that ministers be politically active in a party sense, or
whether the church should rise above party sectarianism and
give a 'Christian response' to the burning political and social
questions of the day. Although one suspects that they preferred
the former option, that does not make this incident any the less
significant. Young people, at least in Ynysmeudwy, believed that
the church's role was to voice an opinion in political matters
even if it could not provide leadership. The fact is that, by then,
the battle was being lost. Elements within the churches were
beginning to stress its primary task of saving souls[165] or, in liberal
theological terms, of encouraging people to recognize their
responsibility in the light of their personal experience.[166] A new
man would make new surroundings.[167] At the same time some
within the congregations were rejecting ministerial involvement
in politics.[168] This simply added to the confusion and left
Nonconformists ultimately unable to offer a clear definition of
purpose. This was an accusation made against the church by

---

[164] *Labour Voice*, 10 December 1927, p.6.

[165] Ibid., 1 October 1927, p.1.

[166] *Y Tyst*, 14 April 1927, p.3; 21 April 1927, p.3; 15 August 1935, p.9; 6 April, 1936,
p.8; *Y Goleuad*, 3 August 1927, p.10; Herbert Morgan, 'Cynhadledd Urdd y Deyrnas', *Yr
Efrydydd*, III/10 (July 1928), 262–4; 'G.J.', 'Bywyd personol a threfn cymdeithas', *Yr
Efrydydd*, XI/2 (November 1934), 30–4; W. D. Davies, *Datguddiad Duw Efrydiau Diwinyddol*
(Caernarfon, 1934), p.180.

[167] *Y Goleuad*, 25 May 1932, p.7.

[168] A. H. Jones, *Obedient Servant*, p.35.

Table 5.2 Membership figures for the three main Nonconformist denominations in Wales, 1926–1939

Year	Baptists	Independents	Calvinistic Methodists
1926	130,098	–	189,727
1927	129,758	134,971	189,132
1928	128,747	129,732	187,892
1929	126,203	129,382	186,194
1930	125,704	125,806	185,827
1931	124,891	124,083	185,239
1932	124,134	121,070	184,257
1933	123,068	120,140	183,044
1934	122,840	117,483	182,608
1935	122,375	117,961	182,221
1936	120,595	115,716	180,999
1937	118,580	108,320	179,880
1938	117,018	107,735	179,386
1939	116,813	105,576	177,448

Source: John Williams, *Digest of Welsh Historical Statistics*, II (Cardiff, 1985), pp.249–345.

some within its ranks: that the service and function of the church were unclear to its members.[169]

In some respects by this time the writing was on the wall. Welsh Nonconformity at the end of the 1920s was plagued by mounting confusion concerning both its theology and its social role. The adoption of Liberal Theology and social concern had not had the desired effect. They had neither reformed society nor revived the church. In 1933 John Morgan Jones, Bangor, who was by that time the leading Welsh exponent of Liberal Modernism and also a keen supporter of the Labour Party, noted that the churches were no longer central to the national life.[170] Actual membership of the main Nonconformist denominations had been declining since 1926 (see table 5.2) and the

[169] *Seren Cymru*, 12 August 1932, p.2.
[170] John Morgan Jones, 'Religion', *The Welsh Outlook* (1933), 323.

denominational press bemoaned both the numerical decline and the loss of Nonconformist influence in society.[171] The declining interest in religion is perhaps demonstrated by the fate of a column in the *Labour Voice* entitled 'Around the churches'. Introduced from July 1933, the column reported sermons preached at the various churches in the Swansea valley.[172] In less than a year it had disappeared.

Almost as soon as the fires of the 1904–5 revival had died down, Nonconformists had begun to express concern at falling congregations. By the late 1920s they were positing several reasons for the decline in chapel allegiance. Scientific advance had offered new pursuits to fill leisure time, while new approaches to concepts of sin and salvation had led to some departing from the churches.[173] Alternative sources for the religious spirit had been discovered, and Nonconformists expressed alarm about the increasing interest, particularly amongst cultured and literary circles, in pseudo-religious movements such as Humanism, Spiritualism, Communism and the New Morality, while they also recognized the labour movement's religious appeal.[174] On a more personal level, the economic depression and consequent unemployment were blamed for the decline in church attendance. Ordinary people felt that they had no suitable apparel to attend chapel services or that they could not contribute to the funds as they would have liked. They questioned why the church did not condemn capitalism as the cause of their poverty and asked why God did not give them a job.[175] The church was condemned for preaching an irrelevant message and not taking practical measures to meet the needs of society that had been rapidly transformed from those of post-war optimism to those of economic depression and collapse. Nonconformists themselves were quick to point out that the weaknesses lay with the church and not Christ himself.[176] It was claimed that men had not drifted from religion because they

---

[171] E.g. Brinley Thomas, 'The organisation of religion in Wales', *The Welsh Outlook* (1929), 364; D. Glyndwr Richards, 'Yr Eglwys a phroblemau heddiw', *Y Dysgedydd* (1932), 193–204; *Seren Cymru*, 14 August 1936, p.2; 12 July 1935, p.2; *Y Tyst*, 18 July 1939, p.8.

[172] *Labour Voice*, 8 July 1933, p.1.

[173] Brinley Thomas, 'Organisation', p.365.

[174] D. Tecwyn Evans, 'Crefydd Cymru heddiw', *Yr Eurgrawn* (1929), 281; R. Jones Williams, 'Cristionogaeth a gwareiddiad', *Yr Eurgrawn* (1935), 325ff.; W. R. Williams, 'Yr Eglwys, cymdeithas a'r wladwriaeth', *Yr Efrydydd* (1937), 57; *Seren Cymru*, 26 July 1935, p.8.

[175] Morgan Watcyn-Williams, *When the Shoe Pinches*, p.78.

[176] *Seren Cymru*, 12 July 1935, p.2; *Y Tyst*, 26 July 1934, p.3.

had lost their religious beliefs.[177] Other reasons, therefore, had to
be offered which often centred on the inadequacies of the church's
witness in the world. It was posited that many had lost faith in the
ability of the church to preach the true gospel[178] or even that
religion was so far separated from the realities of life itself as to be
an irrelevance.[179] Flight from the chapels, liberal Nonconformists
believed, stemmed from the general disappointment over the lack
of an effective Christian contribution to the social debate.[180]
Ordinary people were beginning to perceive that the social
message of the church did not accord with that of the New
Testament, a point which fuelled the claim that a theological
reinterpretation along liberal lines was essential. Nonconformists
were prepared to accept that much true religion existed outside
the church,[181] although most rejected outright the idea that the
highest religious life could be lived apart from the church.[182] In
some respects, such a notion was inevitable given the current
theological presuppositions. If the goal of religion was the
development of character and personality, there was nothing to
stop people developing their characters outside the church.
Indeed, the popular belief in immanence maintained that
character development was inevitable. These points are highly
significant. They do not prove beyond doubt that the inadequacy
of the church's social witness had caused the masses to forsake
religious observance in the chapels. They do show, however, that
while Nonconformists were aware of many possible causes for the
dwindling congregations, they could discover no satisfactory
means of redeeming the situation.

10. The principles and theology of Nonconformist social concern

From as early as 1910 the agenda was set for Nonconformist
social concern and the development of a Nonconformist social

---

[177] Morgan Watcyn-Williams, *From Khaki to Cloth*, p.171.
[178] John Morgan Jones, 'Ymneilltuaeth yng Nghymru heddiw', *Yr Efrydydd*, IV/6 (March 1928), 158.
[179] *Seren Cymru*, 18 September 1936, p.6.
[180] D. R. Jones, 'Yr Eglwys', p.181.
[181] John Morgan Jones, 'Ymneilltuaeth', p.157.
[182] *Y Tyst*, 31 March 1927, p.3.

conscience. Direct political action, except on the part of certain individuals, was eschewed in favour of a rediscovery of the church's spiritual mission. Liberal Theology, particularly that of Albrecht Ritschl and Adolf Harnack, provided its doctrinal underpinning. It was considered natural to criticize the status quo and to seek the removal of all things that hindered the development of personality and character. The status of the individual still remained foremost even within the Kingdom of God which, when finally established, would be the environment where individuals could flourish rather than the perfect society understood in a corporate sense.

It was generally accepted that, in spite of the inherent value of human personality, differences in natural ability made social distinctions inevitable.[183] The Nonconformist argument was that, although social differences would almost certainly continue to exist, they would no longer divide humankind. In the Christian Commonwealth there would be a full opportunity for everyone to reach his or her potential regardless of social standing and financial position. This could only be achieved through individuals 'living along the lines of sacrificial love'.[184] Thus would the Kingdom of God emerge, and the hope for the future of both the labour movement and the church was bound up in their ability to co-operate in its establishment.[185]

The Kingdom was propagated as an ethically induced social state. Thus, human effort and service, the highest moral function, were believed to reveal the Kingdom on earth. This concept came increasingly to the fore during the 1930s. The Kingdom would be established on earth through the dedicated service of mankind.[186] It was posited by many that, more than anything else, the need of the age was for a spirit of service in all aspects of life.[187] Liberal Theology was still sufficiently strong to insist that service, and not the accuracy of its creeds, would ultimately measure the church's value.[188] W. D. Davies insisted

[183] J. H. Howard, *Which Jesus? Young Britain's Choice* (Dolgellau, 1926), p.60.
[184] Ibid., p.74.
[185] Ibid., p.100.
[186] Edward Jones, 'Pethau Cesar a phethau Duw', in E. Curig Davies (ed.), *Llef y Gwyliedydd* (Llanelli, 1927), p.59.
[187] *Labour Voice*, 27 January 1934, p.4; *Y Tyst*, 21 April 1927, p.3; 6 April 1936, p.8; *Y Goleuad*, 10 April 1929, p.9; J. Dyfnallt Owen, Union of Welsh Independents Report, 1936, Bangor, p.135.
[188] J. H. Howard, *Jesus the Agitator* (Wrexham, 1934), p.9.

that the individual could discover 'contentment' (*dedwyddwch*) through service alone: 'Religion is the service of man in the power of the vision of the Divine Value. And in this consecration to the great aims of Freedom, Health, a Fair Opportunity for All, Peace and Goodwill on earth, man grasps contentment.'[189] Such a quotation demonstrates how the nature of religion itself had changed. Some Nonconformists now perceived it exclusively as the service of man. *Seren Cymru*, the organ of the Welsh Baptists, seemed particularly predisposed at this time to emphasize service. It presented the ideal of ethical stewardship[190] which required that service should not be compulsory. Rather it should be offered freely from the 'inducement of the love of Christ'.[191] Christ called people out of the world in order to send them back to purify the world through their good works. 'We should try to leave the world a little better than when we came to it, and who is to bring this about—who but we?'[192]

This appeal for service was one that was made to each individual Christian. Although these articles did not explain why service was necessary, they hinted at a theological rather than a humanitarian answer; service was to be a fruit of the believer's love for Christ. As a result, they offered no explicit social advice; they only stated that something should be done. *Seren Cymru* further emphasized the need for service by reprinting articles by Wyre Lewis.[193]

Service as the expected result of individual conversion continued to be promulgated in the pages of *Seren Cymru* during the 1930s.[194] Although this appeared to be the same message as had previously been promulgated by Nonconformists, *Seren Cymru* now appeared to be emphasizing Jesus's supernatural ideal rather than the social. In this scheme, Jesus was primarily regarded not as teacher but as saviour.[195] Thus it was that the Nonconformist churches tended to return to a wholly individualistic gospel. They could not ignore the claim that regenerated

---

[189] W. D. Davies, *Cristnogaeth a Meddwl yr Oes* (Caernarfon, 1932), p.220.
[190] *Seren Cymru*, 18 December 1936, p.2.
[191] Ibid., 18 February 1927, p.2; 5 February 1937, p.8.
[192] Ibid., 25 February 1927, p.2.
[193] Ibid., 31 October 1930, p.2; for Wyre Lewis, ibid., 5 September 1937, p.8; 12 February 1937, p.8; 26 March 1937, p.8.
[194] Ibid., 14 November 1930, p.4; 28 August 1931, p.4.
[195] Ibid., 28 August 1931, p.4.

people would form a better society, but they were increasingly calling for the church to concentrate on its primary task of preaching the gospel. The redemption wrought in Christ, however that was understood, was thought of in essentially individual terms. As religion had been interpreted as the moral dynamic which would encourage men to live lives dedicated to serve each other, it is hardly surprising that a theological reaction would ensue. By the end of the 1930s there was a hint that although individual redemption had been stressed because it led to a better society, Nonconformists were coming to realize that they had over-emphasized the importance of the latter to the detriment of the former.

Inspired by the conclusions of biblical criticism, it was continually stressed during these years that because the words of Jesus were not directly relevant to the peculiar problems of post-war industrial society, an effort, both intellectual and physical, was required on the part of each individual to discover the main principles of his teaching in order to apply them to human life. As has been noted, the principal element of Christ's teaching was recognized as the principle of service. This would bring about a revolution in the concept of Christian witness which would continue to play a part in church life throughout the twentieth century. Hitherto, the sole purpose of Christian witness had been the conviction of sin leading to specific Christian conversion. Certainly from 1911, Welsh Nonconformist theologians were formulating a concept of Christian service to which conversion would no longer be deemed essential. The aim of Christian witness became service of fellow human beings rather than the conviction of sin and the preaching of salvation in Christ. The emphasis on 'service' led to a redefining of Nonconformist social effort, and as social problems were discussed it gradually became clear that the whole ethos of the church's mission had been called in question. Nonconformists were trying to interpret the church's social role in the context, first, of rapid industrialization and, then, of the horrors of war. They had departed from their traditional view that the church existed merely to convert men and women to Christianity. Instead, Nonconformists adopted the wider responsibility of providing the vision and inspiration of a better society, with the corroborative task of educating the population in its values. The continued emphasis on personal responsibility did not merely illustrate a retention of the conservatism of previous years but formed part of a wider vision of a new, redeemed society. It also meant that the responsibility for practical measures lay firmly with individuals. The church would inspire enthusiasm for social reform but not direct it in any particular way. Because they did not promise the immediate creation of a fair and just society, the Nonconformists' aims were almost totally ignored by the labour movement. Even the possibility of Nonconformist success in solving the social problem was vitiated later in the decade by a theological reaction that undermined the ideological basis of chapel religion.

The difficulty with the churches' policy arose because it depended, first, on ministers encouraging their congregations to believe that these principles would lead to social improvement, and, then, on members' enactment of those principles in their daily lives. Those who promulgated the ideals and principles of the Kingdom had no control over their implementation. Furthermore, nobody explained how this could best be effected. Thus, the inspiring imagery of the Kingdom of God remained an abstract concept doomed ultimately not to be embodied in a fair and just social system.

In the light of all this, the question of labour's withdrawal from the churches very quickly disappeared from view as Nonconformists tried to make their voices heard in the social debate. The question of Socialism was virtually ignored, reflecting the fact that it was considered too overtly political an issue. The Nonconformists were trying to create their own niche from which to develop a unique contribution to the nation's social well-being. In so doing their priorities, and their view of mission, changed. Where Nonconformists made their greatest mistake was not to realize that the war had decisively challenged the prevailing theological view of the dignity of man and his ability to construct the Kingdom of God on earth, in favour of the more traditional view of man's utter depravity.

11. CONCLUSIONS

By the 1920s, four main characteristics of Nonconformist social concern in Wales had become obvious. Although they had been expressed before the Great War, they all gained a wider acceptance and a more definite expression following the cessation of hostilities.

First, there was the growing conviction that social work, particularly among the young, needed to be an inter-denominational affair. The social problem was considered too great an issue to be the subject of religious sectarianism. This would result in fervent interdenominational activity in the 1920s and pave the way for the ecumenical movement after the Second World War. In practice this required the establishment of organizations which were inter-church and non-political. The whole involvement of the church in the discussion of social problems was constantly threatened by one underlying question: what is the role of the church in society? The rationale of the Welsh School of Social Service would insist that the church had no role beyond that of public and corporate worship and the preaching of the gospel. The school's *raison d'être* was to remove the contentious political and social questions of the day from the church and answer them in an agency which, though Christian, was ultimately separate from the church. The establishment of regional committees suggests that Copec, too, must have agreed with this philosophy. In the social and religious context of the 1920s, this appears to have been the only real option. Driven by fear of politically motivated congregational divisions, Non-conformists sought to establish movements other than those already provided by the church. The churches believed that they needed further organizations which would catch the imagination of the young and those who rarely, or never, entered a place of worship. But this also meant that the churches themselves were in danger of being omitted from social affairs. This occurred in the context of ideological developments that promoted a growing acceptance of the idea that the establishment of the Kingdom would occur through the work of the Spirit outside the church.[196] With hindsight, this was probably a mistake. Rather than attempt to create a whole new body, the church leaders' goal should have been a wider-ranging sympathy within the church for their social Christianity.

---

[196] E.g. *Glamorgan Free Press*, 2 April 1909, p.3; cf. Owen Jones, 'Perthynas dyn a chymdeithas', *Y Drysorfa* (1921), p.408.

Secondly, the Nonconformists concentrated their social concern on the need for knowledge and education.[197] Fundamental to the underlying ideology of the period was man's potential for self-redemption through moral and intellectual effort. The stress on education was a natural implication of ethical Idealism. It was not merely self-redemption through the immanent God which philosophical Idealism had brought to theology but also the conviction that ultimate reality was to be found in the realm of moral ideas. It was the dissemination of these ideas which would result in the enlightenment and conversion of men, followed by their commitment to embody such ideas in their everyday lives. Training was vital to this scheme. Despite recognizing this fact, little was actually produced to encourage the process. Denominational meetings tended simply to repeat the need for adequate handbooks without ensuring that they were ever produced.

Thirdly, and most importantly, Nonconformists realized that this should be the task of every high-minded citizen. Even when interpreted in social terms, individual personality remained the principal element in the scheme of salvation. Thus, it was the dehumanizing effect of industry that motivated the church's concern.[198] Society could only be reformed through the moral renewal of individuals and it was that, rather than direct social reform, which was the church's goal.[199] The imagery contained in the introduction to Blake's poem *Milton* fitted the period best. It reflected both the optimism of post-war Britain as well as the liberal theological scheme for social reform. For this very reason it was adopted as the SCM's anthem and was quoted by many, in the labour movement and in the church, who supported social reform.[200] Its imagery was deemed sufficiently important for D. Miall Edwards to translate it into Welsh in 1921, thereby pledging himself and all the liberal theological establishment in Wales to the task ahead.

[197] E.g. D. R. Jones, 'Yr Eglwys', p.179.
[198] E.g. Morgan Watcyn-Williams, *Khaki to Cloth*, p.24.
[199] E.g. *Seren Cymru*, 30 August 1912, p.3; 10 January 1913, p.3; 21 February 1913, p.3.
[200] E.g. Owen Griffith, 'Glasgow 1921', *Yr Efrydydd*, I/3 (March 1921), 67; 'Church and labour', lecture notes, Bala-Bangor Collection, Principal John Morgan Jones Papers, UW Bangor; A. J. Davies, *To Build a New Jerusalem: The Labour Movement from the 1880s to the 1990s* (London, 1992), p.6.

> I will not cease from mental fight,
> Nor shall my sword sleep in my hand,
> Till we have built Jerusalem,
> In England's green and pleasant land.

> Ni chwsg fy nghleddyf yn fy llaw,
> Ni ddianc f'enaid rhag y gad,
> Nes codir muriau Dinas Duw,
> Ar feysydd gwyrddlas Cymru fad.[201]

Society was to be transformed by large-scale individual effort. The churches did not turn their attention away from the individual to society but approached social betterment through individual regeneration and effort. Once individuals had recognized their responsibilities as members of the one brotherhood, they would collectively, though independently, create a new society. In Blake's poem the personal activities of the second stanza are exchanged for communal awareness in the penultimate line, 'Till *we* have built Jerusalem'. Ironically, this was not repeated in the plural form in Miall Edwards's translation, which used the impersonal *codir* ('until the walls are built'), and this despite his concurring wholeheartedly with such an ideology. The responsibilities of individual citizenship were held to be sufficiently vital to both social reform and character development that there is almost an acceptance of works-based salvation. This was the result of the adoption of Ritschl's idea that justification came through the fulfilment of moral duty.

It has to be admitted that the reasoning behind Nonconformist social thinking, though probably naïve, was in many ways accurate. The training of a population which recognized the eternal value of their fellows should create a better environment and social system. Furthermore, it conserved the importance and vitality of the church's unique message. Even when social concern was at its height, Welsh Nonconformists still claimed that the vital element in their work was the ethical salvation of souls and that their efforts should be concentrated on individuals. Through such an ideology they retained a link with their past and affirmed that their purpose was to effect the

---

[201] D. Miall Edwards, 'Gweledigaeth a brwydr', *Yr Efrydydd*, III/1 (October, 1922), 28.

salvation of Christ. However, it was inadequate for the interim period between the present unjust state and the creation of such a population. It fell foul of the labour movement simply because the Socialists sought from the church explicit political support for their policies to the same degree that the chapels had supported the Liberal Party.

Fourthly, Nonconformists were convinced by now that the social problem pointed to a far wider issue than justice for the working class. They were convinced that impure and unjust principles lay at the heart of civilization itself, although this was usually explained as the result of moral (or immoral) choice as opposed to original sin. The principles of brotherly love, service, justice and co-operation were needed to form the basis of a new society. But even this was only a part of the task ahead. The efforts of the churches had to deal not merely with the direct problems of industrial society but with the spread of culture and higher principles in all areas of life.

It is certain that the overriding emphasis on the individual, the vital aspect of Nonconformist theology since the time of the early Dissenters, prevented a truly social exposition of Christianity. This was where the liberal Nonconformists rejected Ritschlian social extremism. There was a tendency in Ritschl's thought to make society, rather than the individual person, the object of God's love.[202] In rejecting this socialistic object of divine love the Nonconformists merely created more problems for themselves. If the individual were still of greatest importance in the scheme of redemption, and if, as Miall Edwards insisted, society were more than a mere conglomeration of individuals,[203] the question of how to define society and the Kingdom of God remained. Nonconformist theology lacked a detailed and distinct definition of either at this time. This was its basic ideological difficulty. Many of the representatives at the conferences in the 1920s held the view that the church was the protector of sacred and eternal ideals and principles. Its role was therefore no more than to explain those principles and present them to the congregations

---

[202] A. E. Garvie, *The Ritschlian Theology* (Edinburgh, 1899), pp.251–2; James Orr, *The Ritschlian Theology and the Evangelical Faith* (London, 1898), p.169.
[203] D. Miall Edwards, 'Christianity and the social problem in industrial areas', *The Welsh Outlook* (1921), 129.

and the public.[204] Apart from the criticism that can be made of the liberal-theological view of the church—was it not there to preach salvation through Christ?—this opinion would lead to the church's undoing and to the ultimate failure of all the great conferences of the 1920s. Ideals and principles need to be given a concrete expression in the reality of everyday life. Neither Copec nor the Welsh School of Social Service attempted to establish any mechanism to accomplish that task. They depended on the goodwill of a congregation to accept the findings of their discussions and then implement them on their behalf. Criticizing the church for failing to secure social reform may appear harsh. It was not the sole nor the most powerful agency involved in the debate and there were many political and social factors beyond its direct control which influenced economic policy and ensured that no lasting reforms could be instigated. However, Nonconformists, through the various means at their disposal, had set as their goal that they should keep social issues before the public and before the politicians and ensure that injustice was not tolerated. But creating a public conscience and opinion proved far more difficult than Lloyd George had assumed in 1911.

---

[204] E.g. *Seren Cymru*, 25 August 1922, p.4, on the need to enlighten the mind.

VI

LOSING THE BATTLE

The International Conference on Life and Work held at
Stockholm in 1925 marked the high point of both Christian
optimism and Liberal Theology's endeavour to provide a
relevant social interpretation of Christianity. Ironically, it was to
sound the first real warning that the principles propounded by
this theology were in fact insufficient, if not invalid, as
foundations for any social interpretation of the Christian faith.
Theological differences between the German delegation and the
delegations of America and Britain were particularly evident
over the doctrine of the Kingdom of God and man's part in
establishing it. Behind this difference lay a feeling that
theological liberalism was an inadequate expression of Christian
truth, a claim which seemed to receive support from the
outbreak of war in 1914. Far more than revealing man's
incessant, progressive development towards perfection, the war
had revealed the primitive corruption at the root of his being that
had traditionally been described in Christian theology as 'sin'.
This had tremendous consequences for the social application of
Christianity. Mankind could no longer be relied on to create a
better environment, while the existence of sin once again became
the most urgent problem facing the church.

Although, following the Stockholm conference, Miall Edwards
believed that Wales would take its rightful place on the world
stage, the gathering in fact signalled the almost total collapse of
social thought within Welsh Nonconformity. The theological
debate surrounding the social application of the gospel had been
propounded by a caucus of Modernist Nonconformists, several
of whom held the responsibility for training future ministers of
religion. By the end of 1926 this group, for various reasons,
appeared to have left this issue behind. In that year Thomas
Rees died. He had concentrated on completing his task as editor-
in-chief of *Y Geiriadur Beiblaidd* over the previous two years and
thus social issues had not been uppermost in his mind, certainly

not since the Copec conference. John Morgan Jones and
D. Miall Edwards tended to turn to more didactic tasks. It was
the exposition of the teaching of Jesus which kept Jones busy,
while Edwards was more concerned with doctrinal and
philosophical issues. Herbert Morgan focused almost exclusively
on his work as Director of the Extra-Mural Department at the
University in Aberystwyth. Gwilym Davies spent more time in
the early 1920s as an observer to the League of Nations in
Geneva and concentrated, first, on the problem of adolescence,
which saw the introduction of the 'Goodwill Message of the
Youth of Wales to the Youth of the World', and thereafter on the
problems of peace and the rise of Fascism.[1]

Perhaps as significant as the loss of the main liberal and social
protagonists was the dissemination of neo-orthodox theological
ideas, particularly by Professor J. E. Daniel of Bala-Bangor
Independent College, and the Revd J. D. Vernon Lewis who in
1934 would join the staff of the Memorial College, Brecon, as
Miall Edwards's successor. The reaction against the prevailing
theological liberalism is usually dated to the publication of Karl
Barth's 1919 commentary on St Paul's Epistle to the Romans.
Barth sought to return theology to its only true subject-matter,
namely God, and he devised a dialectic system for doing so.
Thus, he emphasized the complete contrast between the holy,
eternal God on the one hand, and sinful, finite man, on the
other. This natural difference between man and God could only
be bridged by God himself, and nothing within man could
successfully reach outwards and upwards towards him. Man
depended entirely on revelation for his knowledge of God.
Vernon Lewis first drew attention to Barth's work in an exposition of his thought in the students' periodical, *Yr Efrydydd*.[2] J. E.
Daniel had replaced Thomas Rees as Professor of Christian
Doctrine and Philosophy of Religion at Bala-Bangor in 1926.[3] It
is perhaps symbolic of the theological transition taking place in

[1] E.g. his collection of essays, *Y Byd Ddoe a Heddiw* (Denbigh, 1938); cf. Gwilym Davies,
'A Welsh social diary', *The Welsh Outlook* (1920), 40.
[2] J. D. Vernon Lewis, 'Diwinyddiaeth Karl Barth', *Yr Efrydydd*, III/10 (July 1927),
254–8; III/11 (August 1927), 281–7. For J. D. Vernon Lewis (1879–1970), see E. Lewis
Evans, 'John Daniel Vernon Lewis, 1879–1970', in W. T. Pennar Davies (ed.), *Athrawon
ac Annibynwyr* (Swansea, 1971), pp.79–88.
[3] For J. E. Daniel (1902–1962), see R. Tudur Jones, 'J. E. Daniel', in W. T. Pennar
Davies (ed.), *Athrawon*, pp.128–42; D. Densil Morgan (ed.), *Torri'r Seiliau Sicr* (Llandysul,
1993), introduction, pp.9–91.

this period that Wales's foremost liberal theologians were both succeeded by younger men whose theological convictions lay in a different direction. For these men, the Kingdom of God belonged to a completely different realm of existence from the 'kingdoms of this world'. It could never be secured by human effort at social justice and reform but was the gift of God. Although already dissatisfied with Liberal Theology, Daniel failed to discern a valid alternative.[4] By the end of the 1920s, the prevailing Liberal Theology was facing an ideological challenge which would undermine its humanistic premiss and would ensure that theological exactitude and doctrinal accuracy became an important issue for Welsh Nonconformists.

1. RELIGIOUS DISCONTENT

It was not Barthian theology alone that caused men to question the sufficiency of liberalism. As early as 1922 there had been a growing disquiet that the church was neglecting its true and proper task by concentrating on the problems inherent in contemporary society. There had always been a pietistic and even fundamentalist strain within Welsh Nonconformity, represented by the periodical *Yr Efengylydd*. This journal had continued to emphasize the need for personal conversion, while others had encouraged their readers to study the social problem and work for its solution. Perhaps the Revd R. B. Jones, Baptist pastor at Porth in the Rhondda, best epitomizes this strain. He was searching for a more adequate religious experience and intellectual formulation of faith at the turn of the century. Although initially attracted to the 'New Theology' movement, he came to see this as inadequate and the religious revival of 1904–5 gave him the tonic he needed. After that he persistently offered a fundamentalist, almost sectarian, view of Christian faith in the pages of *Yr Efengylydd* and elsewhere. To this was added the voice of those who had begun to perceive liberalism's basic inadequacy to meet human need, spiritual and temporal. During a sermon to a Swansea valley congregation, J. Lewis Williams stated that only God could remove 'the slums in the souls of the people'.[5] The

---

[4] J. E. Daniel, 'Diwinyddiaeth Cymru', *Yr Efrydydd*, VI/7 (April 1930), 174.
[5] *Labour Voice*, 25 May 1922, p.1.

implication was clear. The use of the word 'slums' was meant to contrast with the concentration on social issues, while at the same time pointing the congregation towards the need for personal regeneration that could only be effected by God. Lewis Williams did not belong to the pietistic strand within Welsh Nonconformity. In fact, he had considered himself to be a 'Christian Socialist' who held a great compassion for the plight of the ordinary people alongside a belief that the religion of Jesus could bring something more to the debate than mere housing reform and just wages. His was not a wholesale rejection of liberalism. But in lending his voice to this opinion, he ensured that attention would be drawn away from the idea of personal effort and development to the need for direct intervention by God. There would be other calls, reported in the once totally socially orientated *Labour Voice* over the next few years, that called on the church to return to its proper task, away from social questions to 'saving souls', away from this life to the life of the hereafter.[6] These were the first signs among labour people of unhappiness with the religious content of the church's message. At the time they appeared merely reactionary, but in fact they pointed to a far deeper question and a far greater problem that was beginning to be recognized and addressed, namely that Liberal Theology had been misleading. It had failed to present a true and accurate account of the Christian gospel and had caused men to depend on their own powers and ability to effect salvation. Rather than reform, it was claimed that such an idea had led to greater social problems and even to war itself, as it had dethroned God in the universe, replacing his sovereignty with the dominion of man.

It was primarily the issue of exact definition of the motif of the Kingdom of God which became paramount after Stockholm. It was still commonly maintained that the main principles of the Kingdom, love, forgiveness and service, were social.[7] The Revd Oswald Davies insisted that individual fulfilment could never occur without the establishment of a society congenial to character development. The Kingdom of God alone could offer such an environment as it represented the social aspect of

---

[6] Ibid., 7 June 1924, p.7; 14 June 1924, p.8; 1 October 1927, p.1.
[7] 'G.J.', 'Yr Eglwys a threfn cymdeithas', *Yr Efrydydd*, X/12 (September 1934), 331.

Christ's teaching.[8] Despite this, during the 1930s the social interpretation of the Kingdom of God was gradually being superseded by the apocalyptic as a result of Dialectic Theology's increasing popularity. The Kingdom was the eschatological gift of God's grace and not therefore to be confused with the idea of an earthly utopia.[9] It rightly belonged to the realm of the divine and to eternity and could not therefore be established by man's moral effort. Men such as Morgan Watcyn-Williams recognized this, but could not break completely from the belief that moral principles lay at the heart of God's Kingdom and that such principles could be adopted and practised by men. 'We must not identify the Kingdom of God with our achievements', he wrote in 1938, 'but we can always seek to realise what we attempt in the light of the Kingdom.'[10]

The Calvinistic Methodists' 'Davies Lectures' for 1933 were entitled *Teyrnas Dduw yng Ngoleuni Syniadau Apocalyptig yr Efengylau* (The Kingdom of God in the Light of the Gospel's Apocalyptic Ideas). The lecturer, the Revd G. A. Edwards, had been involved in the Welsh School of Social Service, Copec and in the Bangor Copec group. It is therefore hardly surprising that his lecture described the Kingdom as a moral task to be realized in the world. He did, however, claim that the moral task depended on individuals receiving the Kingdom as a gift in the present.

> If the Kingdom is already a personal possession, then man has both the responsibility and the honour of sharing it with his fellows. He must realize it increasingly in his commerce, in his work and his leisure and in every other connection—and do what he can to found it in the life of the world around him, until the whole world is put under its rule.[11]

Thus, the character reform accomplished by Jesus would centre on human ethics. To live for the Kingdom was described as the goal of all true life.[12] Christ reformed the moral outlook of the individual who would then attempt gradually to apply moral

[8] *Y Tyst*, 28 July 1938, p.10.
[9] G. A. Edwards, *Y Beibl Heddiw* (Bala, 1932), p.188.
[10] Morgan Watcyn-Williams, 'Jesus Christ and modern tendencies', *The Treasury* (1938), 185.
[11] G. A. Edwards, *Teyrnas Dduw yng Ngoleuni Syniadau Apocalyptig yr Efengylau* (Caernarfon, 1935), p.73.
[12] *Y Beibl Heddiw*, p.187.

standards to every aspect of his life. For the Revd R. E. Owen, who was, like Edwards, a Calvinistic Methodist, the Kingdom was a matter of relationships: between God and people and among people themselves. It consequently had no external political form but was a matter of ethical orientation.[13] It was to be found 'within' Christ's followers.[14] It became clearer that to interpret the Kingdom in terms of a social utopia was not the same as the concept of the Kingdom as taught by Jesus. For him the Kingdom was supernatural and not synonymous with human progress. Fundamentally, then, the need was to regenerate individuals,[15] but this was now to be guarded by the eschatological element in Christ's teaching, for although his followers see the Kingdom as present, it would only be fulfilled in the future.[16]

It is surprising that consideration of eschatology was not more common amongst Welsh Nonconformists at this time. Albert Schweitzer's *Von Reimarus zu Wrede* had reached Britain in 1910 as *The Quest of the Historical Jesus*, and had interpreted Jesus's whole ministry in eschatological terms. Yet Schweitzer was rarely, if ever, mentioned by the Welsh liberal theologians. Leonard Smith has argued that the publication of Schweitzer's book virtually destroyed the foundations of Modernism, in turn affecting the relationship between the church and the labour movement. The church sought to reinterpret its message in eschatological terms by positing that the Kingdom primarily belonged to the eschatological and not to the ethical realm. This would unquestionably undermine the emphasis on this world popular in contemporary theology.[17] In Wales at least this can hardly have been the case. Schweitzer's book was either unheard of or deliberately ignored. The apocalyptic view of God's Kingdom consequently did not receive a full treatment in Welsh for a further quarter-century.

---

[13] *Y Goleuad*, 1 December 1937, p.9.
[14] W. O. Jones, 'Teyrnas Nefoedd', *Y Dysgedydd* (1934), 170; W. D. Davies, Union of Welsh Independents Reports, 1928, Machynlleth, p.755.
[15] E. G. Jones, 'Tlodi', *Y Traethodydd*, 1926, p.238; R. J. Pritchard, Union of Welsh Independents Reports, 1930, Caernarfon, p.112; R. H. Davies, Union of Welsh Independents Reports, 1935, Aberdare, pp.102, 104.
[16] G. A. Edwards, *Y Beibl Heddiw*, p.187.
[17] Leonard Smith, *Religion and the Rise of Labour* (Keele, 1993), pp.21, 171.

2. THEOLOGICAL REACTION

After 1925 Welsh Nonconformists were being confronted with a powerful argument against liberalism. This argument was beginning to appear in denominational periodicals and had also reached the pulpit. Although there were others, two Welshmen in particular personify this reaction to liberalism's inadequacy: D. Martyn Lloyd-Jones and J. E. Daniel.

Martyn Lloyd-Jones[18] left a promising career as a surgeon to become pastor of Bethlehem Forward Movement Church, Aberavon, in the conviction that Wales needed to hear the true gospel. He was scathing about the church's attitude to social issues and the adoption of social theology.

> Such were the results of the much-vaunted social gospel—empty chapels and churches, a spineless Christianity, a War, a phenomenal rise in the number of cases of infidelity and divorce, gambling and sport of all descriptions more popular than ever before, indeed, all the present muddled state of society which we are witnessing.[19]

Liberalism had been characterized by an over-idealized view of humankind which encouraged the individual to believe that the power for both social and personal redemption was within him, the result of a natural, evolutionary process. Lloyd-Jones had come to believe in the total depravity of man and the consequent need of God's specific and individual intervention on his behalf.[20] He was completely sceptical about the church's apparent obsession with social problems, believing that it drew attention away from humanity's real need, which was for personal repentance and regeneration. The experience of one of his principal converts, the church's secretary, E. T. Rees, is instructive.

Rees was a schoolmaster who had been utterly convinced by the Socialist message and had unsuccessfully stood for election to the council. He liked to address ILP meetings and to preach a

---

[18] For D. Martyn Lloyd-Jones (1899–1981), see Iain H. Murray, *D. Martyn Lloyd-Jones: The First Forty Years 1899–1939* (Edinburgh, 1982); *idem, D. Martyn Lloyd-Jones: The Fight of Faith 1939–1981* (Edinburgh, 1990).

[19] D. Martyn Lloyd-Jones, *Evangelistic Sermons at Aberavon* (Edinburgh, 1983), p.177.

[20] Ibid., pp.1, 3.

message of social redemption from the pulpit at Aberavon. Lloyd-Jones challenged the congregation over its confusion between politics and the nature of the Christian gospel which concerned the eternal fate of humankind. His question to E. T. Rees was simply 'After death, what?' By October 1927 Rees had resolved to abandon Socialism and he resigned his membership of the Labour Party. Lloyd-Jones had made him realize that he had 'put politics before the gospel and environmental change before personal change'.[21] He had convinced Rees that Christ had not come to establish a political or social system but to regenerate individuals and reconcile them to God.

Lloyd-Jones pointed to what he perceived to be the liberals' mistaken interpretation of Christianity. In its place he preached a fundamentalism which held tightly to the inspiration of the whole of scripture and to the total depravity of man, both of which required the direct intervention of God. This had been a peripheral aspect within Welsh Nonconformity throughout the period of the liberal ascendancy,[22] but in Lloyd-Jones it achieved a remarkable level of popularity. Congregations increased at Bethlehem, Aberavon, and Lloyd-Jones was invited to preach all over Wales. It went against the grain for the generation of leaders in Welsh chapel circles who were the main protagonists of liberalism, but there was a public for whom this message struck the right note and who had been left untouched by the liberal hegemony.

Concurrent with Lloyd-Jones's fundamentalism was J. E. Daniel's more reasoned and balanced objection to liberalism. Appointed to the chair of Christian Doctrine at the Bala-Bangor theological college on the death of Thomas Rees in 1926, Daniel's ideas proved to be far removed from the theological standpoint of his predecessor. Daniel wished to emphasize Christianity's supernatural nature; it could never adequately be interpreted in terms of human morality or religiosity. It was not innate in man, rather it had to come from God. The crux of liberalism's weakness was that it replaced God with man.[23] Furthermore, the liberal stress on the enunciation of moral

---

[21] *D. Martyn Lloyd-Jones: The First Forty Years*, pp.116, 143–4.
[22] See B. P. Jones, *The King's Champions, 1863–1933* (Redhill, 1968).
[23] J. E. Daniel, 'Pwyslais diwinyddiaeth heddiw', in John Wyn Roberts (ed.), *Sylfeini'r Ffydd Ddoe a Heddiw* (London, 1942), p.84.

principles was not only an inaccurate interpretation of Jesus's message but it undermined the gospel itself. The gospel was a personal message of individual redemption, not the embodiment of abstract principles in personal or social life.[24]

Daniel's most damning criticism of the prevailing theology came over the issue of the nature of the Kingdom of God. It came in an address to the Union of Welsh Independents at Caernarfon in 1930 and made 'the strongest threat to date to the liberal standpoint'.[25] Just as it was God and not man who was responsible for human salvation, so God was also responsible for the coming of the Kingdom. The Kingdom was completely supernatural and thus could not be established by men. It was not fundamentally ethical but apocalyptic: the gift of God which would be ushered in at the *eschaton*. For Daniel, the Kingdom had nothing to do intrinsically with improved social conditions; rather, it had everything to do with individuals' relationship with God.

> I believe that the great danger for us today is to identify the Gospel with social improvement, and believe that it succeeds to the extent that wages are raised, or houses built, or illnesses abolished, or ministers learn the craft of the psycho-analyst.[26]

It was the church's task not to reform society but to save it. Its role was to call men to the Kingdom, not to attempt to build it. In Liberal Theology the church had become just one means of salvation amongst many, while for Daniel the church remained unique, as it alone could preach the word of salvation. It existed in a different realm from that of this world. To do the church justice it should not be viewed in its relationship to society, but in its relationship to God.

Despite his undoubted ability and his sharp insight into both the weaknesses of liberalism and the promise of Dialectic Theology, Daniel failed to produce an extensive body of work to serve as an antidote to the predominant Modernism. His chief

---

[24] J. E. Daniel, 'Gwaed y teulu', in Simon B. Jones and E. Lewis Evans (eds.), *Sylfeini Heddwch* (London, 1944), p.11.
[25] R. Tudur Jones, *Yr Undeb* (Swansea, 1975), p.238.
[26] J. E. Daniel, 'Eglwys Crist yn hanfodol i efengyl Crist', Union of Welsh Independents Reports, 1930, Caernarfon, p.109.

importance was exerted as tutor in a theological college and as
an important figure in the Nationalist Party. Daniel influenced,
both theologically and politically, generations of ministers of all
denominations who passed through the School of Theology at
Bangor. Most notable among his disciples, perhaps, was his
successor in the chair of Christian Doctrine, the Revd Gwilym
Bowyer. When Bowyer first went to Bangor, his mentor was the
extreme liberal, John Morgan Jones. By the time he left, Bowyer
had accepted Daniel's standpoint.[27]

The popularity of this 'new theology' is difficult to assess. The
gospel of individual repentance and regeneration had remained
part of the Welsh tradition and, as has been mentioned, it was
given a certain prominence through the pages of *Yr Efengylydd*
even when liberalism was at its height. There is a sense in which
this strain tended to be restricted to the periphery of church life
and certainly, while the older generation held sway in the
churches, Welsh Nonconformity remained within the liberal
orbit. At the same time, however, the younger generation of men
training for the ministry was more attracted to Barth and a
Theology of Revelation.[28] This new theology only really gained
an ascendancy after the Second World War, partly because the
younger generation had by then become the denominational and
theological leaders and partly because the main protagonists of
the Liberal Theology were dead.

What perhaps is most significant is the effect which the new
emphasis in theology had on social issues. None of those who were
at the forefront of the theological reaction denied the need for a
better society; they merely questioned the nature and orientation of
the church's involvement in social concern. In some respects, there
was a similarity between these theologians and the early Welsh
liberal theologians who had emphasized the need for individual
regeneration as a precondition of social reform. They differed in
interpreting the nature of that regeneration. The liberals saw it as
an ethical orientation towards a higher morality. The Revelation
Theologians saw it as a recognition of sin, repentance and the need
for salvation through God's redeeming grace. The differences,
though, were manifest. Men and women were no longer totally in

---

[27] W. Eifion Powell, *Bywyd a Gwaith Gwilym Bowyer* (Swansea, 1968), p.100.
[28] E.g. D. R. Davies, *In Search of Myself* (London, 1961), pp.202–3.

control of their own destinies, for they needed God to intervene in their life and redeem them. They no longer had the ability, as part of an evolutionary system ever developing towards perfection, to create a social utopia. The Kingdom of God had been removed from the realm of human activity and returned to the realm of apocalyptic. All this had tremendous implications for social concern within the church. Ministers and theologians, following the lead of Reinhold Niebuhr, began to offer an alternative vision, namely, that while people should struggle for social reform they must be aware that a perfect social system was an impossibility in history.[29] Thus, in a matter of forty years or so theology had come almost full circle. Under constant pressure for social reform, from the turn of the century ministers and theologians had argued against the other-worldly elements in religion, believing that they caused men to ignore the problems of this world. Now theologians and ministers were beginning to claim that overconcentration on this world had turned attention away from the next and from the need for individual conversion.[30]

3. Conclusions

Post-1926 Welsh Nonconformity lived in a state of tension between the existing liberal emphasis on the Fatherhood of God, the brotherhood of man and the ethical task of building the Kingdom, and the new ideas which questioned this emphasis and sought to concentrate on the individual's need of redemption. Thus, when it spoke of social responsibility at all, Welsh Nonconformity between the General Strike and the Second World War did so in the same terminology as it had done since 1910, though it was always open to the criticism that the Kingdom was not quite the right image to use. The church's fervent activity at Copec and Stockholm, as well as the localized effort in Wales through the Welsh School of Social Service and the denominational reports, partially obscured the inadequacy of theological liberalism. The Barthian theology on the continent had subjected liberalism to a biting critique and replaced its basic premisses of experience and immanence with those of revelation and transcendence. The preconceptions which had

---

[29] E.g. D. R. Davies, *On to Orthodoxy* (London, 1939), p.114.
[30] Cf. e.g. *Labour Voice*, 7 June 1924, p.7; 14 June 1924, p.8.

prevailed for a quarter of a century were no longer considered appropriate by a new generation of theologians and ministers. It was thus the true nature, purpose and content of theology which became important, as demonstrated by the Tom Nefyn Williams controversy, the response to J. E. Daniel's enthusiastic adoption of Revelation Theology[31] and even in articles published by the arch-liberal, John Morgan Jones.[32]

The social consequence of individual conversion was still being emphasized, although it seemed increasingly to be the case that individual conversion was considered more important than the social outcome of such a moral regeneration. This, too, was ironic. Far from recognizing the needs and possibilities of society *per se*, Nonconformists concerned themselves exclusively with the individual. No adequate social philosophy or theology was developed apart from the claim that social improvement was an implicit factor in individual regeneration. Welsh Nonconformists had never really had a specifically social *theology*. They had depended largely on certain liberal theologians to make a Christian contribution to the social debate. By the end of the 1920s, most of the sympathetic protagonists were either concentrating on other issues, waylaid by illness, or dead. After 1926 Welsh Nonconformity lacked a giant personality or individual theologian prominent enough to keep a social interpretation of Christianity before the church. Thus, the principles were never translated into a practical plan for improvement, nor was the opportunity taken to clarify theology and produce a specifically social interpretation of it. At the same time, chapel membership declined and the international situation deteriorated. Fascism grew in influence, civil war broke out in Spain and there were rumours of wars closer to home. Overall, the situation in which Welsh Nonconformists found themselves appeared very bleak. If, by 1939, social Christianity had not altogether disappeared, its authority was diminished and its power dissipated. Different theological conceptions came to the fore, while a greater pessimism abounded as Europe and the world resumed hostilities and went once more to the slaughter.

[31] See D. Densil Morgan, *Torri'r Seiliau Sicr*, pp.36–8.
[32] See John Morgan Jones, 'Anghenion crefyddol Cymru', *Y Dysgedydd* (1933), 292–7; John Morgan Jones, 'Beth yw diwinyddiaeth Gristionogol?', *Yr Efrydydd*, IX/7 (April 1933), 181–4 and IX/8 (May 1933), 211–14.

CONCLUSION

The advent of the labour movement at the turn of the twentieth century marked a watershed in modern Welsh history. Even if it did owe more to a religious and ethical zeal than to Marxist economic theory, it challenged, and ultimately replaced, the Nonconformist hegemony in Welsh life. Exactly why this occurred is still not clear. A commitment to labour politics did not necessarily mean a departure from organized religion, and many men recognized a parity of aim and ideal between their religious and political creeds. The decline in church attendance which occurred by the late 1920s was caused by various factors. Changing working practices, greater leisure opportunities, the aftermath of war and plain apathy all played a part. What is certain is that very often men had personal and individual reasons for forsaking Nonconformity and Christian practice generally. That some left religion to concentrate on political agitation and social reform is undeniable. That others did not is an equally important fact. The chapels grew increasingly concerned about falling congregations in this period, yet they maintained a strong presence and influence in society until the 1950s. Welsh society was thus an amalgam of various social factors in which the chapel, though gradually losing adherents, was still a strong and influential force in the community, while the labour movement concurrently grew and increased in confidence. Neither ever held the allegiance of all Welshmen, while many amongst the working class felt at home in both. These were perhaps the two strongest social influences in Wales; but there were others, such as sport and the public house, which could claim the primary allegiance of many working men.

The labour movement certainly played an important role in giving working men an opening to air their grievances. In this it largely assumed a unique position in Welsh society. While the chapels had offered the working class the opportunity to practise their oratorical skill in the society meeting, in debating societies and as lay preachers, the topics chosen were respectable and usually religious. They generally gave no opportunity for the working class to discuss the matters which concerned them most, such as fair working practices, wage agreements, victimization and the rapaciousness of their bosses. It is significant that when religious organizations did offer the working class an opportunity to discuss issues close to their hearts, those organizations achieved a remarkable level of support, as did David Pughe's Brotherhood Movement in Merthyr, R. J. Barker's Community House in Trealaw, and Leon Atkin's weekly debates at Risca. This implied that the chapels were unable to reach at least some of the populace unless they were willing to experiment with new religious forms. Perhaps it is the case that while the Nonconformists knew what the working men needed, the labour movement knew what they wanted.

The practical concern about losing adherents and appealing to working men was accompanied by the ideological problem of religious witness in the modern scientific world. The 'New Theology' was one attempt to come to terms with the contemporary situation. It was the natural consequence of a synthesis between the philosophical and theological trends and a consideration of the social and political needs of the time. Its effect on the Nonconformist churches was minimal. It was the influence of Hegelian philosophy, the Kantian emphasis on practical and ethical purpose for religion, and Ritschlian theology which really account for the wider Nonconformist social concern. Thus, the advent of the labour movement, with its Socialist agitators inspired by righteous zeal, together with developments within prevailing theological liberalism, created the ideological basis from which the Nonconformists attempted to develop a distinctly social understanding of the gospel. The achievements of this generation should not be dismissed or discounted. The interwar period was a golden age in Welsh intellectual, literary and theological life. There can have been few periods before or since when quite so many able men were involved in religious life and the theological debate. Their crowning achievement was surely *Y Geiriadur Beiblaidd*, a remarkable work despite the scepticism of succeeding generations regarding its theological stance.[1]

[1] See Gwilym H. Jones, *Geiriadura'r Gair* (Caernarfon, 1993), pp.30–51.

Certainly, the denominations at this time established particular principles in two main areas that would be adopted by the church as almost axiomatic for its witness later in the century. First, their attempts at answering the social problem gave Christianity a say in all questions concerning justice, freedom from oppression and issues of health and fair working practice in both national and international debates. The condition of one's neighbour in this life, regardless of his political or religious creed, became a matter of conscience which resulted in social amelioration and the principle of service being embedded in the church's witness. To insist that Christianity provided the inspiration and dynamic for a social reconstruction on fair and just lines was the church's first great accomplishment during this period. The second was to give this such vital and central importance as to consider ecumenical activity the only means to guarantee a solution. Ecumenism had not been born directly out of social concern. Instead, it had arisen partly to gain Nonconformist political goals through the Liberal Party, as the Free Church Councils had done in the nineteenth century, and partly as the need for evangelism in the world had grown into a challenge beyond the ability of individual denominations, culminating in a great conference in Edinburgh in 1910. But as social reform became an inherent part of the church's message and witness, it naturally became an ecumenical issue. The Nonconformists' willingness to cast aside denominational differences in search of a genuinely Christian answer to society's problems was particularly admirable at a time when the disestablishment campaign was at its most fervent. This certainly paved the way for further ecumenism later in the century.

The prevailing theological liberalism, its weaknesses notwithstanding, also contributed ideological factors of lasting significance. Man's status as a member of the human brotherhood stemming from God's Fatherhood laid the only moral basis for true social righteousness. It also provided a justification for insisting on human value and the consequent need for better housing and working conditions, and also for the divine command of justice for the oppressed. While it promoted individualism far more than sociality, it has to be recognized that the Nonconformists were seeking to be both pragmatic and true to their traditions. They had recognized that the difficulty would always be to effectualize social reform, particularly as they had very little or no political power. Thus, they concentrated on each individual's ethical responsibility towards his neighbour which required that the innate value of personality be recognized by all people. Making this a matter of conscience would ensure that the church could never again neglect its witness for justice in the world.

Above all else, the period is marked by a positive individualism, in an ideological and a pragmatic sense, both in the Socialist movement and within Nonconformity. Ideologically, the Nonconformists had pinned their hopes on the moral regeneration of the individual to lead to a personal dedication to social improvement. Both the chapels and the labour movement emphasized the value of the individual as the seminal precept for social reform. Pragmatically, both had depended on the absolute commitment, intellect and strength of character of certain individuals. The labour movement's dependence on Keir Hardie is particularly striking. The indigenous Socialists almost invariably echoed his message, stressing high ethical standards in individual and social life, and calling for a true practice of religion. Significantly, the men who had advocated a synthesis between the church and the labour movement before the Great War, with the exception of Herbert Morgan, did not exchange this politically orientated effort for a social interpretation of Christianity after the war. Several of them were lost to the Nonconformist ministry. The advocacy of a social Christianity largely depended on Herbert Morgan, John Morgan Jones, D. Miall Edwards and Thomas Rees. Although not alone in calling for a Christian response to the social need, more than anyone else it was they who kept the issues alive in the denominational press, at religious meetings, in movements such as *Urdd y Deyrnas* and the Welsh School of Social Service, and in books and pamphlets. The social problem was undoubtedly the most important issue facing Nonconformists at this time, and the fate of the chapels themselves was recognized to lie in its solution. But important as social reconstruction was, particularly in the 1920s, it was only one issue amongst many for the majority of Nonconformists. Issues of temperance, the problems of adolescence (perceived as directly part of the social problem from around 1912), the Sunday School, disestablishment (achieved in

1920), falling congregations and the task of biblical exposition generally, all caused great concern as witnessed by the various articles in contemporary denominational periodicals.

It is unclear whether Nonconformity contributed anything unique to the social debate. Certainly its insistence that individual morality would create a better society, and that recognition of personal value would provide an inspiration for improvement, was a theoretical protection against the establishment of a state Socialism in which personal freedom would be withdrawn. Individual conversion remained the vital aspect in Nonconformist theology, although by this time the emphasis on the individual owed more to ethical considerations than to traditional soteriology. Nonconformity's principal contribution was made in the work of individual theologians who enthusiastically promoted the adoption of Christian principles within social structures.

In some respects this social ideology, depending on mutual recognition of value and duty, can be said to have succeeded. The unwavering belief in human responsibility to others, and the perceived ability to practise it, were certainly at the heart of the Welfare State established by the Labour government after the Second World War. Salvation would now be realized through the provision of comprehensive and free education and health care, with the state directly responsible for the material and moral welfare of its citizens. On the whole, Nonconformists were unaware of the ideological implications involved in recognizing the state's responsibility towards its citizens. They left unanswered questions pertaining to the relationship between the state and the individual and also to the relationship between the state and the church, even though the former had assumed an ethical role. Nevertheless, had they lived to see its establishment, those theologians who sought a social understanding of Christianity would almost certainly have welcomed the development of the Welfare State.

Contemporary Nonconformists, however, suffered from fatal ideological weaknesses due to the theological and philosophical preconceptions of the age. Doctrinally, their position rested far more on the claim to a moral imperative, borrowed from Hegelian and Kantian philosophy and implied in the Ritschlian concept of 'value', and on the propounding of familiar and homely phrases such as the Fatherhood of God, the brotherhood of man and the Kingdom of God, than on firm theological argument. By treating immanence as their basic premiss, Nonconformist preachers tended to disparage the status and importance of the Creator, replacing it with the ultimate value of the creature. Immanence made this an inherent value, vital to the individual's humanity. Such an anthropology was vital to their call for social reform along lines of justice and fairness, but it depreciated traditional theological formulae. In practice, man's brotherhood was propounded, if not to the exclusion, at least to the detriment of God's Fatherhood. Seeing God as part of his creation implied that the highest examples of human life reflected the divine. This theory found its paragon in Jesus of Nazareth, interpreted as the most ethically perfect example of the race yet to have evolved. Furthermore, the adoption of thoroughgoing theological immanence had resulted in an understanding of God's loving and redemptive action *extra muros ecclesiae*. God's *presence* in the world was not the issue. But the validation of God's activity beyond the visible church in secular movements led inevitably to a devaluing of the church and worship, and to a secularizing of religion and society. It is not surprising that some men found a 'spiritual' home in the labour movement. God had become so ordinary that he could be ignored. A man's religiosity would be measured by his willingness to serve his fellow men rather than by his allegiance to organized religion. Such doctrinal developments would not bode well for Nonconformity's future, particularly at a time when its leaders were all too aware of the gradual withdrawal of many young men from its ranks.

Considering the centrality of the concept of righteousness within the biblical scheme, as well as the command that it should be made concrete,[2] the paucity of scriptural references by the Socialists and Nonconformists alike is striking. Apart from constantly repeating the verse, 'seek ye first the Kingdom of God and his righteousness', and continually claiming that the Lord's

---

[2] See R. E. C. Browne, 'Righteousness', in John Macquarrie (ed.), *A Dictionary of Christian Ethics* (London, 1967), pp.299–300; W. O. Evans, 'Cyfiawnder', in Thomas Rees *et al.* (eds.), *Y Geiriadur Beiblaidd* (Wrexham, 1924–6), pp.335–7; W. O. Evans, 'Cyfiawnder Duw', in *Y Geiriadur Beiblaidd*, p.337; R. G. Roberts, 'Cyfiawnhau, -had', in *Y Geiriadur Beiblaidd*, pp.337–8.

Prayer itself contained the call for God's will to be established on earth, little scripture was quoted. This was the result of Idealism: the belief that moral principles lay at the heart of the gospel message and at the base of reality. The discovery and implementation of such principles would encourage the evolutionary process or, in religious terms, would result in the fulfilment of God's will and the establishment of his Kingdom. Thus, moral principles held the key to both social improvement and religious truth. Inevitably this would undermine the traditional authority of scripture and replace it with the authority of individual conscience and experience, a move which left all religious exposition open to arbitrary interpretation.

The emphasis on principles, the inheritance of philosophical Idealism, also led to a lack of practical measures designed to ensure social improvement. There is sufficient evidence to show that chapels were often at the forefront of relief activity in times of social hardship, such as during the lock-out following the General Strike in 1926. But the various meetings convened to extrapolate the social implications of Christianity never translated the principles that the Nonconformist theologians had succeeded in delineating into practical advice for their implementation within social structures. The absolute dependence on principles as the sole means to effect social renewal was probably misplaced. As Herbert Morgan had insisted, principles were far too abstract unless practical advice for their application was also given. The saddest indictment of Nonconformist activity during the period is that, despite the optimism, the successful identification of necessary principles and the general acceptance that social reform was the greatest need of the age, very little was actually accomplished. This was due, at least in part, to Nonconformity's ideological position.

While Nonconformists had established the propriety of the church's involvement in social issues, they lacked the wider influence that would see their principles embodied in society. They held no direct political influence, which was certainly a deliberate policy from at least 1910. This was a great weakness as they sought to influence a fundamentally political topic. It also left the issue of religion's relationship with politics unanswered. The nature of that relationship, even when despised, had at least previously been taken for granted. The Liberal Party was

synonymous with Nonconformity, while the Anglican Church
was the 'Tory Party at prayer'. In eschewing politics Nonconformists failed to leave a positive foundation for future
generations to define the relationship between religion and
politics.

The return to Jesus and to his teaching had occupied
theologians for over a century and had influenced Welsh
Nonconformists. Such an inquiry had far-reaching implications
for theology and Christian witness. Certainly it led to the
development of an anthropology which stressed the ethical
potential of each human being to reach the moral heights of the
'historical Jesus', however elusive a figure he proved to be.
Moreover, the recognition that the Kingdom formed the centre
of his teaching provided the inspirational focus for men in the
quest for social improvement. However, their expositions were
invariably one-sided and dependent on the exigencies of their
philosophical preconceptions. Unity, goodness and progressive
perfection formed the heart of their world-view, which produced
an ideological difficulty in defining such doctrinal issues as sin—a
fact all the more significant as Nonconformists insisted that sin
was the ultimate cause of social problems. The war should at
least have posed searching questions for this philosophy and
probably should have swept it aside. That it did not left Welsh
Nonconformist theology the victim of a philosophical trend that
was elsewhere losing favour.

Overall, however, the period should be viewed in the context
of the ongoing Christian pilgrimage. A social understanding of
Christianity and the necessity of the church's involvement in
social reform were two factors which were only just emerging in
the witness and practice of the church. It would therefore be
foolish to expect men of the time to have spoken the
authoritative word on the subject. As they sought to make their
witness ever more relevant to their time, their legacy for future
generations is great. They demonstrated the need for the church
to respond to social needs and to the way in which those needs
were perceived by ordinary people. Their mistake was to
concentrate their efforts on providing moral improvement and
regeneration, which tended to exclude God from social
discussions. Their theology of the Kingdom, for example, did
just that, making it a human concept and virtually ignoring the

apocalyptic, the direct and gracious intervention of God which alone could bring it about. While they emphasized the moral imperative at the heart of Christian ethics, namely love of neighbour and love of God, they neglected to see it in the context of God's gracious and redeeming act in Christ. They lacked a definite theology, one which recognized that while mankind's actions should be interpreted according to the principles of the Kingdom, and man's efforts geared towards ever more just systems of society, God's intervention would always be regarded as essential. Man's absolute need of God in Christ should therefore have been axiomatic. Without God there was nothing to differentiate the church from other movements which advocated human effort, such as the Socialist or labour movement. In searching for an adequate social ideology, the Nonconformists tended to ignore the unique and inspirational elements of the traditional Christian message. The principal achievement of this generation of Nonconformists was to ground the Christian faith in the reality of life on this earth, in the conviction that Jesus's teaching had a vital message for this life *per se* and not simply as a preparation for the next. Their ultimate failure was an inability, for a multitude of reasons, to retain the interest and allegiance of the working class.

SOURCES AND BIBLIOGRAPHY

1. PERSONAL PAPERS
2. JOURNALS, PERIODICALS AND NEWSPAPERS
3. REPORTS
4. RECORDED INTERVIEWS
5. BOOKS AND PAMPHLETS
   (i)   Contemporary Publications
   (ii)   Autobiography and Biography
   (iii) History
   (iv)   Reference
6. ARTICLES
7. UNPUBLISHED THESES

1. PERSONAL PAPERS

University of Wales, Bangor
Bala-Bangor Collection, Principal Thomas Rees Papers, Principal John Morgan Jones Papers
Bangor Collection (General), Revd T. E. Nicholas Papers, David Thomas Papers, R. Silyn Roberts Papers

National Library of Wales
Revd Gwilym Davies Papers
Professor D. Miall Edwards Papers
Revd H. M. Hughes Papers
E. Cefni Jones, 'Gwili a'i Waith', MSS 19397C
Revd E. K. Jones Papers
Principal Thomas Rees Papers
Daniel Lleufer Thomas Papers

Private Collection
Revd Leon Atkin

2. JOURNALS, PERIODICALS AND NEWSPAPERS

Y Beirniad, 1911–19
Blwyddiadur y Methodistiaid Calfinaidd, 1910–40
The Congregational Quarterly, 1923–46
Y Cronicl, 1900–14
Y Darian, 1914–34
Y Deyrnas, 1916–19
Y Dinesydd Cymreig, 1912–29
Y Diwygiwr, 1900–7
Y Drysorfa, 1900–39
Y Dysgedydd, 1900–39

Yr Efengylydd, 1900–26
Yr Efrydydd, 1920–39
Yr Eurgrawn Wesleaidd, 1900–39
Y Geninen, 1900–24 and 1928
Y Goleuad, 1906–39
Y Greal, 1900–17
Heddiw, 1936–39
The Hibbert Journal, 1923–46
The Labour Leader, 1908–22.
Llais Llafur, 1906–39 (including *The Labour Voice*, 1915–27 and *The South Wales Voice*, 1927–39)
Y Llenor, 1923–46
The Merthyr Pioneer, 1911–22
The Pilgrim, 1920–6 (London)
Seren Cymru, 1906–39
Seren Gomer, 1900–39
Tarian y Gweithiwr, 1906–14
Theology, 1920–39 (London)
Y Traethodydd, 1900–39
The Treasury, 1912–39 (Caernarfon)
Y Tyst, 1906–39
The Welsh Outlook, 1914–34 (Cardiff)

3. REPORTS

Reports of the Annual Meetings of the Union of Welsh Independents, 1910–39.
Reports of the Baptist Union of Wales, 1910–12, 1917–20, 1929, 1937, 1938
(important addresses were usually published in *Seren Cymru* or *Seren Gomer*).
Adroddiad Pwyllgor V, Comisiwn Ad-drefnu Cymdeithasfa Methodistiaid Calfinaidd Gogledd Cymru, Yr Eglwys a Chwestiynau Cymdeithasol (Caernarfon, 1921).
South Wales Calvinistic Methodist Association Reconstruction Commission, the Report of the Fifth Committee on the Church and Social Questions (Cardiff, 1921).
Cenadwri Cymdeithasol yr Efengyl (Report of the sub-council of the Union of Welsh Independents) (Swansea, 1923).
Copec Reports 1924
    1. *The Nature of God and His Purpose for the World* (London, 1924)
    2. *Education* (London, 1924)
    3. *The Home* (London, 1924)
    4. *The Relation of the Sexes* (London, 1924)
    5. *Leisure* (London, 1924)
    6. *The Treatment of Crime* (London, 1924)
    7. *International Relations* (London, 1924)
    8. *Christianity and War* (London, 1924)
    9. *Industry and Property* (London, 1924)
    10. *Politics and Citizenship* (London, 1924)
    11. *The Social Function of the Church* (London, 1924)
    12. *Historical Illustrations of the Social Effects of Christianity* (London, 1924)
The Proceedings of Copec (London, 1924)
G. K. A. Bell (ed.), *Universal Christian Conference on Life and Work: Stockholm 1925* (London, 1925).
J. H. Oldham (ed.), *Oxford Conference on Church, Community and State 1937: The Churches Survey Their Task* (London, 1937).
Men Without Work: A Report made to the Pilgrim Trust (Cambridge, 1938).

4. Recorded Interviews held at the South Wales Miners' Library, Swansea
   (SOUTH WALES COALFIELD PROJECT)

Phil Abrahams, 14 January 1974.
R. Page Arnot, 6 March 1973.
Will Arthur, 24 May 1973.
Will Arthur, 13 June 1973.
James Brewer, 29 November 1969.
David Brown, 2 July 1973.
Jesse Clark, 14 February 1973.
Dick Cook, 24 January 1974.
Idris Cox, 9 June 1972.
Ben Davies, 11 June 1973.
David John Davies, 3 January 1972.
John Davies, 26 July 1973.
Penry Davies, 20 October 1973.
Tom Davies, December 1973.
Trevor Davies, 3 July 1972.
William Davies, 4 October 1972.
Henry Edwards, June 1973.
Dai Dan Evans, 3 December 1972.
Dai Dan Evans, 7 August 1973.
Edgar Evans, 14 July 1973.
Edgar Evans, 30 November 1973.
Ernest Evans, October 1972.
Glyn Evans, 5 July 1973.
Mrs J. Evans, 11 June 1973.
Jim Evans, 29 January 1972.
John Evans, 13 June 1973.
Ned Gittins, August 1973.
James Griffiths, 20 November 1972.

Len Jeffreys, 12 September 1972.
T. Jenkins, 28 May 1972.
Henry John, 1 December 1972.
Jack John, 1 February 1973.
Josiah Jones, 23 October 1972.
Henry Lewis, 4 December 1972.
Clarence Lloyd, 17 May 1974.
A. J. Martin, 11 July 1973.
Abel Morgan, 9 October 1972.
Abel Morgan, 19 October 1972.
Bob Morris, 19 November 1973.
G. C. Nelmew, 13 August 1973.
T. Nicholas, 16 March 1973.
Will Paynter, 18 April 1969.
Will Paynter, 6 March 1973.
Myrddin H. Powell, 19 September 1975.
George Protheroe, October 1972.
Mrs Rees, Briton Ferry, November 1973.
Claude Stanfield, November 1972.
W. H. Taylor, August 1973.
Bryn Thomas, 23 January 1972.
W. C. Thomas, 9 July 1973.
Rhys Watkins, 13 December 1972.
Tom Watkins, 23 October 1972.
J. L. Williams, 24 April 1974.
John Williams, 23 July 1974.
Len Williams, 21 May 1974.

5. Books and Pamphlets

(i) Contemporary Publications

Anon., *The Tom Nefyn Controversy: An Account of the Crisis in Welsh Calvinistic Methodism* (Port Talbot, 1929).
Anon., *The United School of Social Service for Wales* (n.d.).
Anon., *Ymgyrch Moes a Chrefydd: Galwad i'r Gad* (Caernarfon, 1921).
Adams, David, *Datblygiad yn ei Berthynas a'r Cwymp, Yr Ymgnawdoliad a'r Adgyfodiad* (Caernarfon, 1893).
Idem, Moeseg Cristionogol (Dolgellau, 1901).
Idem, Paul yng Ngoleuni'r Iesu (Dolgellau, 1907).
Idem, Yr Hen a'r Newydd Mewn Duwinyddiaeth (Dolgellau, 1907).
Idem, Yr Eglwys a Gwareiddiad Diweddar (Merthyr Tydfil, 1914).
Barker, R. J., *Christ in the Valley of Unemployment* (London, 1936).
Campbell, R. J., *The New Theology* (London, 1907).
Davies, D. J. and Noëlle, *Cymoedd Tan Gwmwl* (Denbigh, 1938).
Davies, D. R., *On to Orthodoxy* (London, 1939).
Davies, E. Curig (ed.), *Llef y Gwyliedydd* (Llanelli, 1927).
Davies, George M. Ll., *Cenhadon Hedd*, Pamffledi Heddychwyr Cymru, 2nd ser., no. 8 (Denbigh, 1943).

Idem, Essays Towards Peace (London, 1946).

Davies, Gwilym (ed.), *Social Problems in Wales* (Swansea, 1913).

Idem, Twenty Five Years of the Welsh School of Social Service 1911–1936 (n.d.).

Idem, Y Byd Ddoe a Heddiw (Denbigh, 1938).

Davies, Rhys, *My Wales* (London, 1937).

Davies, W. D., *Cristnogaeth a Meddwl yr Oes* (Caernarfon, 1932).

Idem, Datguddiad Duw: Efrydiau Diwinyddol (Caernarfon, 1934).

Dodd, C. H., *The Parables of the Kingdom* (London, 1935).

Edwards, D.Miall (ed.), *Efengyl y Deyrnas* (Bala, 1927).

Idem, Epistol Cyffredinol Iago (Aberdare, 1910).

Idem, Crefydd a Bywyd (Dolgellau, 1915).

Idem, Crist a Gwareiddiad (Dolgellau, 1921).

Idem, Epistol Cyffredinol Iago (2nd edn., Swansea, 1922).

Idem, Yr Efengyl Gymdeithasol (published by the Welsh School of Social Service, n.d.).

Idem, The Philosophy of Religion (London, 1924).

Idem, Religion in Wales, Traethodau'r Deyrnas, English ser., no. 3 (Wrexham, 1926).

Idem, Iaith a Diwylliant Cenedl (Dolgellau, 1927).

Idem, Bannau'r Ffydd (Wrexham, 1929).

Idem, Christianity and Philosophy (Edinburgh, 1932).

Idem, Yr Antur Fawr: Pregethau (Wrexham, 1932).

Idem, Crefydd a Diwylliant (Wrexham, 1934).

Edwards, D. Miall and M. E. Davies, *Cyflwr Crefydd yng Nghymru*, Traethodau'r Deyrnas, 1 (Wrexham, 1924).

Edwards, D. Miall and Thomas Rees, *COPEC* (articles from *Y Tyst* published as a pamphlet by the Welsh School of Social Service, n.d.).

Edwards, G. A., *Hanes Gwareiddiad* (Wrexham, 1927).

Idem, Y Beibl Heddiw (Bala, 1932).

Idem, Teyrnas Dduw yng Ngoleuni Syniadau Apocalyptig yr Efengylau (Y Ddarlith Davies 1933) (Caernarfon, 1935).

Edwards, G. A. and John Morgan Jones, *Diwinyddiaeth yng Nghymru*, Traethodau'r Deyrnas, no. 4 (Wrexham, 1924).

Evans, David, *Labour Strife in the South Wales Coalfield 1910–1911* (Cardiff, 1911).

Evans, D. Emrys, *Crefydd a Chymdeithas*, Cyfres y Brifysgol a'r Werin, no. 15 (Cardiff, 1933).

Evans, D. Tudwal, *Sosialaeth* (Barmouth, 1911).

Evans, J. R., *Cristionogaeth a'r Bywyd Da* (Y Ddarlith Davies 1938) (Llandysul, 1941).

Evans, James, *Moeseg*, Cyfres y Brifysgol a'r Werin, no. 5 (Cardiff, 1930).

Evans, Owen, *Diwinyddiaeth Gristionogol* (Bangor, 1906).

Idem, Diwinyddiaeth Gristionogol, II (Bangor, 1911).

Evans, William, *An Outline of the History of Welsh Theology* (London, 1900).

Fleure, H. J., *Wales and Her People*, Traethodau'r Deyrnas, English ser., no. 2 (Wrexham, 1926).

Forsyth, P. T., *Socialism, the Church and the Poor* (London, 1908).

Idem, The Church, the Gospel and Society (London, 1962).

Garvie, A. E., *The Ritschlian Theology* (Edinburgh, 1899).

Griffith, D. M., *Nationality in the Sunday School Movement* (Bangor, 1925).

Griffith-Jones, E., *The Ascent Through Christ* (7th edn., London, 1901).

Gwyther, C. E., *The Valley Shall Be Exalted: Light Shines in the Rhondda* (London, 1949).

Hardie, J. Keir, *Can a Man Be a Christian on a Pound a Week?* (London, n.d.).

Idem, The Red Dragon and the Red Flag (Merthyr Tydfil, 1912).

Harnack, A., *What is Christianity?* (London, 1901).

Howard, J. H., *Cristionogaeth a Chymdeithas* (Liverpool, 1914).

Idem, Which Jesus? Young Britain's Choice (Dolgellau, 1926).

Idem, Jesus the Agitator (Wrexham, 1934).

Hughes, J. G. Moelwyn, *Addoli* (Y Ddarlith Davies 1935) (Liverpool, 1937).

Hughes, R. R., *Dyn a'i Dynged* (Y Ddarlith Davies 1931) (Llangefni, 1939).

Humphreys, E. Morgan, *Cymru a'r Wasg*, Traethodau'r Deyrnas, no. 10 (Wrexham, 1924).

Hyde, William DeWitte, *Outlines of Social Theology* (London, 1895).

Jenkins, J. Gwili, *Y Ddwy Efengyl a Phethau Eraill* (Carmarthen, 1915).

Jones, Gwenan, *Addysg yng Nghymru*, Traethodau'r Deyrnas, no. 2 (Wrexham, 1924).

Idem, Cymru a'i Chymdogion, Traethodau'r Deyrnas, nos. 11–12 (Wrexham, 1924).

Jones, Henry, *Social Responsibilities: Lectures to Business Men* (2nd edn., Glasgow, 1906).

Idem, Dinasyddiaeth Bur ac Areithiau Eraill (Caernarfon, 1911).

Jones, John Morgan (Bangor), *Politics in Wales*, Free Lectures for the People (Aberdare, 1902).

Idem, Cymdeithas Addysg y Gweithwyr: Sgwrs (1940).

Jones, John Morgan (Merthyr Tydfil), *Religion and Socialism* (Merthyr Tydfil, 1910).

Idem, Y Datguddiad o Dduw yn yr Hen Destament (Caernarfon, 1936).

Jones, John Puleston, *Epistol Iago* (Caernarfon, 1898).

Idem, Epistol Iago (2nd edn., Caernarfon, 1922).

Jones, J. R., *Sosialaeth yng Ngoleuni'r Beibl*, Fabian Tract no. 143 (London, 1909).

Jones, R. Merfyn (ed.), *The Miners' Next Step* (Shoreditch, 1982).

Jones, T.Gwynn, *The Culture and Tradition of Wales*, Traethodau'r Deyrnas, English ser., no. 5 (Wrexham, 1926).

Jones, Thomas, *A Theme with Variations* (Gregynog, 1930).

Keeble, S. E. (ed.), *The Social Teaching of the Bible* (London, 1909).

Idem, Towards the New Era: A Draft Scheme of Industrial Reconstruction (London, 1917).

Idem, Christian Responsibility for the Social Order (London, 1922).

Idem, Copec: An Account of the Christian Conference on Politics, Economics and Citizenship (London, n.d.).

Lewis, Saunders, *An Introduction to Welsh Literature*, Traethodau'r Deyrnas, English ser., no. 1 (Wrexham, 1926).

Lewis, Thomas, *Yr Hen Destament a Beirniadaeth Ddiweddar*, Traethodau'r Deyrnas, 2nd ser., no. 1 (Wrexham, 1930).

Lloyd George, David *The Relation of the Churches to Social Questions*, Christian Commonwealth Sermon Supplements, no. 58, 17 January 1912 (London, 1912).

Lloyd-Jones, D. Martyn, *Evangelistic Sermons at Aberavon* (Edinburgh, 1983).

Machen, J. Gresham, *Christianity and Liberalism* (Grand Rapids, Mich., 1968).

Mess, H. A.,*The Message of Copec* (London, 1924).

Micklem, Nathaniel and Herbert Morgan, *Christ and Caesar* (London, 1921).

Morgan, Herbert, *The Church and the Social Problem* (Carmarthen, 1911).

Idem, The Social Task in Wales (London, 1919).

Idem, Diwydiant yng Nghymru, Traethodau'r Deyrnas, no. 3 (Wrexham, 1924).

Morgan, J. Vyrnwy (Viator Cambrensis), *The Rise and Decline of Welsh Nonconformity* (London, 1912).

Idem, The Welsh Mind in Evolution (London, 1925).

Morgan, Richard, *Cristionogaeth yn Iachawdwriaeth Dynoliaeth* (Bangor, 1912).

Morris, Richard, *Person Crist*, Llawlyfrau Diwinyddol i'r Werin, no. 2 (Wrexham, 1911).

Morris, R. Hopkin, *Welsh Politics*, Traethodau'r Deyrnas, English ser., no. 6 (Wrexham, 1927).

Morris, W., *Esboniad ar Epistol Iago* (2nd edn.,Tonypandy, 1922).

Orr, James, *The Ritschlian Theology and the Evangelical Faith* (London, 1898).

Owen, John, *Gwybodaeth y Sanctaidd* (Y Ddarlith Davies 1923) (Caernarfon, 1923).

Phillips, D. M., *Esboniad ar Epistol Iago* (Cardiff, 1922).

Phillips, Thomas, *Social Unrest*, Christian Commonwealth Sermon Supplements, no. 75, 15 May 1912 (London, 1912).

Phillips, W. F., *Y Ddraig Goch ynte'r Faner Goch ac Ysgrifau Eraill* (Cardiff, 1913).
Powell, D., *Yr Ail Ddyfodiad* (Carmarthen, 1921).
Price, W., *Sosialaeth: A Ddylid ei Chefnogi?* (Holyhead, 1908).
Raven, Charles E., *The Meaning of Copec* (published by the Welsh School of Social Service, n.d.).
Reason, Will, *The Social Problem for Christian Citizens* (2nd edn., London, 1913).
Idem, The Issues of Personal Faith in Social Service (London, 1916).
Idem, Christianity and Social Renewal (London, 1919).
Rees, John Morgan, *An Introduction to the Industrial Revolution in South Wales*, Traethodau'r Deyrnas, English ser., no. 4 (Wrexham, 1926).
Rees, Thomas, *Dinasyddiaeth Bur* (address given in the Gwynedd Temperance Association, Bangor, 18 October 1923, Liverpool, 1923).
Idem, Cenadwri'r Eglwys a Phroblemau'r Dydd (Wrexham, 1923).
Idem, Gwleidyddiaeth yng Nghymru, Traethodau'r Deyrnas, no. 7 (Wrexham, 1924).
Rees, W. J., *Egwyddor Ganolog yr Efengyl* (Penmaenmawr, 1931).
Roberts, Dorothy E., *Oriau Hamdden ac Adloniant*, Traethodau'r Deyrnas, no. 9 (Wrexham, 1924).
Roberts, Robert Alun, *Bywyd Gwledig Cymru*, Traethodau'r Deyrnas, no. 5 (Wrexham, 1924).
Roberts, R.G. (ed.), *Crist a Chwestiynau'r Dydd* (Blaenau Ffestiniog, 1908).
Roberts, R. Silyn, *Y Blaid Lafur Annibynol: Ei Hanes a'i Hamcan* (Blaenau Ffestiniog, 1908).
Rowlands, T., *Gwerslyfr Epistol Iago* (Bangor, 1922).
Schweitzer, Albert, *The Quest of the Historical Jesus* (London, 1952).
Shillito, E., *The Hope and Mission of the Free Churches* (London, 1912).
Idem, Christian Citizenship: The Story and Meaning of Copec (London, 1924).
Idem, Life and Work: The Universal Christian Conference on Life and Work held in Stockholm 1925 (London, 1925).
Stead, F. H., *The Story of Social Christianity*, I (London, 1924).
Idem, The Story of Social Christianity, II (London, 1924).
Thomas, Ben Bowen, *Cenadwri Copec* (Wrexham, 1924).
Thomas, Daniel Lleufer, *Labour Unions in Wales: Their Early Struggle for Existence* (Swansea, 1901).
Thomas, David, *Y Werin a'i Theyrnas* (Caernarfon, 1910).
Idem, Y Blaid Lafur a Dinasyddiaeth y Gweithiwr (Manchester, c.1911).
Idem, Y Deyrnas a Phroblemau Cymdeithasol, Traethodau'r Deyrnas, no. 6 (Wrexham, 1924).
Idem, Y Ddinasyddiaeth Fawr (Wrexham, 1938).
Thomas, David S., *Dylanwad Cymdeithasol Cristionogaeth* (New York, 1883).
Thomas, D. L. and Herbert Morgan, *Housing Conditions in Wales* (London, 1911).
Thomas, E. Gwynhefin, *Yr Eglwys a'r Amseroedd Enbyd* (Blaenau Ffestiniog, 1928).
Watcyn-Williams, M., *The Beatitudes in the Modern World* (London, 1935).
Idem, When the Shoe Pinches (London, 1936).
Williams, D. Llewelyn, *Cyflwr Iechyd yng Nghymru*, Traethodau'r Deyrnas, 2nd ser., no. 3 (Wrexham, 1930).
Williams, E., *Perthynas Duw a'r Byd* (Caernarfon, 1927).
Williams, Ifor, *Llenyddiaeth Gymraeg Fore*, Traethodau'r Deyrnas, no. 8 (Wrexham, 1924).
Idem, Llenyddiaeth Gymraeg a Chrefydd, Traethodau'r Deyrnas, 2nd ser., no. 2 (Wrexham, 1930).
Williams, J. Lewis (ed.), *Seiliau'r Ffydd* (Merthyr Tydfil, 1909).
Williams, Tom Nefyn, *Y Ffordd yr Edrychaf ar Bethau* (Dolgellau, 1928).
Williams, T. Rhondda, *The Social Gospel* (London, 1902).
Idem, The New Theology: An Exposition (London, 1907).
Idem, The Church and the Labour Cause, Christian Commonwealth Sermon Supplements, no. 26, 7 June 1911 (London, 1911).

Idem, The Working Faith of a Liberal Theologian (London, 1914).
Idem, Christian Belief in the Modern World (London, 1929).
Idem, Making the Better World (London, 1929).
Idem, Faith Without Fear (London, 1933).
Williams, W. J., *Teyrnas Dduw yn yr Hen Destament* (Y Ddarlith Davies 1910) (Caernarfon, 1913).

(ii) Autobiography and Biography
Anon., *Herbert Morgan 1875–1946* (Carmarthen, 1946).
Anon., *Thomas Phillips 1868–1936* (London, 1937).
Benn, Caroline, *Keir Hardie* (London, 1992).
Coombes, B. L., *These Poor Hands* (London, 1939).
Davies, D. R., *In Search of Myself* (London, 1961).
Davies, E. Tegla, *Gyda'r Blynyddoedd* (Liverpool, 1952).
Davies, Ieuan, *Joseph James* (Swansea, 1983).
Idem, Lewis, Tymbl (Swansea, 1989).
Davies, P., *A. J. Cook* (Manchester, 1987).
Davies, Rhys, *Print of a Hare's Foot* (London, 1969).
Davies, T. Eirug (ed.), *Y Prifathro Thomas Rees: Ei Fywyd a'i Waith* (Llandysul, 1939).
Davies, Walter Haydn, *The Right Place, the Right Time: Memories of Boyhood Days in a Welsh Mining Community* (Llandybïe, 1972).
Idem, Ups and Downs (Swansea, 1975).
Davies, W. T. Pennar (ed.), *Athrawon ac Annibynwyr* (Swansea, 1971).
Edwards, W. J., *From the Valley I Came* (London, 1956).
Ellis, E. J., *T.J. A Life of Dr. Thomas Jones C.H.* (Cardiff, 1992).
Evans, D. Tecwyn, *Atgofion Cynnar* (Tywyn, 1950).
Evans, E. Keri and W. Pari Huws, *Cofiant y Parch. David Adams* (Liverpool, 1924).
Evans, R. Wallis (ed.), *Syr Ben Bowen Thomas 1899–1977: Teyrnged* (Aberystwyth, 1978).
Foot, Paul, *'An Agitator of the Worst Kind': A Portrait of Miners' Leader A. J. Cook* (London, 1986).
Griffiths, James, *Pages from Memory* (London, 1969).
Griffiths, Robert, *S. O. Davies: A Socialist Faith* (Llandysul, 1983).
Gruffydd, W. J., *Hen Atgofion* (Aberystwyth, 1936).
Hamilton-Fyfe, H., *Keir Hardie* (London, 1935).
Hodges, Frank, *My Adventures as a Labour Leader* (London, 1925).
Horner, Arthur, *Incorrigible Rebel* (London, 1960).
Howard, J. H., *Winding Lanes* (Caernarfon, 1938).
Howell, D., *Nicholas of Glais: The People's Champion* (Clydach, 1991).
Hughes, Emrys (ed.), *Keir Hardie: His Writings and Speeches* (Glasgow, 1928).
Hughes, G. R., *Y Parch. Rhys J. Huws* (Caernarfon, 1917).
Hughes, R. R., *John Williams Brynsiencyn* (Caernarfon, 1929).
Jenkins, R. T., *Edrych yn Ôl* (London, 1968).
Idem, Cyfoedion (London, 1974).
Jones, A. H., *His Lordship's Obedient Servant: Recollections of a South Wales Borderer* (Llandysul, 1987).
Jones, D. James (Gwenallt), *Detholiad o Ryddiaith Gymraeg R. J. Derfel* (Denbigh, 1945).
Idem, Detholiad o Ryddiaith Gymraeg R. J. Derfel, II (Llandysul, 1945).
Jones, E. Cefni, *Gwili: Cofiant a Phregethau* (Llandysul, 1937).
Jones, Henry, *Old Memories* (Cardiff, 1922).
Jones, Ieuan Gwynedd (ed.), *Gwilym Davies: A Tribute* (Llandysul, 1981).
Jones, Jack, *Jack Jones' Unfinished Journey* (London, 1937).
Jones, R. J., *Troi'r Dail* (Swansea, 1962).
Jones, R. Tudur (ed.), *Credu a Chofio: Ysgrifau Edwin Pryce Jones* (Swansea, 1991).

Jones, R. W. (ed.), *Ysgrifau Puleston* (Bala, 1926).
Idem, Meddyliau Puleston (Caernarfon, 1934).
Idem, John Puleston Jones M.A. D.D. (Caernarfon, 1929).
Jones, Thomas, *Welsh Broth* (London, 1951).
Idem, Rhymney Memories (2nd edn., Llandysul, 1970).
Jones, W. Glasnant, *Cyn Cof Gennyf a Wedyn* (Swansea, 1949).
Lloyd-Jones, Bethan, *Memories of Sandfields 1927–1938* (Edinburgh, 1983).
Lloyd-Jones, E. R., *Niebuhr*, Cyfres y Meddwl Modern (Denbigh, 1989).
Matthews, E. Gwynn, *Hegel*, Cyfres y Meddwl Modern (Denbigh, 1984).
Morgan, D. Densil (ed.), *Torri'r Seiliau Sicr: Detholiad o Ysgrifau J. E. Daniel* (Llandysul, 1993).
Idem, Barth, Cyfres y Meddwl Modern (Denbigh, 1992).
Morgan, Kenneth O., *David Lloyd George: Welsh Radical as World Statesman* (Cardiff, 1963).
Idem, Keir Hardie: Radical and Socialist (London, 1975).
Morgan, Robert, *My Lamp Still Burns* (Llandysul, 1981).
Mor O'Brien, A. (ed.), *An Autobiography of Edmund Stonelake* (Cardiff, 1981).
Morris, W. (ed.), *Tom Nefyn* (Caernarfon, 1962).
Murray, Iain H., *D. Martyn Lloyd-Jones: The First Forty Years* (Edinburgh, 1982).
Owen, John (ed.), *Pregethau'r Diweddar Barch. John Williams D.D., Brynsiencyn* (Caernarfon, 1922).
Idem, Pregethau'r Diweddar Barch. John Williams D.D., Brynsiencyn, II (Caernarfon, 1923).
Nicholas, Islwyn ap, *R. J. Derfel* (London, 1945).
Nicholas, James, *Pan Oeddwn Grwt Diniwed yn y Wlad* (Llandysul, 1979).
Paynter, Will, *My Generation* (London, 1972).
Powell, W. Eifion, *Bywyd a Gwaith Gwilym Bowyer* (Swansea, 1968).
Prothero, Cliff, *Recount* (Ormskirk, 1982).
Rees, D. Ben (ed.), *Herio'r Byd* (Liverpool, 1980).
Idem, Dal i Herio'r Byd (Liverpool, 1983).
Idem, Dal Ati i Herio'r Byd (Liverpool, 1988).
Roberts, D. J., *Peter Price* (Swansea, 1970).
Roberts, R. Gwylfa (ed.), *Gweithiau Rhys J. Huws* (Llanelli, 1932).
Singer, Peter, *Hegel* (Oxford, 1983).
Smith, Dai, *Aneurin Bevan and the World of South Wales* (Cardiff, 1993).
Smith, J. Beverley (ed.), *James Griffiths and his Times* (Ferndale, 1978).
Thomas, Ben Bowen (ed.), *Lleufer y Werin, Cyfrol Deyrnged i David Thomas M.A.* (Caernarfon, 1965).
Thomas, David, *Silyn* (Liverpool, 1956).
Idem, Diolch am Gael Byw: Rhai o f'Atgofion (Liverpool, 1968).
Thomas, George, *George Thomas, Mr Speaker* (London, 1985).
Watcyn-Williams, M., *From Khaki to Cloth* (Caernarfon, 1949).
Watkins, Harold M., *Unusual Students* (Liverpool, 1947).
Williams, J. Roose (ed.), *T. E. Nicholas: Proffwyd Sosialaeth a Bardd Gwrthryfel* (Bangor, 1971).
Williams, Tom Nefyn, *Yr Ymchwil* (Denbigh, 1949).
Williams, T. Rhondda, *How I Found My Faith* (London, 1938).
Williams, W. Nantlais, *O Gopa Bryn Nebo* (Llandysul, 1967).

(iii) History
Arnot, R. Page, *The South Wales Miners 1898–1914* (London, 1967).
Idem, The South Wales Miners 1914–1926 (Cardiff, 1975).
Awbery, S., *Labour's Early Struggles in Swansea* (Swansea, 1949).
Ballard, P. H. and E. Jones (eds.), *The Valley's Call* (Ferndale, 1975).
Bassett, T. M., *Bedyddwyr Cymru* (Swansea, 1977).
Bebbington, D. W., *The Nonconformist Conscience* (London, 1982).

Bickerstaff, Mabel, *Something Wonderful Happened* (Liverpool, 1954).
Brennan, T., E. W. Cooney and H. Pollins, *Social Change in South West Wales* (London, 1954).
Cox, Idris, *The Fight for Socialism in Wales 1848–1948* (Cardiff, 1948).
Davies, A. J., *To Build a New Jerusalem: The Labour Movement from the 1880s to the 1990s* (London, 1992).
Davies, Dewi Eirug, *Hoff Ddysgedig Nyth: Cyfraniad Coleg Presbyteraidd Caerfyrddin i Fywyd Cymru* (Swansea, 1976).
Idem, Diwinyddiaeth yng Nghymru 1927–1977 (Llandysul, 1984).
Idem, Byddin y Brenin: Cymru a'i Chrefydd yn y Rhyfel Mawr (Swansea, 1988).
Davies, D. Hywel, *The Welsh National Party 1925–1945: A Call to Nationhood* (Cardiff, 1983).
Davies, John, *Hanes Cymru* (London, 1990).
Dodd, A. H., *The Industrial Revolution in North Wales* (3rd edn., Cardiff, 1971).
Edwards, Hywel Teifi (ed.), *Cwm Tawe* (Llandysul, 1993).
Idem, Arwr Glew Erwau'r Glo (Llandysul, 1994).
Idem, Nedd a Dulais (Llandysul, 1994).
Evans, Eric Wyn, *The Miners of South Wales* (Cardiff, 1961).
Foote, Geoffrey, *The Labour Party's Political Thought: A History* (London, 1985).
Francis, Hywel and David Smith, *The Fed* (London, 1980).
Herbert, T. and G. E. Jones, *Wales 1880–1914* (Cardiff, 1988).
Hopkins, K. S. (ed.), *Rhondda Past and Future* (Ferndale, 1975).
Hughes, G. A., *Men of No Property* (Caerwys, 1971).
Inglis, K. S., *Churches and the Working Classes in Victorian England* (London, 1963).
Jenkins, Geraint H. and J. Beverley Smith (eds.), *Politics and Society in Wales, 1840–1922* (Cardiff, 1988).
Jenkins, Philip, *A History of Modern Wales 1536–1990* (London, 1992).
Johnson, M. D., *The Dissolution of Dissent 1850–1918* (New York, 1987).
Jones, B. P., *The King's Champions 1863–1933* (Redhill, 1968).
Jones, Emyr, *Canrif y Chwarelwyr* (Denbigh, 1963).
Jones, Gwilym H., *Geiriadura'r Gair* (Caernarfon, 1993).
Jones, Peter d'A., *The Christian Socialist Revival 1877–1914* (Princeton, 1968).
Jones, Peter Ellis, *Bangor 1883–1983: A Study in Municipal Government* (Cardiff, 1986).
Jones, R. Merfyn, *The North Wales Quarrymen, 1874–1922* (Cardiff, 1981).
Jones, R. Tudur, *Congregationalism in England 1662–1962* (London, 1962).
Idem, Hanes Annibynwyr Cymru (Swansea, 1966).
Idem, Diwinyddiaeth ym Mangor 1922–1972 (Cardiff, 1972).
Idem, Yr Undeb (Swansea, 1975).
Idem, Ffydd ac Argyfwng Cenedl, I, Prysurdeb a Phryder (Swansea, 1981).
Idem, Ffydd ac Argyfwng Cenedl, II, Dryswch a Diwygiad (Swansea, 1982).
Jones, V. (ed.), *The Church in a Mobile Society* (Swansea, 1969).
Koss, S., *Nonconformity in Modern British Politics* (London, 1975).
Lewis, E. D., *The Rhondda Valleys* (London, 1959).
Lewis, Richard, *Leaders and Teachers: Adult Education and the Challenge of Labour in South Wales 1906–1940* (Cardiff, 1993).
Lieven, Michael, *Senghennydd: The Universal Pit Village* (Llandysul, 1994).
Macintyre, Stuart, *Little Moscows: Communism and Working Class Militancy in Inter-War Britain* (London, 1980).
Macquarrie, John, *Twentieth Century Religious Thought* (4th edn., London, 1989).
Mayor, S., *The Churches and the Labour Movement* (London, 1967).
Millar, J. P. M., *The Labour College Movement* (London, 1979).
Moore, Robert, *Pitmen, Preachers and Politics* (Cambridge, 1974).
Morgan, Kenneth O., *Wales in British Politics 1868–1922* (Oxford, 1963; 2nd edn. Cardiff, 1991).
Idem, Rebirth of a Nation: Wales 1880–1980 (Oxford, 1981).

Idem, The Red Dragon and the Red Flag: The Case of James Griffiths and Aneurin Bevan (Aberystwyth, 1989).

Munson, James, *The Nonconformists: In Search of a Lost Culture* (London, 1991).

Neill, Stephen and Tom Wright, *The Interpretation of the New Testament 1861–1986* (Oxford, 1988).

Parry, Cyril, *The Radical Tradition in Welsh Politics: A Study of Liberal and Labour Politics in Gwynedd 1900–1920* (Hull, 1970).

Parry, R. Ifor, *Ymneilltuaeth* (Llandysul, 1962).

Preston, Ronald, *Church and Society in the Late Twentieth Century* (London, 1983).

Raven, Charles E., *Christian Socialism 1848–1854* (London, 1920; new impression, 1968).

Rees, D. Ben, *Chapels in the Valley* (Upton, 1975).

Idem, Wales: The Cultural Heritage (Ormskirk, 1981).

Richards, Glyn, *Datblygiad Rhyddfrydiaeth Ddiwinyddol ymhlith yr Annibynwyr* (Swansea, 1957).

Roberts, Dafydd, *Y Chwarelwyr a'r Sowth* (Caernarfon, 1982).

Smith, Dai, *Wales! Wales?* (London, 1984).

Smith, David (ed.), *A People and a Proletariat: Essays in the History of Wales 1780–1980* (London, 1980).

Smith, Leonard, *Religion and the Rise of Labour* (Keele, 1993).

Stephens, Meic (ed.), *A Rhondda Anthology* (Bridgend, 1993).

Walters, Huw, *Canu'r Pwll a'r Pulpud* (Denbigh, 1987).

Williams, A. Tudno, *Mudiad Rhydychen a Chymru* (Y Ddarlith Davies 1983) (Denbigh, 1983).

Williams, Glanmor (ed.), *Merthyr Politics: The Making of a Working Class Tradition* (Cardiff, 1966).

Williams, Gwyn A., *When Was Wales?* (London, 1985).

Williams, Harri, *Duw Daeareg a Darwin* (Y Ddarlith Davies 1979) (Llandysul, 1979).

Wilson, Bryan R., *Religion in a Secular Society* (London, 1966).

(iv) Reference

Jenkins, R. T. and E. D. Jones (eds.), *Y Bywgraffiadur Cymreig 1940–1950* (London, 1970).

Lloyd, J. E. and R. T. Jenkins (eds.), *Y Bywgraffiadur Cymreig Hyd 1940* (London, 1953).

Idem, The Dictionary of National Biography Down to 1940 (London, 1959).

6. ARTICLES

Use was made of relevant historical articles in: *Diwinyddiaeth, Llafur, Y Traethodydd, The Welsh History Review*, and the various editions of Geraint H. Jenkins (ed.), *Cof Cenedl*, published (Llandysul) annually since 1986. The more important articles are listed in the footnotes above. The following also were used:

Evans, Trebor Lloyd, 'Diwinyddiaeth yng Nghymru', *Y Dysgedydd* (1940), 197–200, 223–6.

Hall, Basil, 'The Welsh Revival of 1904–5: a critique', in G. J. Cuming and D. Baker (eds.), *Studies in Church History*, VIII (Cambridge, 1972).

Harries, C. C., 'Churches, chapels and the Welsh', *New Society*, XXI (21 February 1963).

Howell D. and C. Barber, 'Wales', in F. M. L. Thompson (ed.), *The Cambridge Social History of Britain, 1750–1950*, I, *Regions and Communities* (Cambridge 1990), pp.281–354.

Jenkins, Gwyn, 'The Welsh Outlook 1914–1933', *The National Library of Wales Journal*, XXIV/4 (1986), 463–92.

Jones, J. Graham, 'Welsh politics between the wars: the personnel of labour', *Transactions of the Honourable Society of Cymmrodorion* (1983), 164–83.

Kent, John, 'Hugh Price Hughes and the Nonconformist conscience', in G. V. Bennett and J. D. Walsh (eds.), *Essays in Modern English Church History* (London, 1966), pp.181–205.

Leech, Ken, 'The Christian Left in Britain (1850–1950)', in R. Ambler and D. Haslam (eds.), *Agenda for Prophets* (London, 1980).

Lloyd, D. Tecwyn, 'T. E. Nicholas', in Aneirin Talfan Davies (ed.), *Gwŷr Llên* (London, 1948), pp.143–64.

Morgan, Prys, 'Gwerin Cymru—Y Ffaith a'r Delfryd', *Transactions of the Honourable Society of Cymmrodorion* (1967), 117–31.

Robbins, Keith, 'The spiritual pilgrimage of the Rev. R. J. Campbell', *The Journal of Ecclesiastical History*, XXX/2 (1979), 261–76.

Smith, J. Beverley, 'John Gwili Jenkins', *Transactions of the Honourable Society of Cymmrodorion* (1974–5), 191–214.

Stead, Peter, 'Vernon Hartshorn: miners' agent and Cabinet Minister', in S. Williams (ed.), *Glamorgan Historian*, VI (Cowbridge, 1969), pp.83–94.

Idem, 'Establishing a heartland—the Labour Party in Wales', in K. D. Brown (ed.), *The First Labour Party 1906–1914* (London, 1985).

Thompson, David M., 'The emergence of the Nonconformist social gospel in England', in Keith Robbins (ed.), *Studies in English Church History*, subsidia 7, *Protestant Evangelicalism in Britain, Ireland, Germany and America c.1750–c.1950* (Oxford, 1990).

Turner, Christopher B., 'Conflicts of faith? Religion and labour in Wales 1890–1914', in D. R. Hopkin and G. Kealey (eds.), *Class, Community and the Labour Movement: Wales and Canada 1850–1930* (Aberystwyth, 1989), pp.67–85.

Williams, C. R., 'The Welsh religious revival, 1904–5', *British Journal of Sociology*, III/3 (1952), 242–59.

Yeo, S., 'A new life: the religion of Socialism in Britain, 1883–1896', *History Workshop Journal*, IV (1977), 5–56.

7. UNPUBLISHED THESES

Fox, K. O., 'The emergence of the political labour movement in the eastern section of the south Wales coalfield 1894–1910' (MA thesis, University of Wales, 1965).

Gwyther, C. E., 'Methodism and Syndicalism in the Rhondda Valley 1906–1926' (Ph.D. thesis, University of Sheffield, 1967).

Howys, Siân, 'Bywyd a gwaith T. E. Nicholas' (MA thesis, University of Wales, 1985).

Jackson, P. W., 'The interaction of industry and organised religion in a changing cultural pattern' (MA thesis, University of Wales, 1957).

Lewis, E. T., 'Religious organisations in Wales considered in relation to economic conditions 1850–1930' (MA thesis, University of Wales, 1965).

Parry, Cyril, 'Socialism in Gwynedd' (Ph.D. thesis, University of Wales, 1967).

Roberts, Dafydd, 'The slate quarrying communities of Caernarvonshire and Meirionethshire 1911–1929' (Ph.D. thesis, University of Wales, 1982).

Smith, David, 'The rebuilding of the South Wales Miners Federation 1927–1939: a trade union and its society' (Ph.D. thesis, University of Wales, 1976).

Turner, Christopher B., 'Revivals and popular religion in Victorian and Edwardian Wales' (Ph.D. thesis, University of Wales, 1979).

Williams, Christopher Mark, 'Democratic Rhondda: politics and society 1885–1951' (Ph.D. thesis, University of Wales, 1991).

INDEX

Aberaman, 117
Aberavon, 112
    Bethlehem Forward Movement
        Church, 235, 236
Aber-craf, 39, 84, 110
Aberdare, 13, 54, 68, 70, 117, 118, 170,
    191
Aberystwyth, 62, 66
    United Theological College, 135, 192
    University College of Wales, 168, 230
Ablett, Noah, 98, 99
Abrahams, Phil, 96
Abrahams, William (Mabon), 9
Adams, Revd David, 154
America, 13
Amman valley, 92, 105, 107, 108, 112,
    117, 118
Ammanford, 37, 118, 137, 186
Anglican Church (and the Church in
    Wales), 1, 54, 88, 212, 248
    clergy, 139
Anglo-Catholicism, 54
apocalyptic ideal, 79, 160,179, 233, 234,
    237, 239, 249
Arthur, Will, 93, 94, 117
Ashley, T., 105
Atkin, Revd Leon, 204, 205, 213, 242

Bala, 62
    Theological College, 177, 192, 197
Bangor, 40, 49, 68, 132, 192
    Bala-Bangor Theological College, 16,
        132, 162, 230, 236
    Copec group, 198, 199
    North Wales Baptist College, 42
    School of Theology, 238
Banwen Colliery, 106
Baptists, 2, 23, 36, 59, 60, 102, 116, 128,
    133, 136, 162, 186, 187, 193, 221
    Baptist Union, 60, 136, 144, 169
    Baptist Union Social Service League,
        136
    Monmouthshire Baptist Association, 2
Bargoed, 60, 110
    Central Hall, 204

Barker, Revd R. J., 202, 203, 213, 242
Barth, Karl, 211, 230, 237, 239
Bax, E. Belfort, 62
Bedlinog
    Moriah chapel, 106, 113, 114
Bedwellty, 107
Benn, Caroline, 11
Berlin, 156
Bethesda, 127
Bibbings, G. H., 62
Bible, 53, 87, 101, 130, 131
    Acts of the Apostles, 27
    biblical criticism, 139, 188, 222
    biblical scholarship, 13, 39, 51, 52
    biblical studies, 68, 131, 160
    Book of Isaiah, 41
    Epistle of St James, 187, 188, 189
    Epistle to the Romans, 230
    Gospel of St Mark, 158
    Gospel of St Matthew, 86, 158
    New Testament, 20, 41, 42, 47, 56, 86,
        165, 219, 231, 242
    Old Testament, 27, 51
Birmingham
    Copec Conference, 195
Blaenau Ffestiniog, 37, 38, 127
Blake, William
    poem *Milton*, 225, 226
Blatchford, Robert, 3, 62
    Merrie England, 55
Bolwell, Hector, 106, 113
Bowyer, Revd Gwilym, 238
Boyer, Revd Llewellyn, 215
Brace, William, 136
Bradford, 8, 14, 19
Branch, Joseph, 102
Brecon
    Memorial College, 18, 132, 162, 230
Bridgend, 128
Briton Ferry, 102
Brockway, Fenner, 7
brotherhood
    brotherhood of man, 32, 41, 55, 56, 68,
        119, 135, 155, 157, 158, 159, 161,
        176, 180, 181, 211, 239, 243, 246

Brotherhood Meetings, 148, 149, 150, 242
general, 134, 139
Socialist, 9, 20, 23, 25, 28, 41, 52, 64, 68, 76, 103, 159
Brunner, Emil, 211
Brymbo, 127
Brynaman, 170
Brynsiencyn, 57, 58

Caerleon College, 190, 194
Caernarfon, 127, 132, 236
Calvinistic Methodists, 4, 37, 49, 52, 57, 58, 64, 102, 116, 121, 128, 136, 137, 177, 185, 186, 187, 192, 193, 210, 211, 212, 233, 234
Campaign for Morals and Religion, 182, 183, 184, 189
Presbyterian Church of Wales, 199
Reconstruction Commission, 58, 179, 180, 181, 182, 184
Cambrian Combine (liquidation, 1928–9), 203
Campbell, Revd R. J., 9, 13, 14, 15, 16, 17, 18, 19, 20, 21, 22, 29, 31, 46, 47, 51, 102, 103, 105, 107, 141
capitalism, 3, 13, 25, 34, 85, 103, 218
capitalist, 3, 25, 45, 48, 49, 71, 72
Cardiff, 56, 62, 205, 206
conference December 1911, 138, 139, 140, 141, 142, 143, 144, 145, 146, 147, 150, 168, 169, 187, 188, 213
Park Hall, 138, 139, 144
Religion and Labour Week, 145, 146
South Wales Baptist College, 132, 182
Carmarthen, 28, 114, 115, 116, 117, 132
Presbyterian College, 128
'Carwr Cyfiawnder', 173, 174
Cenadwri Cymdeithasol yr Efengyl, 185
Central Labour College, 99, 112
Chamberlain, Neville, 207
chapel
general decline in attendance, 1, 183, 217, 218, 219, 241, 245
hostility towards the labour movement, 59, 60, 61, 80, 88, 89, 90, 124, 126, 171, 172
opposed to Socialism, 61, 62, 63, 64, 65, 66, 67
working-class women remaining faithful, 73, 91, 94
working men leaving, 18, 73, 79, 84, 91, 93, 94, 95, 96, 98, 99, 100, 101,

102, 105, 109, 110, 114, 117, 121, 123, 125, 128, 129, 139, 140, 147, 148, 149, 150, 160, 161, 162, 164, 166, 167, 169, 173, 213, 223
character, 10, 11, 33, 51, 63, 66, 154, 179, 182, 219, 220, 232, 233
Christian Commonwealth, 141
Christian Social Union, 54
Christian Socialism, 54, 55, 56, 57, 58
Christian Socialist, 232
Church Socialist League, 54
citizenship
Christian, 177, 189, 197
class
consciousness, 4, 55, 56, 113
middle class, 14
system, 3, 4, 56, 125
war, 4, 9, 18, 55, 76, 166
working class, 13, 14, 15, 17, 30, 35, 38, 44, 45, 48, 49, 61, 69, 70
Clydach, 112
co-operation
church and the labour movement, 26, 27, 37, 44, 45, 49, 80, 82, 90, 145, 146, 147, 166, 168, 170, 220, 244
ecumenical, 131, 132, 133, 134, 135, 136, 182, 189–202, 224, 243
general, 7, 20, 23, 25, 26, 32, 53, 63, 176, 198, 227
in industry, 179, 200
politics and religion, 214, 215
collectivism, 7, 123
communism, 10, 11, 27, 48, 111, 112, 175, 204, 206, 215, 218
Bolshevism, 173
Communist Party, 96, 99, 104
competition, 7, 20, 130, 178
Congregational Union of England and Wales, 206
Congregationalist/ism, 18, 20, 37, 112, 162, 188, see also Independents
conscience, 21, 32, 38, 45, 51, 55, 67, 90, 141, 160, 172, 182, 198, 209, 220, 228, 243, 244, 247
church as society's, 182, 200
the Nonconformist conscience, 108
Conservatism
Conservative Party (Tory Party), 34, 73, 88, 248
political, 171
Cook, A. J., 79, 95, 102, 104, 112, 117
Coombs, B. L., 80, 81
Cooperative Magazine, 6

Copec, 184, 187, 195–9, 200, 208, 224, 228, 229, 233, 239
Cox, Idris, 98, 99, 100
Cristionogaeth a Chymdeithas, 55
Cristionogaeth yn Iachawdwriaeth Dynoliaeth, 66
Cwmafan, 55
Cwmaman, 41
Cwmcynon, 106
Cwmgors, 127
Cwmllynfell, 170
Cwmtwrch, 106
Cyngor Cymdeithasol Eglwysi'r Rhondda, 207

Daniel, J. E., 230, 231, 235, 236, 237, 238, 240
Darwin, Charles, 5, 101, 154
Das Kapital, 99
Davies, D. J., 119
Davies, Revd Gwilym, 28, 132, 133, 137, 197, 230
Davies, Revd Professor J. M., 132
Davies, Revd J. Park, 128
Davies, Revd J. T., 60
Davies, John, 96
Davies, Noëlle, 119
Davies, Revd Oswald, 232
Davies, Paul, 95
Davies, Rhys, 111
Davies, Rhys J., 170, 171
Davies, S. O., 18, 79, 112, 117
Davies, Samuel, 107
Davies, Revd Thomas Alban, 206, 207, 208, 213
Davies, Trevor, 100
Davies, Revd W. D., 220
Davies, W. M., 106.
Davies, Walter Haydn, 78, 94
deacons (diaconate), 36, 59, 78, 88, 106, 107, 113, 117, 125
Derfel, Robert Jones, 23
'Dewi Vychan', 143
Dialectic Theology, 208, 211, 230, 233, 237
disestablishment, 27, 131, 134, 195, 212, 243, 244
Dowlais, 19, 148

Edinburgh, 243
Edwards, Charles, 107
Edwards, Professor D. Miall, 132, 133, 135, 162, 165, 177, 178, 184, 185, 188, 190, 197, 199, 200, 201, 225, 226, 227, 229, 230, 244

Edwards, Revd G. A., 192, 193, 195, 198, 233, 234
Edwards, W. J., 12
Edwards, Principal William, 182
Efengyl y Deyrnas, 178
Eisteddfod, 5, 28, 38
Ellis, William, 127
eschatology, 11, 26, 160, 233, 234, 237
Evans, Beriah Gwynfe, 171, 174
Evans, Christmas, 2
Evans, D. Tecwyn, 2
Evans, Revd D. Tudwal, 49, 52, 53
Evans, Dai Dan, 104
Evans, Revd J. Derlwyn, 173
Evans, John, 105
Evans, Revd Owen, 33, 34
Evans, Revd W. O., 34
Evans, W. T. Glyn, 152
evolution, 5, 15, 20, 21, 35, 36, 39, 45

Fabian Tracts, 37
Fascism, 230, 240
Ferndale, 100, 105, 110
Fishguard, 137
Free Church Councils, 243
freedom, 3, 23, 33, 35, 38, 41, 45, 55, 56
Freeman, Revd George, 60

'Galileo', 87
Garnant, 127
Garvie, Alfred E., 195
George, David Lloyd, 23, 72, 138, 141, 142, 145, 147, 150, 187, 228
George, William, 133
Gittins, Ned, 108
Glais, 4, 16, 37, 42, 43, 127
Glamorgan, 114, 115, 116, 117
Glynneath, 93, 106
    Empire Colliery, 117
Glyntaff, 140
God
    Fatherhood of, 32, 34, 41, 50, 53, 56, 64, 68, 119, 135, 155, 156, 157, 158, 159, 176, 180, 181, 185, 193, 196, 211, 239, 243, 246
    immanence of, 5, 15, 21, 131, 154, 159, 181, 210, 219, 225, 239, 246
    Trinity, 181, 210
Gower, 62
Great War, 4, 42, 43, 47, 49, 57, 58, 70, 72, 74, 76, 80, 85, 89, 93, 94, 100, 112, 116, 137, 138, 162, 163, 165, 166, 170, 172, 179, 183, 191, 202,

213, 223, 229, 239, 241, 248, 244
Griffith-Jones, Revd Ebenezer, 5
Griffiths, Revd J., 118, 119, 137,186
Griffiths, James, 12, 17, 39, 41, 79, 92, 93, 102, 103, 105, 117
Guild of St Matthew, 54
Gwaelod y Garth, 106
Gwauncaegurwen, 103
    Carmel chapel, 96
Gwendraeth valley, 92, 105, 118, 208
gwerin, 4, 22, 24, 38, 42, 46, 80, 118, 125, 171, 209
'Gwilym Hiraethog', 23
Gwynedd, 24, 28
Gwynfryn Academy, 37

Hallding, Revd Percy, 148
Hardie, James Keir, 3, 8, 9, 10, 11, 12, 13, 14, 17, 18, 22, 24, 28, 29, 31, 35, 39, 41, 46, 48, 57, 65, 68, 71, 72, 74, 78, 81, 84, 103, 104, 105, 107, 124, 127, 135, 145, 146, 161, 244
Harnack, Adolf, 32, 68, 156, 161, 220
Hartshorn, Vernon, 89, 138, 143, 145, 146
Headlam, Stewart, 54
Hegel, G. W. F., 154
Hegelian philosophy, 5, 15, 20, 242, 245, 285
higher criticism, 5, 41, 65
Hinds, John, 136
Hodges, Frank, 79, 97, 98, 100, 102, 112, 117
Holyhead, 60
Horner, Arthur, 79, 97, 98, 99, 100, 102, 104, 112, 117
Howard, Revd J. H., 55
Hughes, Revd Daniel, 59, 127, 172
Hughes, Revd H. M., 139, 185
Hughes, Revd H. Maldwyn, 32, 33, 34
Huws, Revd Rhys J., 68, 127, 172
Huws, Revd W. Parri, 185

Independent Labour Party (ILP), 8, 16, 19, 20, 24, 25, 31, 36, 37, 38, 39, 41, 43, 48, 59, 60, 62, 68, 71, 72, 79, 85, 88, 93, 102, 112, 123, 124, 128, 168, 170, 235
Independents, 2, 114, 116, 128, 132, 136, 186, 193
    Association of Glamorgan, 173, 214
    Union of Welsh, 130, 131, 132, 151, 178, 184, 199, 236

individual regeneration bringing social renewal, 54, 63–4, 67, 119, 151, 152, 153, 154, 161, 178, 180, 182, 185, 186, 187, 188, 189, 196, 214, 215, 216, 222, 226, 238, 240, 244, 245
individual responsibility, 6, 10, 33, 34, 36, 41, 43, 63, 68, 75, 76, 141, 142, 153, 155, 157, 160, 161, 176, 178, 183, 184, 185, 186, 189, 193, 196, 200, 220, 222, 223, 225, 226, 227, 244, 245
industrial unrest
    Cambrian Combine dispute, 128, 129
    coalfield strike and lock-out (1898), 71, 187
    general labour, 173, 202
    General Strike and lock-out (1926), 109, 173, 174, 175, 202, 203, 206, 213, 239, 247
    Penrhyn strike and lock-out, 5, 71, 76
    railway dispute (1911), 71, 129
    Royal Commission into Industrial Unrest (Report, 1917), 111, 112
    strike Brymbo Steel Works (1896), 4
    strike and lock-out (1921), 103, 109, 187, 202, 206
    Taff Merthyr dispute (1934), 106, 113, 114
industry
    as a service for mankind, 180, 185, 186, 192, 200
    the need to recognize personality, 178, 192
injustice, 10, 13, 15, 34, 40, 51, 67, 72, 83, 91, 95, 106, 129, 130, 141, 165, 175, 202, 228

Jeffreys, Len, 96
Jenkins, Canon J. D., 54
Jenkins, John (Gwili), 28, 37, 40, 41, 42, 48, 127, 172
Jenkins, William, 107
Jerusalem, the Holy City, 215
Jesus Christ, 27, 32, 34, 37, 40, 51, 52, 54, 57, 64, 86, 140, 158, 203, 210, 214, 218, 221, 233, 236, 237, 246
    atoning sacrifice, 52
    cross of, 13, 44
    example, 15, 20
    founded kingdom, 178, 187
    gospel, 119, 173, 180
    ideals and principles, 36, 44, 61, 81, 173, 185, 202, 221

lordship, 176, 190
mission, 194
not a Socialist, 55
religion of, 15, 55, 87, 120, 146, 232
saviour, 35, 52, 59, 69, 160, 221, 227,
   228, 249
Son of Man, 118
teaching, 13, 26, 28, 43, 49, 50, 53, 63,
   76, 80, 82, 83, 87, 88, 90, 149, 155,
   156, 159, 160, 165, 180, 181, 184,
   185, 190, 196, 197, 208, 222, 230,
   233, 234, 248, 249
working-class, Socialist, 12, 13, 17, 35,
   53, 81
John, Will, 107
Jones, Revd Buckley, 114
Jones, Revd E. K., 4, 127
Jones, Gwenan, 177
Jones, H. Cefni, 174
Jones, Revd J. Edryd, 28, 127
Jones, J. Graham, 107
Jones, J. Gwynedd, 40
Jones, Revd J. Puleston, 181, 187
Jones, J. R., 37
Jones, Revd J. Towyn, 68
Jones, Revd J. Tywi, 56, 137
Jones, Jack, 11, 122
Jones, Revd James, 132
Jones, Revd John Morgan (Bangor), 16,
   68, 162, 165, 177, 197, 217, 230,
   238, 240, 244
Jones, Revd John Morgan (Cardiff), 145
Jones, Revd John Morgan (Merthyr
   Tydfil), 49, 50, 51, 52, 54, 139, 140,
   177
Jones, Michael D., 23
Jones, Revd R. B., 231
Jones, Revd Stanley, 127, 132
Jones, T. E., 66
Jones, Revd V. Gower, 140
Jones, Revd W. Rowland, 28, 36, 37, 48,
   69, 127
justice, 18, 20, 23, 25, 27, 31, 35, 45, 55,
   63, 67, 68, 79, 92, 123, 134, 165,
   171, 173, 175, 176, 193, 227, 243,
   244

Kant, Immanuel, 180, 242, 245
Kantian philosophy, 155
Kingdom of God, Heaven, 9, 12, 13, 17, 27,
   34, 37, 51, 55, 60, 66, 68, 69, 76, 81,
   83, 86, 87, 119, 131, 136, 148, 155,
   156, 159, 160, 161, 162, 165, 166, 176,
177, 178, 179, 180, 181, 182, 184, 185,
   186, 190, 191, 196, 197, 200, 201, 205,
   206, 208, 211, 215, 220, 223, 224, 227,
   229, 231, 232, 233, 234, 236, 239, 246,
   247, 248, 249

Labour Church, 8, 58
Labour Leader, 28, 142
labour movement
   as a religion, 9, 11, 12, 13, 14, 79, 81,
      102, 103, 104, 120, 121, 128, 218
   hostility to chapels, 80, 81, 82, 83, 84,
      85, 86, 87, 88, 89, 90, 91, 100, 121,
      126, 127
   Sunday meetings, 60, 88
Labour Party, 1, 72, 73, 84, 96, 99, 103,
   114, 120, 126, 138, 169, 171, 172,
   205, 207, 209, 217, 235
Labour Voice, 74, 104, 105, 108, 170, 217,
   232
Lampeter, 130
League for Progressive Thought, 15, 16
League of Nations, 230
Levi, Professor Thomas, 66
Lewis, Revd D. J., 151
Lewis, Revd D. Wyre, 186, 187, 193
Lewis, Revd E. D., 60, 136
Lewis, Revd H. Elfed, 182, 184
Lewis, Henry, 84, 110
Lewis, Revd J. D. Vernon, 230
Liberal Party, 1, 2, 3, 6, 7, 17, 28, 55, 56,
   58, 59, 65, 68, 69, 70, 72, 73, 84, 88,
   89, 112, 124, 125, 126, 138, 143,
   163, 169, 171, 172, 227, 243, 247
Liberal Theology, 21, 130, 131, 139, 155,
   161, 177, 178, 179, 183, 193, 200,
   201, 207, 208, 211, 213, 217, 220,
   229, 231, 232, 237, 238
liberalism
   political, 3, 34, 59, 60, 74, 76, 90, 123,
      125, 171, 172, 209
   reaction to theological, 200, 201, 222,
      223, 230, 235, 236, 237, 238, 239
   theological, 31, 40, 45, 69, 176, 183,
      184, 186, 188, 190, 193, 196, 202,
      206, 208, 209, 211, 212, 216, 219,
      228, 229, 232, 235, 236, 237, 239,
      242, 243
Llais Llafur, 17, 23, 35, 39, 57, 74, 80, 82,
   84, 86, 87, 125, 128, 140, 141, 144,
   162
Llandaf
   bishop of, 141, 212

Industrial Committee, 212
Llandrindod Wells, 132, 138, 182
Llanelli, 2, 17, 71, 79, 128, 129, 172
Lloyd, D. Tecwyn, 42
Lloyd-Jones, D. Martyn, 235, 236
London, 14, 16, 22, 46, 99, 127, 152
     Castle Street Baptist chapel, 172
     City Temple, 14
Lord Penrhyn, 71
Lord's Prayer, 13, 50, 215, 246, 247

MacDonald, Ramsay, 112, 206, 207
Maerdy, 105, 174
     Siloa Congregational church, 107
Manchester, 8
Marx, Marxism, Marxist, 43, 82, 99, 100,
     107, 112, 173, 241
materialism, 21, 28, 31, 38, 43, 63, 67, 76,
     88, 94, 98, 105, 118, 119, 122, 165
Maurice, F. D., 54
means test, 202, 204
Men Without Work, 110
Merthyr Express, 3
Merthyr Pioneer, 23, 74, 86, 118, 148, 149
Merthyr Tydfil, 13, 36, 49, 51, 52, 72, 79,
     110, 121, 127, 140, 147, 148, 149,
     206, 242
     Hope chapel, 49
Meyer, Revd F. B., 141
Miners' Federation of Great Britain
     (MFGB), 79, 97, 112
Miskin, 36, 58
Monism, 15, 18
Monmouth, 114, 115, 116, 117
Monthly Democrat, 124
Morgan, Abel, 102
Morgan, Revd Herbert, 16, 28, 41, 132,
     133, 137, 151, 155, 162, 163, 165,
     166, 167, 168, 169, 170, 172, 177,
     179, 191, 192, 193, 197, 216, 230,
     244, 247
Morgan, J. Vyrnwy, 112
Morgan, Kenneth O., 11, 70
Morgan, R. Price, 171
Morgan, Richard, 66
Morris, Revd William, 187
Moses, 12, 13, 168
Mountain Ash, 136, 205
My Adventures as a Labour Leader, 97

Nantymoel, 60
National Union of Mineworkers (NUM),
     79, 97

nationalism, 119, 120, 207
     Nationalist Party, 238
nationalization, 7, 11, 20, 25, 27, 31, 33,
     37, 38, 39, 43
Neath, 19, 90, 107, 168, 170
     Gnoll Road Congregational church,
     131
Neath Abbey, 55
Neighbour, Revd George, 36, 58
Neo-Hegelian Idealism, 155
New Theology, 9, 14, 15, 17, 18, 19, 21,
     22, 47, 51, 141
Newcastle Emlyn, 128
Newport, Monmouthshire, 52, 62, 132
Nicholas, Revd James, 36, 37, 48, 69, 127,
     172
Nicholas, T., 90
Nicholas, Revd T. E., 4, 16, 28, 37, 42,
     43, 44, 45, 46, 47, 48, 65, 69, 74,
     127, 165, 170, 172
Niebuhr, Reinhold, 239
Noel, Conrad, 54
Nonconformist Liberal hegemony
     end of, 70, 133, 147
Nonconformity
     allied to the Liberal Party, 2, 3, 248
     importance of social problems, 129
     withdrawal from politics, 126, 150, 163,
     164, 169, 170, 171, 185, 209, 214,
     215, 216, 247-8
north Wales, 24, 43, 74, 75, 76, 77, 92,
     117, 118
North Wales Quarrymen's Union, 74, 92
nystagmus, 111

Owen, Revd R. E., 234
Owen, Robert, 23
Oxford, 62
     Conference on Church, Community
     and State (1937), 202

pacifism, 46, 49, 165, 168, 170
Paris, 202
Parliament, 13, 57, 74, 141, 173, 191,
     195, 214
Parri, H. Monfa, 119
Parry, Dr Cyril, 75
Parry-Williams, T. H., 177
Paynter, Will, 92, 101, 109, 117
Peel, Robert, 2
Penmaen-mawr, 62
Penrhyndeudraeth, 40
Penygroes, Caernarfon, 132

Peregrine, Revd R. E., 184
personality
    human, 36, 51, 63, 64, 121, 134, 154,
        177, 197, 219, 220, 225
    value of, 103, 139, 180, 181, 185, 190,
        200, 208, 214, 220, 244
Phillips, Professor David, 177, 197
Phillips, Revd W. F., 56, 61, 62, 63, 64,
    65, 74, 124, 138, 145
Philosophical Idealism, 15, 21, 154, 155,
    159, 161, 169, 188, 211, 225, 247
Pilgrim Trust, 110, 112, 120
Pontyclun, 36, 58
Pontypool, 59, 127
Pontypridd
    Board of Guardians, 174
Porth, 130, 231
'Port Talbot', 86, 87
private ownership, 7, 8, 67
Progressive Theology Leagues, 130, 131
Prothero, Cliff, 79, 103
Prys, Principal Owen, 135, 197
public house, 93, 122, 241
Pughe, Revd David, 147, 148, 149, 150,
    212, 242

radical politics, 2, 7, 48, 95
Rank, Joseph, 204
Reade, H. Musgrave, 60, 62
Reason, Revd Will, 132
Rebecca riots, 2
redistribution of wealth, 23, 24, 37
Rees, Revd D. G., 128
Rees, David, 2
Rees, E. T., 235, 236
Rees, Ebenezer, 74
Rees, Principal Thomas, 132, 154, 162,
    165, 171, 184, 185, 197, 198, 229,
    230, 236, 244
Rees, Timothy, 212, 213
Reformation
    Protestant, 3
Religion and Socialism, 49
Rengsdorf, 202
revival (1859), 1
    (1904), 6, 42, 43, 71, 95, 97, 103, 105,
        114, 116, 125, 126, 188, 218, 231
revolution, 20, 25
Rhiwfawr, 127
Rhondda, 70, 92, 102, 105, 107, 112, 117,
    129, 130, 203, 206, 207, 208, 231
Rhosllannerchrugog, 186
Richard, Henry, 23

Richards, Revd Thomas, 132
Risca, 204, 242
Ritschl, Albrecht, 68, 156, 160, 161, 220,
    226, 227, 242, 245
Roberts, Revd Bedford, 55
Roberts, Revd E. Wyn, 214
Roberts, Evan, 39, 103
Roberts, Revd O. L., 185
Roberts, Revd R. Silyn, 28, 37, 38, 39, 40,
    41, 48, 62, 69, 127, 172
Roberts, Samuel, 23
Roderick, Revd T. M., 108, 127, 172
Roderick, Revd W. D., 28, 127, 172
Roman Catholic Church, 134, 195
Rowlands, David (Dewi Môn), 2
Rowlands, Revd Thomas, 188

sacrifice, 10, 15, 23, 44, 47, 48, 52, 53, 76,
    119, 154, 158
Saunders, Revd W., 60
Schweitzer, Albert, 234
Second World War, 117, 120, 201, 224,
    238, 239, 245
Seren Cymru, 40, 52, 136, 186, 221
Sermon on the Mount, 9, 10, 17, 50, 61,
    76, 86, 140, 189
service, 20, 33, 44, 51, 53, 56, 76, 81, 104,
    134, 140, 154, 158, 185, 186, 191,
    203, 220, 221, 222, 232, 243
Shankland, Revd Thomas, 171
Shrewsbury, 137
silicosis, 111
sin, 10, 15, 16, 19, 36, 49, 61, 67, 91, 124,
    201, 218, 222, 223, 227, 229, 230,
    235, 236, 238, 248
slavery, 35
slums, 10, 15, 24, 46, 83, 127, 130, 151,
    231, 232
Smith, Leonard, 121
social problems, 45, 50, 51, 58, 59, 64, 70,
    133, 140, 141, 151, 160, 163, 164,
    168, 170, 172, 178, 179, 183, 184,
    186, 188, 189, 190, 191, 195, 197,
    201, 213, 222, 224, 227, 232, 235,
    243, 244, 248
    character development, 184
    health, 141, 243, 245
    housing, 27, 44, 57, 129, 140, 141, 151,
        153, 156, 157, 175, 184, 197, 209,
        232, 237, 243
    international issues, 70, 178, 197,
        240
    leisure time, 14, 141, 183, 213

solutions to
  eugenics, 181
  stewardship, 181, 186, 200, 221
  temperance, 78, 107, 108, 109, 151,
    183, 192, 205, 244
  uneven distribution of wealth, 24, 46, 130
  wages, 27, 44, 57, 184, 213, 232, 237,
    241
social reform, 16, 18, 21, 31, 32, 34, 35, 36,
    37, 50, 56, 57, 67, 68, 88, 97, 129,
    133, 147, 150, 151, 152, 153, 156,
    161, 163, 169, 170, 173, 178, 179,
    183, 184, 186, 188, 190, 191, 195,
    197, 201, 213, 222, 224, 227, 232,
    237, 238, 239, 241, 243, 244, 247, 248
  leading to individual salvation, 10, 11,
    19, 34, 36, 45, 46, 66, 151, 152, 184,
    232
Socialism
  as a religion, 7, 8, 17, 22, 25, 26, 28, 29,
    30, 31, 38, 104, 122, 126
  as practical application of Christianity,
    43, 44, 58, 81, 84, 88, 103, 110, 122
South Wales Coalfield Project, 75, 109
South Wales Daily News (SWDN), 124, 125,
    127, 134, 143, 146
South Wales Miners' Federation (SWMF),
    71, 92, 93, 99, 105, 107, 112, 113,
    124, 125, 174
South Wales Voice, 74
spiritual
  as contrasted with material, 7, 31, 33,
    34, 44, 49, 50, 54, 61
Stockholm
  Cathedral, 200
  International Conference on Life and
    Work, 199–202, 208, 229, 232, 239
Student Christian Movement (SCM), 176,
    225
Swansea, 56, 105, 106, 130
  Mynydd Newydd Colliery, 105
  St Paul's Congregational Church, 205
  Swansea (Tawe) valley, 43, 47, 74, 105,
    108, 117, 118, 218, 231
Syndicalism, 98

Tai'r Gwaith, 108, 109
Talysarn, 24, 197
Tanygrisiau, 37
Tarian y Gweithiwr, 73, 105, 137
Tawney, R. H., 3
Taylor, W. H., 100, 101
Temple, William, 195

Teyrnas Dduw yng Ngoleuni Syniadau
  Apocalyptig yr Efengylau, 233
The Miners' Next Step, 98
The Quest of the Historical Jesus, 234
Thomas, Ben Bowen, 190
Thomas, Daniel Lleufer, 5, 130, 131, 132,
    134, 142, 190
Thomas, David (Talysarn), 24, 25, 26, 27,
    29, 31, 197
Thomas, Dylan, 205
Thomas, George, 202
Thomas, Revd Keinion, 5
Thomas, Morgan (Lord Mayor of
    Cardiff), 56
Thomas, W. C., 106
Ton Pentre (Bethesda Church), 206
Tonypandy, 36, 127
  Central Hall, 202, 203
  riots, 71, 129, 188
'Toplis', 134
trade unions, 4, 25, 51, 92, 97, 106, 112,
    122, 143
Traethodau'r Deyrnas, 177
Trealaw
  Community House, 203, 242
Trevor, Revd John, 8
Tumble, 151, 208

unemployment, 110, 121, 183, 202, 204,
    205, 206, 207, 213–19
Union of Welsh Independents, see
  Independents
Unitarian, 128
Universal Council for Life and Work, 202
Urdd y Deyrnas, 176, 177, 244

Walters, Revd D. D. (Gwallter Ddu), 28,
    35, 69, 127, 128, 171
Watcyn-Williams, Revd Morgan, 121,
    214, 215, 233
Watkins, Harold M., 93
Watkins, Tom, 95
Welfare State, 245
Welsh Outlook, 163, 166, 169
Welsh School of Social Service, 132, 133,
    134, 135, 136, 137, 138, 142, 150,
    188, 189–95, 197, 198, 199, 224,
    228, 233, 239, 244
Wesleyan Methodism, 24, 97, 148, 188,
    202, 204
Westhoughton, 170
Whiteing, Richard, 7
Williams, C. R., 1

Williams, David (Mayor of Swansea), 56
Williams, Professor David, 177
Williams, Revd Iona, 127, 172
Williams, Revd J. Lewis, 55, 231, 232
Williams, John, 106
Williams, Revd John, Brynsiencyn, 57, 58
Williams, Silas, 144
Williams, Revd Thomas Rhondda, 14, 15, 19, 20, 21, 22, 29, 31, 84
Williams, Revd Tom Nefyn, 52, 208–12, 213, 240
Williams, W. O., 34
Wilson, Revd Ben, 13, 14, 29, 44, 170
Wilson, Revd Stitt, 13, 14, 29, 44
Woods, Bishop F. T., 200
Workers' Educational Association (WEA), 40, 93
working class, 71, 78, 80, 88, 93, 98, 113, 122, 124, 125, 126, 134, 139, 143, 149, 150, 163, 166, 167, 169, 170, 173, 183, 213, 227, 241, 242, 249
Workingman's Club, *see* Tai'r Gwaith

Y Blaid Lafur Annibynnol:
    Ei Hanes a'i Hamcan, 38

Y Cronicl, 126
Y Cymro, 23
Y Darian, 73, 105, 118
Y Deyrnas, 165
Y Dinesydd Cymreig, 74, 76, 119
Y Ffordd yr Edrychaf ar Bethau, 210, 211, 212
Y Geiriadur Beiblaidd, 229, 242
Y Geninen, 43
Y Goleuad, 61, 174, 183, 200
Y Tyst, 171, 173, 195, 200
Y Werin a'i Theyrnas, 24
Ynysmeudwy
    Bethesda chapel, 173, 216
Ynysybwl, 95, 102
Yorkshire, 19
Yr Efengylydd, 60, 231, 237
Yr Efrydydd, 176, 230
Yr Eurgrawn, 32,
Ystalyfera, 136
    Pant-teg chapel, 17, 103, 173
Ystrad
    Bodringallt Welsh Independent chapel, 60